Designed by Pauline Brown

Set in 12 point Whitman by the Perseus Books Group

Library of Congress Cataloging-in-Publication Data

Shagrin, Jenn.
  Veganize this! : from surf & turf to ice-cream pie—200 animal-free recipes
for people who love to eat / Jenn Shagrin. — 1st Da capo Press ed.
    p. cm.
  Includes index.
  ISBN 978-0-7382-1402-3 (alk. paper)
  1. Vegan cooking. I. Title.
  TX837.S457 2010
  641.5'636—dc22

                                           2010030404

Published by Da Capo Press
A Member of the Perseus Books Group
www.dacapopress.com

Note: The information in this book is true and complete to the best of our knowledge. This book is intended only as an informative guide for those wishing to know more about health issues. In no way is this book intended to replace, countermand, or conflict with the advice given to you by your own physician. The ultimate decision concerning care should be made between you and your doctor. We strongly recommend you follow his or her advice. Information in this book is general and is offered with no guarantees on the part of the authors or Da Capo Press. The authors and publisher disclaim all liability in connection with the use of this book. The names and identifying details of people associated with events described in this book have been changed. Any similarity to actual persons is coincidental.

Da Capo Press books are available at special discounts for bulk purchases in the United States by corporations, institutions, and other organizations. For more information, please contact the Special Markets Department at the Perseus Books Group, 2300 Chestnut Street, Suite 200, Philadelphia, PA 19103, or call (800) 810-4145, extension 5000, or e-mail special.markets@perseusbooks.com.

10 9 8 7 6 5 4 3 2 1

VEGANIZE THIS!

From Surf & Turf to Ice-Cream Pie

200 Animal-Free Recipes for People WHO LOVE to EAT

JENN SHAGRIN

Da Capo
LIFE
LONG

DA CAPO LIFELONG

A Member of the Perseus Books Group

To my wife, Jane—
my muse and the love of my life.

To my mother and father—
my undyingly loving, caring, and ass-saving support system.

To my Grandfather, "Oo-Oo"—
my inspiration for relentless work ethic, drive,
and passion for knowledge.

CONTENTS

Introduction *xiii*

The Shaggy Kitchen Have-to-Have Pantry Essentials *xv*

1 HAIL SEITAN! AND HIS FOLLOWERS . . . 1

THE STAPLE
- MimicCreme and Alternatives *3*

SEITAN RECIPES
- Chicken-Style Seitan *5*
- Beef-Style Seitan *6*
- Pork Chop–Style Seitan *7*
- Turkey-Style Seitan *8*
- Ham-Style Seitan *9*
- Veal Chop–Style Seitan *10*
- Vegan Meatballs *11*
- Vegan Chicken-Apple Sausage *12*
- Crispy Vegan Prosciutto *14*
- Vegan Pancetta *14*
- Vegan Bacon *15*

SEAFOOD
- Basic Seafood Marinade *16*
- Tofu Scallops *17*
- Vegan Clams and Clamshells *18*
- Vegan Canned Tuna Packed in Oil *19*
- Vegan Sea Bass *20*

CHEESES AND OTHER DAIRY PRODUCTS
- DIY Vegan Mozzarella That Melts! *21*
- Vegan Parmesan Blend *22*
- Vegan Ricotta *22*
- Vegan Mascarpone *23*
- Vegan Goat Cheese *23*
- Vegan Fontina *24*
- Vegan Crème Fraîche *25*
- Vegan Cool Whip *25*

EGGS
- Vegan Scrambled Eggs *27*
- Vegan Egg Mix *28*
- Vegan Egg Yolk Mix *28*
- Flaxseed Egg *29*

CONTENTS

2 RECIPES GUARANTEED TO GET YOU LAID . . . 31

JENN SHAGGY'S GUIDE TO COOKING AND SHAGGING

- Heirloom Cannellini Beans with Sage, Crispy Vegan Prosciutto, and Fava Bean Pesto Ragout 33
- Pineapple Five-Spice Bun with Pineapple-Orange Sherry-Glazed Tofu 35
- Vegan Goat Cheese, Spinach, and Sun-Dried Tomato–Stuffed Pork Chops with Roasted Garlic Fingerling Potatoes and Pearl Onions 38
- Orzo with Vegan Chicken-Apple Sausage, Asparagus, Baby Tomatoes, and Vegan Ricotta Salata in a White Tomato Sauce 40
- Coconut Vinegar–Cured Tofu Scallops with Lemongrass-Basil Cream Sauce and Cilantro-Garlic Coconut Rice 42

MAKING FRESH PASTA: BECAUSE EVERYONE LOOKS SEXIER COVERED IN FLOUR

- Basic Pasta Dough 45
- Vegan Eggplant Parmesan Ravioli with Heirloom Tomato, Strawberry, and Chocolate Marinara 46

■ ■ ■

- Pan-Roasted Tempeh with White Bean Broth, Cilantro Pesto, and Roasted Shallots with Sautéed Kale 48

- Vegan Jumbo Lump Jackfruit Crab Cakes with Spanish Garlic Mayonnaise and Warm Saffron Nage 50
- Eggs Benedict Florentine Omelets with Sage Hollandaise Sauce 53

ABOUT THE NEW MEXICAN HATCH CHILE PEPPER

- Hatch Chile Chicken Cacciatore with Black Garlic–Tomato Sauce 56
- Crab and Oyster Mushroom Mezzelune in a Roasted Hatch Chile and Walnut Cream Sauce 58

■ ■ ■

- Saffron, Oregano, and Garlic Chive–Infused Vegan Sea Bass, Clams, Bacon, and Beech Mushrooms in White Wine 61
- Roasted White Eggplant Fettuccine Alfredo with Fresh Fennel and Spinach 62
- Vegan Turkish Pomegranate Meatball Soup 64
- Vegan Veal Chops with Sunchoke Caponata 66

FUNGI? FUNGAL!

- Free-Form Wild Mushroom Lasagne with Champagne-Lemon Cream Sauce and Sun-Dried Tomato and Roasted Red Pepper Salsa 68

- White Lasagne with Basil Ricotta, Spinach, Young Rocket, and Diced Vegan Pancetta 70
- Vegan Chicken Marsala Masala with Fresh Morels 72
- Vegan Escargots à la Bourguignonne en Croûte Vegan Brioche with Café de Paris Butter 73
- Pan-Seared White Pepper Tofu Scallops with Basil Cream Sauce Served over Linguine 74
- Red Chard, Roasted Garlic, and Ricotta-Stuffed Peppers with Sun-Dried Tomato and Toasted Pine Nut Marinara 76
- Lemon-Artichoke Cavatelli in an Heirloom Tomato-Cream Vinaigrette with English Peas and Vegan Prosciutto 78

VEGAN SURF AND TURF
- Lemon-Thyme-Agave-Braised Short Ribs and Seared Tofu Scallops in a Mineola Tangelo–Saffron Sauce 80

■ ■ ■

- Vegan Carnitas, Caramelized Shallot, and Mushroom Enchiladas with Tomatillo, Green Apple, and Avocado Sauce and Lime Crème Fraîche 82
- Quinoalenta and Rosemary Squash Chips with Wild Mushrooms and Vegan Mascarpone 83
- Dijonaise-Crusted Beef Tenderloin Medallions with Vegan Béarnaise Sauce over Roasted Eggplant and Garlic Smashed Potatoes 86

3 SATISFYING THE VEGAN MUNCHIES . . . 89

- Vegan Quattro Formaggio White Truffle Macaroni and Cheese 91
- Morel Mushroom and Bacon White Macaroni and Cheese 92
- Spanish Purple Pepper Vegan Beef Stew 94
- Vegan Sausage and Beer Gravy over Cheddar, Green Onion, and Cilantro Buttermilk Biscuits with Fried Dill and Dandelion Greens 96
- Vegan Braciole 99

PIZZA: THE FANCY WAY AND THE QUICK WAY
- Herbes de Provence and Roasted Garlic Pizza Dough with Melting Vegan Cheese Blend 100
- Eggplant Lasagne-Style Vegan Deep-Dish Pizza 103
- No-Yeast Pizza Crust 104

■ ■ ■

- Coffee-Rubbed Vegan Steak Tacos with Grilled Lobster Mushroom, Heirloom Cherry Tomato, and Corn Salsa 105

CONTENTS

- Vegan Chicken-Fried Tofu Steaks with Rosemary-Thyme Chicken Gravy, Two Ways: Gluten Free and Regular 108
- Louisiana-Style Yellow Rice 111
- Spaghetti and Meatballs with San Marzano and Port Wine Marinara Sauce 112
- Thai Tofu, Vegetable, and Coconut Soup 113
- Green Garlic Gumbo 114
- Belgian Ale and Roasted Garlic-Infused White Chicken Chili Gumbo 116
- Heirloom Bean, Red Russian Kale, and Wheat Berry Chili 117
- Creamy Roasted Pumpkin, Sherry, and Tarragon Soup 119
- Cheesy Sweet Onion and Heirloom Tomato Pie 120
- Chicken Paprikash 122
- Vegan Doritos 123
- Vegan Spicy No-Tuna Sushi Roll 125
- Vegan Pork Chops and Cranberries in Oregon Pinot Noir Reduction with Wild Mushroom, Kale, Beet, and Hazelnut Hash 127
- Taiwanese Minced Pork and Garlic Chive Chow Mein 129

4 VEGAN HOLIDAY SURVIVAL KIT . . . 133

- Vegan Lemongrass, Ginger, and Coriander-Infused Matzo Ball Soup 134
- Vegan Kugel with Broccoli Rabe and Chanterelles 137
- Vegan Sautéed Shallot, Cremini, and Fennel Green Bean Casserole 138
- Roasted Chestnut, Marble Rye, and Pancetta Stuffing with Sherry, Leeks, and Blue Foot and Shiitake Mushrooms 140
- Garlicky White Beans 142
- Oregano and Basil-Rubbed Marsala Flank Steak Stuffed with Saffron Wild Mushrooms 143
- Juniper Berry and White Peppercorn-Rubbed Field Roast with Sage-Infused Vegetables and Balsamic Ale-Cranberry Reduction 144
- Vegan Red Wine and Peppercorn-Braised Brisket 146
- Vegan Matzo Brei 148
- Individual Broccoli, Cheddar, and Rice Casseroles in a Chanterelle and Rosemary Cream Sauce 149
- Butternut Squash and Vanilla Bean Risotto 150
- Quattro Garlic Mashed Potatoes and White Beans 152
- Fennel, Vidalia Onion, and Roasted Garlic Potato Latkes with Mom's Applesauce 153
- Pumpkin Tartare over Chickpea-Black Cumin Crepe Crisps with Vegan Sage and White Ale Browned Butter Sauce 155

5 GRILLIN' & CHILLIN' . . . 159

- Mini Vegan Veal, Black Peppercorn, and Basil Sliders with Artichoke and Avocado Tapenade 160
- Vegan Orange-Sesame Grilled Chicken Tenders 162
- Faux Chicken Coconut-Basil Burgers with Cilantro-Mint Chutney 163
- Grilled Sage-Rubbed Pork Chops with Warm Apple Slaw 165
- Bourbon Buffalo Mole Chicken Wings with Vegan Bleu Cheese–Avocado Oil Aioli 166
- Frisée, Carrot, and Celery Stick Salad with Toasted Garlic and Cumin Vinaigrette 168
- Columbian Ale-Sautéed Vegan Steak with Sweet Onions and Garlic-Ginger-Ají-Avocado Sauce 169
- Curried Pork, Enoki Mushroom, and Purple Basil Pot Stickers with a Porcini, Shoyu, and Sake Reduction 170
- White Pepper Vegan Turkey Shawarma with Chipotle-Tomato Relish and Roasted Garlic, Sage, and Artichoke Tahini Paste 173
- Summertime Heirloom Tomato and Herb Salad 176
- Heirloom Tomato, Black Garlic, and Marsala-Roasted Chickpea Panzanella 177
- Cumin and Avocado Oil–Rubbed Portobello Tortas with Dragon Fruit Pico de Gallo and Purple Basil–White Peppercorn Mayo 178
- Orecchiette and Wild Arugula Salad in Vegan Basil-Mint Aioli 180

LET'S HAVE A KOREAN BARBECUE!

- Vegan Galbi (Korean Short Ribs) and Bulgogi (Grilled Steak) 181
- Black Sesame-Spinach Banchan (Side Dish) Salad 183

■ ■ ■

- Pan-Asian Black Sesame-Cabbage Slaw Tossed with Rose Water, Cilantro, and Mint Pesto 183
- Vegan Black Cumin Crab Tostadas over Cabbage Salad with Lime, Mint, and Wasabi Dressing 185
- Harvest Time Salsa 186
- Vegan Dill and Chive Cashew Cheese 187
- Vegan Tuna and Garlic Cannellini Bean Salad 188
- Chipotle Adobo Barbecued Chicken 188
- Vegan Roasted Garlic Caesar Dressing with Homemade Buttery Croutons 189
- Vegan Ranch Dressing: My Way 191
- Vegan Green Papaya Salad (Som Tum) 192
- Warm Spinach and Red Onion Salad with Green Apple, Meyer Lemon, and Fresh Mint Vinaigrette 193
- Grilled Steak and Creminis with Garlic, Sherry, and Rosemary Sauce 194
- Vegan Prosciutto-Wrapped Greens 195

CONTENTS

6 GET BAKED . . . 197

- Vegan Twinkies *198*
- Vegan Butternut Squash, Apple, and Onion Galette with Blue Cheese *200*
- Rainier Cherry, Lemon, and Sweet Ricotta Gratin *202*
- Vegan Belgian Waffles *203*
- Sweet Baguette Hazelnut French Toast with Vegan Aunt Jemima Syrup *205*
- Garlic French Toast *206*
- Rustic Sunflower Seed and Lime Pesto Quiche Tartlets with Roma Tomatoes and Black Olives *207*
- Mom's Carrot Pudding *209*
- Vegan Brioche *210*
- Fire-Roasted Pumpkin, Hazelnut, and Black Cumin Pie with Vanilla Bean Crème Fraîche *211*
- Vegan Peanut Butter Dream Pie *214*
- Bubbe's Pinwheel Cookies *215*
- Vegan Coconut Ice-Cream Pie *217*
- Homemade Vegan Marshmallows *218*
- Southern Sea Salt–Pecan Pralines *219*

Metric Conversions *221*
Acknowledgments *223*
Index *227*

INTRODUCTION

I could very well start by saying that food and cooking "have always been a huge part of my life" and all that yada yada yada, but I might as well just be honest:

I am a lazy vegan who likes food that really *tastes good* and is simple to make.

True, growing up in a Jewish household, food was an integral part of my childhood. The smell of San Marzano tomatoes simmering with garlic or Chinese take-out will always remind me of lazy Sundays. But when I really get down to the nitty-gritty of my passion for cooking, I simply just *love* food. I love the way it excites my senses. I love seeing a warm smile spread across someone's face when they try one of my culinary creations. But most important, I love conceptualizing cruelty-free versions of my favorite foods for all my fellow vegans to enjoy. Of course, I want all the nonvegans of the world to embrace my recipes as well. To me, it's the deepest compliment when an omnivore exclaims, "This is vegan?!" after biting into something I've prepared.

I find that the voice for animal rights is well received when vegans lead by example rather than preach. I'm not trying to lecture anyone or bully anyone into becoming a vegan, but rather demonstrate that great vegan food most certainly is not tasteless, and neither is a vegan's sense of humor! And just as it's not my intention to criticize carnivores, everyone should give cruelty-free cuisine a chance as well, before passing judgment on the vegan community.

INTRODUCTION

Cooking, to me, is art. It's one of the myriad forms of creativity that's present in my life, along with acting and comedy. Cooking and comedy go hand-in-hand in my mind. Whether it's hearing someone's laughter after telling one of my corny jokes, or reveling in the joy of someone enjoying my food, I'm in the business of helping people smile more. What's not to love about a full belly and a happy face? Just like Buddha! Okay, that was corny. Anyway . . .

My approach to creating recipes centers around developing the most authentic vegan replication of a traditionally nonvegan dish. At times, a recipe may seem complex or impossible. But you have my word that I explain everything in accurate detail so that preparing each dish is fun and easy!

On the easier end of the spectrum, you'll enjoy such recipes as Belgian Ale and Roasted Garlic–Infused White Chicken Chili Gumbo. More complex recipes such as Curried Pork, Enoki Mushroom, and Purple Basil Pot Stickers with a Porcini, Shoyu, and Sake Reduction or Saffron, Oregano, and Garlic Chive–Infused Vegan Sea Bass, Clams, Bacon and Beech Mushrooms in White Wine may seem scary, but I promise that they're fall-off-your-chair delicious and provide you with a chance to learn new skills!

Now, let's get down to business. First, you'll find a list of all my favorite ingredients to have on hand. In the first chapter, you'll find a step-by-step guide to creating all the mock meats used in the recipes. Although these are the backbone of many of my dishes, you can also simplify many of the recipes by substituting prepackaged mock meats or tofu. They'll still, literally or figuratively, impress the pants off of whoever you're feeding.

Now grab yourself a cocktail, cozy up in an armchair, and start reading! There's something in here for everyone, even the Beefy Fried McSteak lover in your life!

Happy veganizing!

Jenn

THE SHAGGY KITCHEN HAVE-TO-HAVE PANTRY ESSENTIALS

What follows is a list of my favorite vegan products that are used throughout the book. Many of the vegan cookbooks already out there cover the basics, so I'm just going to cut the fluff and get down to the nitty-gritty specifics. Bear in mind that they are just suggestions. Different strokes for different folks, right? Substitutions are always allowed, and can even be more fun because you're experimenting. Besides, life's more fun when there aren't any rules.

ALCOHOL

I have two general rules when it comes to the wine, beer, or champagne I use in my recipes:

1. If I won't drink it, I won't use it.
2. If the beverage contains any animal ingredients, I won't use it, either.

To be sure that the brand of alcohol you're using is cruelty free, there's a great online directory of vegan-friendly alcoholic beverages available at www.barnivore.com.

ARROWHEAD MILLS VITAL WHEAT GLUTEN

Visit www.arrowheadmills.com, or check their list of store locations.

BETTER THAN BOUILLON BASES BY SUPERIOR TOUCH

Better Than Bouillon, manufactured by Superior Touch Products, has a line of vegan stocks, including Vegan Beef and Vegan Chicken flavors. They are an amazingly authentic replication of their animal product–filled counterparts. The basic way to turn these pastes into broth is to dissolve 1 teaspoon of Better Than Bouillon Base per 1 cup of warm water. You can find the bases at most health food stores, or buy direct from Better Than Bouillon's Web site (www.superiortouch.com/).

BACON BITS

My favorite brand of vegan bacon bits is Frontier Bac'Uns. The PETA Web site also tells me that Betty Crocker Bac~Os are also vegan.

BARBECUE SAUCE

I just wanted to share my absolute favorite, which is Organicville Original BBQ Sauce. It is out-of-this-world delicious. I eat it with a spoon! They also make amazing vegan ketchup, ranch dressing, salsa, and other condiments to spice up your dinner table.

BOB'S RED MILL PRODUCTS

Bob's Red Mill manufactures just about every type of flour, both regular and gluten free, that's available on this good earth. They also make a variety of premade crust and baking mixes to help you cut corners. Check out their Web site for the lowdown on all that they offer (www.bobsredmill.com).

BRAGG LIQUID AMINOS

A tasty, healthy alternative to soy sauce made from non-GMO soybeans. It's a liquid protein concentrate that contains sixteen essential and nonessential amino acids. Available at many chain grocery stores and health food stores, and also via their Web site (http://bragg.com/).

BREAD

Just a note about breads: read the labels carefully—nonvegan ingredients can show up where you least expect them. My favorite brand is Rudi's Organic Bakery (www.rudisbakery.com)

CHEESE ALTERNATIVES

Here's a basic list of the vegan cheeses you see in many of my recipes. Depending on where you live, they may or may not be readily available for you to purchase. They're all available online either directly on the company Web sites or online vegan storefronts.

- Dr-Cow Aged Tree Nut Cheeses and Natural Organic Foods (www.dr-cow.com)
- The Redwood Co.'s Cheezly vegan cheese. (www.redwoodfoods.es/)
- Daiya vegan cheese (www.daiyafoods.com)
- Follow Your Heart vegan gourmet cheese alternatives, cream cheese, and sour cream. (www.followyourheart.com)
- Sunergia Soyfoods cheese alternatives are great. Try their Soy Bleu or any of their Soy Feta flavors. (www.sunergiasoyfoods.com)
- Teese vegan cheese is made by Chicago Soydairy, which also manufactures a variety of other great vegan goodies. (www.chicagosoydairy.com)

CHICKPEA FLOUR

Chickpea flour, also known as gram or garbanzo bean flour, is flour made from ground garbanzo beans. It's readily available at Whole Food Market, health food markets, and Indian specialty grocers. It is gluten free, which is an additional bonus to its excellent binding abilities. Bob's Red Mill manufactures a great garbanzo bean flour (www.bobs redmill.com).

COLGIN LIQUID SMOKE

Colgin clearly places a lovely little vegan symbol on their packaging that also happens to be part of the bad-ass tattoo on the back of my arm. I had to give them some brand loyalty. Truthfully, their liquid smoke has a great depth of flavor. I use it all the time. You'll notice I list the mesquite flavor, but feel free to experiment with their other varieties (www.colgin.com/).

ENER-G EGG REPLACER

Always use this product dry. Ignore the package directions that instruct you to mix the powder with water to replace an egg. Special shout-out to Jenny Goldberg of the L.A.-based Spork Foods for teaching me this bit of advice. Available at most health food stores, and also via Ener-G's Web site (www.ener-g.com/).

GARDEN TIME ORGANIC PASTAS

They manufacture a great eggless wide ribbon noodle that I use all the time. They don't have a company Web site, but you can buy their products in most health food stores and on Amazon.com.

GARLIC PASTE

Garlic paste is great on just about anything from crackers to pasta. My favorite brand is Majestic Garlic's Creamy Garlic Paste (www.majesticgarlic.com).

IMAGINE FOODS

They make No Chicken Broth, that you can use in place of the Better Than Bouillon brand, and I also use their Creamy Portobello Mushroom Soup in my Vegan Sautéed Shallot, Cremini, and Fennel Green Bean Casserole. Their entire line of cream-free creamy soups are great on a cold night (www.imaginefoods.com).

MEAT ALTERNATIVES

Fake meats may not suit your fancy. I have no shame admitting I'm a faux meat whore . . . as long as no animals are harmed in the preparation process. My favorites include:

- Field Roast Grain Meat Co. (www.fieldroast.com)
- MATCH Meats faux meat products are amazing. If you're feeling too lazy to make vegan ground beef, substitute with their Ground Beef product and use as the recipe indicates (www.matchmeats.com).
- Tofurky products (www.tofurky.com)
- Vegetarian Plus by VegUSA. Check their Web site for which of their products are vegan: www.vegeusa.com.

MIMICCREME

MimicCreme, a vegan substitute for heavy cream, is probably my favorite vegan product on the market. If the health food stores in your area don't carry it yet, kindly ask them to do so. You can check their Web site for store locations, or buy it directly from the company (www.mimiccreme.com). Or see page 3 for MimicCreme alternatives you can make at home.

MISO PASTE

Traditionally made from soybeans or other starters such as rice and barley, miso paste adds a great depth of flavor to any dish. There are many types of miso pastes available, each with their own unique taste. For example, mellow white miso paste has an almost cheeselike flavor, whereas red miso paste has a darker, saltier taste. One of my favorite brands is Miyako Oriental Foods' Cold Mountain Miso Paste (www.cold mountainmiso.com).

MUIR GLEN TOMATO PRODUCTS

Their organic tomato sauces, tomato pastes, and canned tomatoes are delicious. I eat their Organic Fire Roasted Diced Tomatoes out of a can with a spoon, and I don't care what you have to say about it. Available in most chain grocery stores and through their Web site: www.muirglen.com.

NATURE'S FLAVORS FOOD COLORING

Made from all natural ingredients (i.e., none of those nasty chemicals), Nature's Flavors line of food colorings are great for adding a little flair to your dishes. Available at some health foods stores, Whole Foods Market, and through the manufacturer's Web site (www.naturesflavors.com).

NOW FOODS AGAR POWDER

Agar powder (you may also see it as agar-agar or by its Japanese name, kanten) is a powder derived from a bright red sea vegetable and is known for its excellent gelling and thickening properties.

Although Now Foods Agar Powder is only one of the many brands of agar powder available, it is my favorite. Check their Web site for store locations (www.nowfoods .com/). Other brands of agar powder are available at Asian grocers and health food stores.

If you can only locate agar flakes, grind the flakes into a fine powder first using a mortar and pestle or coffee grinder before using in any recipe.

SOY CREAMER, SOY YOGURT, AND SOY MILK BY WILDWOOD ORGANICS

Manufactured by the Pulmuone Company, Wildwood Organics soy products are not only delicious, but 100 percent American organic soybeans. Their tofu is great as well. You can buy Wildwood products at most major chain grocery stores, or check their Web site (www.pulmuonewildwood.com).

TEMPEH

If I can find fresh, locally made tempeh, I buy it. If not, I really like Lightlife Organic Soy Tempeh . . . especially their Smoky Tempeh Strips (http://www.lightlife.com).

TOFU

Fresh tofu is my favorite, but many of my recipes require tofu to "perform." Mori-Nu's silken tofu line is one of my favorites for softer tofu (www.morinu.com). For extra-firm, Wildwood Organics is my go-to brand (www.pulmuonewildwood.com).

VEGAN CREAM CHEESE

See "Follow Your Heart" under Cheese Alternatives.

VEGAN SOUR CREAM

See "Follow Your Heart" under Cheese Alternatives.

VEGAN MARGARINES

Earth Balance tub and stick margarines are two of my refrigerator staples. Know that if you're watching your girlish figure or manly physique, you can always sub equal amounts of canola oil or use cooking spray for sautéing. Just be aware that you may need to adjust the salt content.

VEGETABLE RENNET

Vegetable rennet is an excellent product for turning vegan milks into cheeses, custards, and so on. It's a thickening agent that's completely vegetable based. My favorite is Malaka Liquid Vegetarian Rennet, available on Amazon.com, at natural foods markets, or Whole Foods Market.

1

HAIL SEITAN! AND HIS FOLLOWERS . . .

Even though my passion for cooking sprouted from my family's deep love of food, I never expected it to become my creative priority. If someone had asked me five years ago what I thought I'd be doing today, I probably would have said one of two things:

a. Holding a steady position as an anchorwoman for a snappy news/talk show, or

b. Harvesting a flourishing marijuana farm in Northern California under the code name "Pimpstress of Mystery," surrounded by people named Haze and Blitz, while fighting off the DEA with my wit and charm.

Maybe it's the Gemini in me, but my deep need to cook emerged seemingly overnight about four years ago. I should rephrase that. I don't just "need to cook"; I need to create *great* vegan cuisine. My kitchen became my laboratory and art space; and I, for the first time in my life, became a perfectionist.

First, I was determined to hone the vegan culinary art of making seitan. Tell people you worship Satan, and their eyes will bug out of their head before they turn around and run for their life. Tell them you "hail seitan" and their reaction will be very similar if they've eaten a bad batch. I spent countless hours in my kitchen

"Hail Seitan! And His Followers..." is a set of recipes and explanations for making vegan mock meats. This is more of a resource guide that will be sourced back to from recipes throughout the rest of the book. This chapter also includes a number of vegan cheese and egg recipes.

developing a seitan recipe that is not only delicious to vegans and omnivores, but one that the novice home chef can approach with confidence.

Most vegans that get down with their bad selves in the kitchen have made seitan at least once. The first attempt is usually one that's filled with *schpilkes* (that's my *bubbe*'s snazzy Yiddish terminology for "nervous energy"). But with the right ingredients, equipment, and know-how, even the most devout carnivores will be praising your seitan in no time, instead of bolting for the nearest burger joint.

What follows is, pardon the pun, the "bare bones" set of recipes for all the mock meats, cheeses, egg, and dairy substitutes that are used throughout the book. You'll have the opportunity to use them in almost every recipe in this book, and you can even use them as a replacement for meat in your old favorite carnivore recipes.

Think of this chapter as more of an instruction manual to help you use the rest of the cookbook. My method for making seitan helps you create the most delectable, easy-to-digest wheat meat you'll ever eat!

A GLUTEN-FREE 411 If you're gluten intolerant, you can use any of the seitan broths as marinades for tofu. Just drain the tofu well, cut or slice it into the desired shape, and allow it to marinate, refrigerated, for at least three hours in the seitan broths. Now, let's get started.

MIMICCREME AND ALTERNATIVES

You'll notice that throughout *Veganize This!* I use the ingredient MimicCreme quite often. It's a fantastic product invented by an amazing woman named Rose Anne Jarrett. She's granted me permission to name her product in all my recipes, which you'll see often as it's incredibly useful in preparing great vegan food. If you can't find yourself a carton, use the numbered alternatives below.

Number 1 can be used as an alternative in any and all savory recipes, and numbers 2 through 5 work well in both savory dishes, sweet dishes, and baked goods.

1. Combine ½ cup of raw cashew pieces and ¼ cup of almond slivers in a bowl, then cover with water. Allow them to soak overnight. Then drain well, and puree in a food processor with about ½ cup of water. Keep blending and adding water until it's a completely smooth mixture. The consistency should be similar to that of a milkshake.

2. Take 1 cup of the highest-fat soy or other nondairy milk you can find, and pour into a small saucepan. Mix 2 tablespoons of cornstarch with 2 tablespoons of ice-cold water. Heat the soy milk over medium-high heat, stirring frequently, until it begins to boil, then add the cornstarch mixture. Cook, stirring continually, until reduced by half. Depending on how much MimicCreme the recipe calls for, you may need to double or triple the amounts.

3. Vegan Buttermilk: Use the highest-fat soy or other nondairy milk of choice, combine it with 1 tablespoon white vinegar per cup of milk. Stir well, then set aside to coagulate.

4. Take one 14-ounce can of coconut milk, and pour into a small saucepan. Mix 1 tablespoon of cornstarch with 1 tablespoon of ice-cold water. Heat the coconut milk over medium-high heat, stirring frequently, until it begins to boil, then add the cornstarch mixture. Cook, stirring continually, until reduced by one-third. Depending on how much MimicCreme the recipe calls for, you may need to double or triple the amounts.

5. Take 1 pint of soy creamer, and pour into a small saucepan. Mix 2 tablespoons of cornstarch with 2 tablespoons of ice-cold water. Heat the soy creamer over medium-high heat, stirring frequently, until beginning to boil, then add the cornstarch mixture. Cook until reduced by half. Depending on how much MimicCreme the recipe calls for, you may need to double or triple the amounts.

SEITAN RECIPES

SHAGGY KITCHEN TIP All these broths are reusable; store them in a glass container in your fridge—they'll keep for up to one week. These broths freeze well, too. Throughout *Veganize This!* you'll find tips for using the various broths. Hey—the economy is in shambles. We gotta get by somehow, right?

CHICKEN-STYLE SEITAN

⋺ Makes 6 servings ⋵

CHICKEN BROTH

8 cups prepared Better Than Bouillon No Chicken Base (see page xvi for how to prepare)

1 cup MimicCreme or alternative (page 3)

7 whole white button mushrooms

1 teaspoon shallot powder

1 teaspoon onion powder

1 teaspoon roasted garlic powder

2 bay leaves

Pinch of celery seeds

CHICKEN-STYLE SEITAN DOUGH

1 cup vital wheat gluten

1 cup prepared Better Than Bouillon No Chicken Base (see page xvi for how to prepare)

1½ tablespoons MimicCreme or alternative (page 3)

Prepare the broth: First, take all the chicken broth ingredients and mix them together in a very large pot. Bring to a boil.

Prepare the seitan: While the broth's starting to heat up, make your seitan dough by combining and kneading the vital wheat gluten, No Chicken broth, and MimicCreme until completely mixed. It will be a little wetter than most seitan doughs. Squeeze out the excess liquid and form the mixture into a ball. On a cutting board, flatten out the ball and use a sharp knife or kitchen shears to cut, pie style, into six chicken breast–shaped wedges. Before putting into the boiling broth, flatten each wedge by pressing it firmly between your hands to ⅓ to ¼ inch thick, then drop into the pot of boiling broth.

Cover the pot, lower the heat to a simmer, and let the seitan cook for about an hour, stirring every 10 to 15 minutes.

Don't throw out the broth! Use a slotted spoon to remove each piece of seitan and place in a colander to drain. Let the seitan and the broth cool. Allow the seitan to marinate in the broth until ready to use, if time allows. Drain again before using.

Don't worry if there isn't time to marinate the cooked seitan. You can use it right away if that hot date is waiting on your doorstep.

BEEF-STYLE SEITAN

≷ Makes 6 servings ≸

BEEF BROTH

8 cups prepared Better Than Bouillon
No Beef Base (see page xvi for
how to prepare)

6 dried shiitake mushrooms

2 tablespoons tamari

1 portobello mushroom cap, chopped

1 tablespoon garlic powder

2 teaspoons onion powder

2 bay leaves

BEEF-STYLE SEITAN DOUGH

1 cup vital wheat gluten

1 cup prepared Better Than Bouillon
No Beef Broth Base (see page xvi
for how to prepare)

1 tablespoon MimicCreme or alternative (page 3)

Prepare the broth: First, place all the beef broth ingredients in a large pot and bring to a boil.

Prepare the seitan: While the broth's starting to heat up, make your seitan dough by combining and kneading the vital wheat gluten, No Beef broth, and MimicCreme until completely mixed. It will be a little wetter than most seitan doughs. Squeeze out the excess liquid and form the mixture into a ball. On a cutting board, flatten out the ball and use a sharp knife or kitchen shears to cut, pie style, into six beef-shaped wedges. Before putting into the boiling broth, flatten each wedge by pressing it firmly between your hands to $\frac{1}{3}$ to $\frac{1}{4}$ inch thick, then drop into the pot of boiling broth.

Cover the pot, lower the heat to a simmer, and let the seitan cook for about an hour, stirring every 10 to 15 minutes. Don't throw out the broth! Use a slotted spoon to remove each piece of seitan and place in a colander to drain. Let the seitan and the broth cool. Allow the seitan to marinate in the broth until ready to use, if time allows. Drain again before using.

PORK CHOP-STYLE SEITAN

> Makes 6 servings <

PORK CHOP BROTH

4 cups prepared Better Than Bouillon
    No Chicken Base (see page xvi for
    how to prepare)

½ tablespoon Better Than Bouillon No
    Beef Base (just the paste)

1 cup MimicCreme or alternative (page
    3)

1 cup water

⅛ cup tamari

1 cup pineapple coconut nectar or
    apple juice

½ teaspoon ground ginger

½ teaspoon Chinese five-spice powder

2 teaspoons garlic powder

1 teaspoon shallot powder

4 whole cloves, ground

3 points broken off a whole star anise

1 teaspoon kosher salt

1 teaspoon sugar

PORK CHOP-STYLE SEITAN DOUGH

1 cup vital wheat gluten

1 cup prepared Better Than Bouillon
    No Chicken Base (see page xvi for
    how to prepare)

1 tablespoon MimicCreme or alterna-
    tive (page 3)

Prepare the broth: First, take all the pork chop broth ingredients and mix them together in a very large pot. Bring to a boil.

Prepare the seitan: While the broth's starting to heat up, make your seitan dough by combining and kneading the vital wheat gluten, No Chicken broth, and MimicCreme until completely mixed. It will be a little wetter than most seitan doughs. Squeeze out the excess liquid and form the mixture into a ball. On a cutting board, flatten out the ball and use a sharp knife or kitchen shears to cut, pie style, into six pork chop–shaped wedges. Before putting into the boiling broth, flatten each wedge by pressing it firmly between your hands to ⅓ to ¼ inch thick, then drop into the pot of boiling broth.

Cover the pot, lower the heat to a simmer, and let the seitan cook for about an hour, stirring every 10 to 15 minutes.

Don't throw out the broth! Use a slotted spoon to remove each piece of pork chop and place in a colander to drain. Let the seitan and the broth cool. Allow the seitan to marinate in the broth until ready to use, if time allows. Drain again before using.

TURKEY-STYLE SEITAN

>≡ Makes 6 servings ≡<

TURKEY BROTH

4 cups prepared Better Than Bouillon's No Chicken Base (see page xvi for how to prepare)

2 cups low-sodium vegan vegetable broth

1 cup dry white wine (I use Chardonnay)

½ (12-ounce) can light ale

1¼ cup MimicCreme or alternative (page 3)

1 tablespoon freshly squeezed lemon juice

¼ cup mirin

1 teaspoon onion powder

1 teaspoon garlic powder

½ teaspoon yellow mustard powder

2 bay leaves

2 ribs celery, sliced

1 tablespoon mellow white miso paste

TURKEY-STYLE SEITAN DOUGH

⅓ cup prepared Better Than Bouillon No Chicken Base (see page xvi for how to prepare)

⅓ cup white ale

⅓ cup MimicCreme or alternative (page 3)

1 cup vital wheat gluten

Prepare the broth: Combine all the broth ingredients, *except* the miso paste, in a very large stockpot. Bring to a boil, then add the miso paste and stir until dissolved.

Prepare the seitan: While the broth's starting to heat up, whisk together the No Chicken broth, ale, and MimicCreme, then mix with the vital wheat gluten and knead until it's completely mixed. Squeeze out any excess liquid, then depending on the recipe you're using the vegan turkey for, either shape into one large rectangle or flatten the dough into a circle and use a sharp knife or kitchen shears to cut, pie style, into four turkey breast–shaped wedges.

Drop the dough into the pot of boiling broth, lower the heat to a simmer, and cover the pot with a lid. Let the seitan simmer for about an hour, stirring every 10 to 15 minutes.

Once done cooking, drain the seitan well. Place on a drying rack, then allow to drain for a few hours to achieve that "dry" element that real turkey has.

Use as directed in any of my vegan turkey recipes, or substitute for real turkey in one of your favorites!

HAM-STYLE SEITAN

 Makes 6 servings

HAM-STYLE BROTH

6 cups prepared Better Than Bouillon No Beef Base (see page xvi for how to prepare)

12 ounces hard apple cider, or 1 cup apple juice

¼ cup Bragg Liquid Aminos

3 tablespoons of natural red food coloring, or 1 tablespoon traditional red food coloring (optional)

1 tablespoon brown sugar

15 to 20 drops liquid smoke

¼ cup mirin

1 cup MimicCreme or alternative (page 3)

8 whole cloves, crushed

Pinch of ground ginger

4 to 5 fennel seeds

HAM-STYLE SEITAN DOUGH

1 cup vital wheat gluten

½ teaspoon Better Than Bouillon's No Beef Base (just the paste)

1 scant cup water

1 teaspoon vegan brown sugar

½ tablespoon beet powder (optional, for color)

1 tablespoon MimicCreme or alternative (page 3)

About 10 drops liquid smoke

Prepare the broth: First, take all the ham broth ingredients and mix them together in a very large pot. Bring to a boil.

Prepare the seitan: While the broth's starting to heat up, place the vital wheat gluten in a stand mixer bowl or large bowl. In a measuring cup, dissolve the No Beef Base in the water, then whisk in the remaining ingredients. Knead until completely mixed. It will be a little wetter than most seitan doughs. Squeeze out the excess liquid and form the mixture into a ball. On a cutting board, flatten out the ball and use a sharp knife or kitchen shears to cut into four pieces. Before putting into the boiling broth, flatten each wedge by pressing it firmly between your hands to ⅓ to ¼ inch thick, then drop into the pot of boiling broth.

Cover the pot, lower the heat to a simmer, and let the seitan cook for about an hour, stirring every 10 to 15 minutes.

Don't throw out the broth! Use a slotted spoon to remove each piece of seitan and place in a colander to drain. Let the seitan and the broth cool. Allow the seitan to marinate in the broth until ready to use, if time allows. Drain again before using.

9

VEAL CHOP-STYLE SEITAN

⇉ Makes 6 servings ⇇

VEAL CHOP BROTH

6 cups prepared Better Than Bouillon No Chicken Base (see page xvi for how to prepare)

¼ cup tamari

1 cup prepared Better Than Bouillon No Beef Base (see page xvi for how to prepare)

1 (12-ounce) bottle dark stout ale

1 cup MimicCreme or alternative (page 3)

Handful of dried porcini mushrooms

1 teaspoon garlic powder

1 teaspoon onion powder

VEAL CHOP SEITAN DOUGH

1 cup vital wheat gluten

1 cup prepared Better Than Bouillon No Beef Base (see page xvi for how to prepare)

1½ tablespoons MimicCreme or alternative (page 3)

Prepare the broth: First, take all the veal chop broth ingredients and mix them together in a very large pot. Bring to a boil.

Prepare the seitan: While the broth's starting to heat up, make your seitan dough by combining and kneading the vital wheat gluten, No Beef broth, and MimicCreme until completely mixed. It will be a little wetter than most seitan doughs. Squeeze out the excess liquid and form the mixture into a ball. On a cutting board, flatten out the ball and use a sharp knife or kitchen shears to cut, pie style, into eight veal chop–shaped wedges. Before putting into the boiling broth, flatten each wedge by pressing it firmly between your hands to ⅓ to ¼ inch thick, then drop into the pot of boiling broth.

Cover the pot, lower the heat to a simmer, and let the seitan cook for about an hour, stirring every 10 to 15 minutes.

Don't throw out the broth! Use a slotted spoon to remove each piece of seitan and place in a colander to drain. Let the seitan and the broth cool. Allow the seitan to marinate in the broth until ready to use, if time allows. Drain again before using.

10

VEGAN MEATBALLS

Makes 15 to 20 meatballs

MEATBALL SEITAN DOUGH

1½ cups vital wheat gluten

1½ cups prepared Better Than Bouillon No Beef Base (see page xvi for
how to prepare)

⅓ cup plus 2 tablespoons MimicCreme
or alternative (page 3)

1 tablespoon vegan margarine

3 cloves garlic, minced

1 teaspoon dried oregano

1½ teaspoons dried parsley

⅓ cup vegan bread crumbs

¼ cup wheat germ

3 flaxseed eggs (3 tablespoons ground
flaxseed mixed with 3 tablespoons
water; see page 29 for how to
prepare)

¼ cup Vegan Parmesan Blend (page 22)

MEATBALL BROTH

6 dried shiitake mushrooms rehydrated
in 1 cup water

7 cups prepared Better Than Bouillon
No Beef Base (see page xvi for
how to prepare)

2 tablespoons tamari

1 portobello mushroom cap, chopped

1 tablespoon garlic powder

2 teaspoons onion powder

2 bay leaves

This recipe calls for homemade seitan, but if you don't have time to make it, you can also just use prepackaged vegan beef crumbles (see page xix). Make sure you rehydrate your dried shiitakes in the 1 cup of water 30 minutes prior to making the meatball dough. Don't discard the water once they're hydrated.

Prepare the meatball seitan dough: Using a stand mixer (if you have one; by hand, if not), mix together vital wheat gluten, No Beef broth, and 2 tablespoons of the MimicCreme well.

Prepare the broth: In a large pot, bring all the meatball broth ingredients to a boil. Take the meatball dough and break off little pieces, dropping them into the boiling broth until all the dough has been used.

Cover, lower the heat to a simmer, and let cook for 1 hour. Stir every 10 minutes or so.

Place a large strainer or colander in the sink. Remove the pot from the heat and pour the contents of the pot into the strainer. Remove the bay leaves, then let the seitan and mushrooms cool to room temperature. Once cool enough to touch, use a food processor to grind up the seitan and soaked mushrooms until they're a very fine texture.

(continues)

Vegan Meatballs (continued)

In a small skillet over medium-high heat, melt the margarine and sauté the garlic for about 30 seconds. Add the garlic, oregano, and parsley to the ground seitan mixture and mix in well. Sauté for 2 to 3 minutes, then remove from the heat and set aside to cool.

Preheat the oven to 350°F and grease a baking sheet.

Once cool enough to touch, transfer the ground seitan mixture to a large bowl, then add the remaining MimicCreme, bread crumbs, wheat germ, flaxseed egg, and Parmesan. Use your hands to mix well.

Form the mixture into ½-inch balls, then bake until browned and warmed through, 15 to 20 minutes.

VEGAN CHICKEN-APPLE SAUSAGE

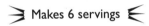
Makes 6 servings

If you lack all the equipment in the recipe, no worries—there are many variations to making the sausages. See the tip for alternative instructions.

Heat the oil in a large skillet over medium-high heat. Add the garlic and sauté 30 seconds. Add the onions, plus a pinch of salt and pepper, then sauté until the onions are translucent and beginning to brown.

Add the chicken, apples, Worcestershire, ground ginger, and lemon juice. Cook until the apples are beginning to soften.

Add the cooked rice and stir well to combine. Cook until the rice has completely warmed through. Remove from the heat.

2 tablespoons canola oil

3 cloves garlic, minced

1/2 white onion, chopped roughly

Salt and freshly ground black pepper

1 batch Chicken-Style Seitan (page 5), drained well and cut into small (1- to 2-inch) pieces

2 Gala apples, cored and chopped roughly

3 tablespoons vegan Worcestershire sauce

1 teaspoon ground ginger

Splash of freshly squeezed lemon juice

3 1/2 cups white rice cooked in prepared Better Than Bouillon No Chicken or Vegetable Base (see page xvi for how to prepare)

5 to 6 feet of vegan sausage casings (optional) (Available on eBay! See tip for alternative instructions.)

Using a meat grinder or food processor, grind the mixture to the texture of ground beef.

Using a sausage maker attachment for a KitchenAid or other sausage maker, take the sausage casings and fill each link, twisting off after each link is 6 to 7 inches long. Your sausage maker should have specific instructions as to how to make the links, so directions may vary depending on what product you use. Use as directed in the recipes throughout the book, or to eat plain, preheat your oven to 350°F. Gently slide the sausages out of their casing, then bake for 20 to 25 minutes, until golden brown.

SHAGGY KITCHEN TIP If you lack any of the equipment listed, shape the sausages by hand by rolling them out on a flat surface, then steam in a steamer basket over boiling water for 35 minutes prior to using as directed in my recipes or in one of your favorites.

CRISPY VEGAN PROSCIUTTO

 Makes about 4 servings

3 tablespoons soy sauce

2 tablespoons mirin

5 to 6 drops mesquite-flavored liquid smoke

½ teaspoon Better Than Bouillon No Beef Base dissolved in 1 tablespoon water

1 teaspoon sugar

1 teaspoon fennel seeds

1 whole star anise

4 whole cloves, crushed

Pinch of Chinese five-spice powder

8 ounces extra-firm tofu, sliced paper thin

Combine all the ingredients, except the tofu, in a large, shallow dish, then add the tofu. Allow the tofu to marinate for a few hours in the fridge.

Once you're ready to use, preheat the oven to 375°F. Lightly grease a sheet pan with olive oil, then spread out the slices of tofu evenly. Bake for 4 to 7 minutes on each side, flipping once, until browned and crispy around the edges.

VEGAN PANCETTA

Makes about 4 servings

12 ounces baked firm tofu, preferably "smoked" flavor

6 tablespoons soy sauce

2 tablespoons Bragg Liquid Aminos

4 teaspoons Better Than Bouillon No Beef Base mixed with ½ cup water

1 to 2 teaspoons Colgin Hickory-Flavored Liquid Smoke

½ teaspoon garlic powder

½ teaspoon onion powder

2 tablespoons olive oil

Slice the baked tofu into very thin slices, then dice the slices into small squares. Place the diced tofu in a shallow, airtight container.

Whisk together the rest of the ingredients very well, then pour over the diced tofu. Allow the tofu to marinate for about 2 hours.

Drain the pancetta well before using.

Keeps covered in the refrigerator for up to one week.

VEGAN BACON

⊰ Makes about 4 servings ⊱

8 ounces baked firm tofu, cut into
   bacon-size slices

4 tablespoons soy sauce

2 tablespoons Bragg Liquid Aminos

2½ tablespoons mirin

¾ teaspoon liquid smoke

½ teaspoon Better Than Bouillon No
   Beef Base mixed with 1 tablespoon water

Pinch of garlic powder

Pinch of onion powder

1 to 2 teaspoons canola oil

½ teaspoon beet powder (optional, for
   color)

Stack the tofu slices in an airtight container. Combine the rest of the ingredients well, then pour over the tofu slices. Cover and allow the tofu to marinate for a few hours in the refrigerator.

Preheat the oven to 375°F. Lightly grease a sheet pan with canola oil, then spread out the slices of tofu evenly. Bake 4 to 7 minutes on each side, flipping once, until browned.

This marinade also works well with tempeh or seitan.

SEAFOOD

SHAGGY KITCHEN TIP Dried seaweeds such as kombu and dulse are great vegan pantry essentials. You can find them at health food stores, Whole Foods Market, and Asian grocers.

BASIC SEAFOOD MARINADE

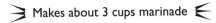 Makes about 3 cups marinade

2 teaspoons freshly squeezed lemon juice
3 cups cold water
½ tablespoon dulse
Large pinch of garlic powder
Large pinch of shallot powder
2 large stalks kombu, cut into 1-inch pieces
1 teaspoon sea salt, plus more for sprinkling over the vegan seafood
2 teaspoons mellow white miso paste

Used for making tofu scallops, vegan clams, vegan sea bass, and so on.

Place the lemon juice, water, dulse, garlic and shallot powder, and kombu in a small saucepan, and bring to a boil. Boil for a minute, then remove the pan from the heat.

Stir in the salt and miso paste until fully dissolved. Allow the mixture to sit until it reaches room temperature.

Use a mesh strainer to catch and discard the dulse and kombu, then pour the broth over the top of the vegan seafood you are using, making sure the seafood is fully submerged. Place in the refrigerator and allow to marinate for 2 to 3 hours.

Once you're ready to use, remove the seafood carefully from the marinade and drain well.

TOFU SCALLOPS

≥ Makes 14 to 16 scallops; about 6 servings ≤

1 pound extra-firm tofu
1 batch Basic Seafood Marinade (page 16)

Remove the block of tofu from its package and wrap with paper towels or highly absorbent cloth towels. Place a heavy object on top of the wrapped tofu and allow to drain for 30 minutes. Flip over the tofu, place the heavy object back on top, and allow to drain for another 30 minutes.

Discard the paper towels and place the tofu on a cutting board. Set the tofu on its long, narrow side, and slice the block into two long slabs like so:

Using half of a tea ball, a small circular cookie cutter, or a steady hand and knife, slice small scallop-shaped rounds out of the tofu as pictured.

The finished scallops should look as sexy as the pictures on the left.

Allow them to marinate overnight in the marinade, then use in any of my recipes requiring tofu scallops, or use as a replacement for real scallops in any nonvegan recipe.

VEGAN CLAMS AND CLAMSHELLS

 Makes about 40 clams, or 6 servings

CLAMS
1 pound extra-firm tofu
1 batch Basic Seafood Marinade (page 16)

CLAMSHELLS
1 batch No-Yeast Pizza Crust (page 104) or premade pizza dough, 1 French baguette, or a batch Basic Pasta Dough (page 45)

If scallops don't float your boat, you can use the same recipe to make clams. But hold onto your hat—you can make clamshells, too.

Prepare the clams: Slice the block of tofu crosswise so that you have three large rectangles. Using either a 1 cm round cookie cutter or a knife, slice small (1 cm wide) circles out of each slab of tofu.

Place the tiny circles of tofu in an airtight container, then fully submerge them in the marinade.

Once you're ready to use, drain the clams well, then use as directed in any recipe that calls for real clams.

You can keep the clams in the marinade in your refrigerator for up to one week.

Prepare the clamshells: There are three ways to make some vegan clamshells. The most important step, used in all three methods, is to find a madeleine baking pan. Then, either:

1. Preheat the oven to 350°F. Make the pizza dough recipe on page 100 or premade pizza dough, press 2 to 3 tablespoons of dough into each madeleine space on the pan, and bake for 12 to 15 minutes. Allow to cool, then slice open like a clam and hollow out each side of the shell.

2. Buy a French baguette, then cut into ½-inch thick slices. Press the slices of baguette into the madeleine mold, then trim off the excess dough to form a shell.

3. Roll out the pasta dough so that it's about $\frac{1}{16}$ inch thick, then press the dough into the madeleine mold. Carefully cut away the excess dough around the edges of the shell. Set on a floured surface to dry for about an hour, then cook in salted, boiling water until al dente.

For usage purposes, these shells are more of a garnish. For example, if you're making the Saffron, Oregano, and Garlic Chive–Infused Vegan Sea Bass, Clams, Bacon, and Beech Mushrooms in White Wine (page 61), you can use any of these methods to make clamshells that can be used for plating decoration. Not to mention they're all pretty darn tasty.

VEGAN CANNED TUNA PACKED IN OIL

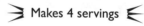 Makes 4 servings

2 (16-ounce) cans young green jackfruit packed in water (see tip)
Juice from 1 (10-ounce) jar kalamata olives (the can should read that 10 ounces is the "drained weight")
½ cup water
⅔ cup extra-virgin olive oil, plus about ¼ cup more for marinating
3 stalks kombu, broken into thirds
1 tablespoon soy sauce

I confess: I miss tuna sandwiches. There's just something about that lunchbox staple that tastes like second grade. Who knew that you could create the taste and texture with a handy li'l item called jackfruit? Jackfruit's flaky texture and flavorless yet absorbent nature makes its versatility almost endless when used as a meat substitute. All you have to do is get creative! The easiest places to find jackfruit are Asian or Indian grocers. You can use either the type that's packed in water or the one packed in brine, but beware of any jackfruit packed in syrup. It's even fruitier than I am!

(continues)

Vegan Canned Tuna Packed in Oil (continued)

Break up the jackfruit well, discarding any tough pieces of core.

Place the jackfruit, kalamata juice, water, ⅔ cup of oil, kombu, and soy sauce in a medium-size saucepan, then bring to a boil.

Boil until the liquid has reduced by half. Remove the pan from the heat and set aside to cool to room temperature.

Once cool, drain through a colander. Leave the pieces of kombu mixed with the jackfruit.

Place the jackfruit and kombu in a shallow, airtight container, then drizzle about ¼ cup more oil over the top.

Allow the tuna to marinate in the fridge for 2 to 3 hours before using.

Keeps refrigerated in an airtight container for up to one week.

VEGAN SEA BASS

 Makes about 4 servings

You'll notice that the ingredient list for this recipe is remarkably similar to that for the earlier scallops and clams recipes. The one big difference here is the type of tofu used. The silken tofu really adds the flaky effect that one would remember from taking a fork to a piece of real fish.

I pound silken tofu, drained well and sliced lengthwise into six pieces
I batch Basic Seafood Marinade (page 16)

Place the slices of tofu in a shallow, airtight container.

Pour the marinade over the top of the tofu, then allow it to marinate in the refrigerator for at least 2 hours prior to using.

Once you're ready to use, drain the tofu well, then use as directed in any recipe that calls for real sea bass.

Keeps in the marinade in your refrigerator for up to one week.

A plethora of vegan cheeses are available for purchase. Not only can they be costly, but if you don't live in the right place, they can be difficult to locate. (Beware of merely lactose-free cheeses, which contain casein [milk protein].) The easy way out is to just make them yourself! It's not only easy, but it's fun. You'll feel incredibly rewarded when you bite into a piece of pizza made entirely from scratch . . . and when your dinner guests give you a big pat on the back. Turn your kitchen into a lab space and get crackin'!

DIY VEGAN MOZZARELLA THAT MELTS!

⇒ Makes about 1½ pounds; about 24 (1-ounce) servings ⇐

1½ (12-ounce) packages silken soft tofu
1 cup MimicCreme or alternative (page 3)
½ tablespoon kosher salt
1 teaspoon garlic powder
1 teaspoon rice vinegar
4 teaspoons agar powder

Enjoy this recipe, kids. Don't be afraid of the cost of agar powder. I cook all the time, and I've yet to go through the entire eight-dollar bottle in one year.

Place the tofu, MimicCreme, salt, garlic powder, and rice vinegar in a blender or food processor, and blend at high speed until it's a completely liquid consistency. Transfer the mixture to a small saucepan, stir in the agar powder, and allow to sit for 5 minutes.

(continues)

21

DIY Vegan Mozzarella That Melts! (continued)

Bring to a boil over medium heat, stirring occasionally, then remove from the heat and pour immediately into a baking dish. Smooth the top of the mixture as if you were making a batch of brownies, then place into the refrigerator for a few hours until completely set.

Use as you would any of your favorite vegan cheeses. It shreds, slices, and even does my taxes.

Keeps covered in the refrigerator for up to eight days.

VEGAN PARMESAN BLEND

 Makes about 2 cups

> 1/3 cup raw walnut pieces
> 1/3 cup raw cashew pieces
> 3 tablespoons raw sunflower seeds
> 1/4 cup roasted sesame seeds
> 1/4 cup nutritional yeast
> 2 to 3 teaspoons kosher salt

Blend all the ingredients together in a food processor until they are completely broken up and fully combined. Taste for salt.

Keeps refrigerated in an airtight container or plastic bag for up to two months.

VEGAN RICOTTA

Makes about 1 pound; 8 servings

> 12 ounces extra-firm tofu
> 1/2 teaspoon dried basil
> 1/2 teaspoon dried oregano
> 2 teaspoons freshly squeezed lemon juice
> 1/2 teaspoon garlic powder
> 1/2 teaspoon salt
> 1/8 cup Vegan Egg Mix (page 28)

Place all ingredients in a food processor and blend until the mixture just comes together. It will be fairly light and fluffy. Be careful not to overmix into a paste.

Keeps covered in the refrigerator for up to one week.

VEGAN MASCARPONE

Makes about ¾ pound; 6 servings

1 (12-ounce) package silken soft tofu
⅛ cup MimicCreme or alternative
    (page 3)
½ teaspoon sugar

A stand mixer with a whisk attachment is ideal for this, but a strong arm and a whisk will do the job as well. Combine all the ingredients and whisk together on the highest setting possible (the setting that doesn't leave you covered in tofu chunks), until light and creamy.

Chill covered in the refrigerator until ready to use. Keeps for up to one week.

VEGAN GOAT CHEESE

Makes about 1 cup; about 6 servings

SPREADABLE CHEESE
½ cup vegan cream cheese
¼ cup vegan sour cream
1 (⅓-inch thick) slice soy feta
½ teaspoon shallot powder
Splash of freshly squeezed lemon juice
Splash of vermouth
Salt

To prepare spreadable goat cheese: Place all the ingredients except the salt in a medium-size bowl and use a spoon to blend together well. Add salt to taste.

Chill covered in the refrigerator until ready to use. Keeps for up to two weeks.

(continues)

Vegan Goat Cheese (continued)

SOLID CHEESE

½ cup vegan cream cheese

¼ cup vegan sour cream

5 ounces extra-firm tofu

1 (⅓-inch thick) slice soy feta

1 teaspoon shallot powder

2 splashes of freshly squeezed lemon juice

2 splashes of vermouth

¼ cup water

½ teaspoon salt

4 teaspoons agar powder

To prepare solid goat cheese: Prepare a greased 8-inch square baking dish or cake pan.

Blend all the ingredients, *except* the agar powder, in a food processor instead of by hand, then place in a small saucepan. Sprinkle the agar powder on top and mix in well.

Let the mixture sit for 5 minutes, then bring to a boil over medium-high heat, stirring constantly.

Remove from the heat, pour into a prepared baking dish, and allow to cool for a few moments. Place in the refrigerator overnight to set.

Keeps covered in the refrigerator for up to one week.

VEGAN FONTINA

Makes about ⅔ cup

½ cup medium-firm tofu, drained well

1 teaspoon Dr-Cow Aged Tree Nut Cheese (any flavor) or homemade nut-based hard cheese

1 teaspoon freshly squeezed lemon juice

⅛ teaspoon jarred minced garlic, or 1 clove pressed or finely minced garlic

¼ teaspoon stone-ground mustard

½ teaspoon salt

Pinch of shallot powder

Grate the block of tofu with a cheese grater, then place in a food processor with all the other ingredients. Use the pulse function of the food processor until the ingredients are fully combined.

Keeps covered in the refrigerator for up to one week.

VEGAN CRÈME FRAÎCHE

≥ Makes 1 cup ≤

⅔ cup MimicCreme or Vegan Buttermilk (page 4)
⅓ cup plain soy yogurt

Mix the MimicCreme and plain soy yogurt together well, and leave out (unrefrigerated) for 12 hours. Yes, you read that correctly. It won't kill you—I promise.

Keeps covered in the refrigerator for up to one week.

VEGAN COOL WHIP

≥ Makes about 1½ cups ≤

5 tablespoons vegan shortening
1 (8-ounce) container vegan cream cheese
⅔ cup cornstarch
¼ cup MimicCreme or alternative (page 3)
¾ cup confectioners' sugar

Using a stand mixer with the whip attachment or a hand mixer, beat all the ingredients in a large bowl at low speed until just combined.

Once the dry ingredients are out of the Danger Zone (a.k.a. mixed in completely), whip the mixture on the highest setting possible for 5 to 10 minutes, or until the mixture forms peaks when whipped.

Chill in the refrigerator for at least an hour to set prior to use. Keeps refrigerated for 7 to 10 days.

Eggs are the quintessential American breakfast food. I can't even count on ten hands how many times I've ordered a tofu scramble, and been served improperly cooked, bland tofu sautéed with a combination of vegetables. If I'm lucky, the chef decided to add some salt. If I'm really lucky, there's some hot sauce on the table.

As you can probably tell, I don't tend to stand by passively. I tinkered around in my kitchen laboratory until I found a method that suited my madness. What follows in this section is not only a recipe that kicks all those supposed tofu scrambles to the curb, but also a useful guide for veganizing your favorite recipes that call for egg yolks.

Here's how to make some really realistic vegan eggs.

VEGAN SCRAMBLED EGGS

≷ Makes 6 servings ≶

If you are using this in place of beaten eggs in a recipe, follow the basic directions. If you are making plain old scrambled "eggs," add the extra-firm tofu to the food processor at the very end, and just pulse a few times until it's broken up.

1 (12-ounce) package silken soft tofu

1 (12-ounce) package silken extra-firm tofu

¼ cup MimicCreme or alternative (page 3)

¾ cup Vegan Egg Mix (page 28)

1 tablespoon mellow white miso paste dissolved in 1 tablespoon hot water

Pinch of garlic powder

Pinch of turmeric

Pinch of yellow mustard powder

2 pinches of curry powder

1½ teaspoons black Indian salt, or to taste

About 1 tablespoon Nature's Flavors orange food coloring (optional)

Blend all the ingredients in a food processor. Taste for salt. Heat a skillet with a little vegan margarine or canola oil over medium-high heat. Sauté some veggies or fake meats of your choosing for a minute or two. Pour in the scrambled egg mixture and cook until it begins to brown and is heated through.

There aren't any rules here. You can use this basic recipe as you would in a quiche, any scramble recipe, you name it! Get creative.

VEGAN EGG MIX

> Makes about 25 servings <

1/3 cup raw walnut pieces
1/3 cup raw cashew pieces
3 tablespoons raw sunflower seeds
1/4 cup roasted sesame seeds
1/4 cup nutritional yeast
2 to 3 teaspoons kosher salt
Pinch of garlic powder
Pinch of turmeric
Pinch of yellow mustard powder

I make big batches of this at once, then store it in airtight bags so I don't have to make it all the time. It's easy and cheap, especially if your local natural foods grocer has a bulk bin section.

Blend all the ingredients in a food processor until they just start to stick together. The mixture should smell and taste "eggy" to you when you're finished. Omit the last three ingredients to make a bitchin' Parmesan substitute. Also great when sprinkled on tofu when making a scramble. Keeps covered in the refrigerator for up to two months.

VEGAN EGG YOLK MIX

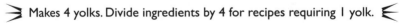

> Makes 4 yolks. Divide ingredients by 4 for recipes requiring 1 yolk. <

1/2 cup MimicCreme or alternative
  (page 3)
8 teaspoons Vegan Egg Mix (page 28)
1/2 teaspoon turmeric
1/2 teaspoon yellow mustard powder

I use this often as a substitution for eggs and their binding effect in my recipes. Like I said: Make a big batch of Vegan Egg Mix. It really comes in handy.

Blend all the ingredients together well. Allow to chill in the refrigerator at least 30 minutes before serving. Keeps for up to one week in the refrigerator.

FLAXSEED EGG

 Makes 1 flaxseed egg (equal to one chicken egg)

1 tablespoon golden/yellow flaxseeds
1 tablespoon water

Flaxseed eggs have been a vegan replacement for ages. They're super easy to make, and can be thrown right into your recipe.

First, you need to grind the flaxseeds into a fine powder. I find that the best kitchen device for doing so is a coffee grinder, but you can also use a mortar and pestle or food processor.

Once the flaxseeds are ground into a powder, combine with the water until a thick (okay, egglike) consistency is obtained.

Use in my recipes as directed, or as a replacement for eggs when they are used within a recipe as a binding agent (not for egg flavor). See Vegan Scrambled Eggs and Vegan Egg Mix (pages 27 and 28) for egg alternatives that can be eaten like eggs.

2

RECIPES GUARANTEED TO GET YOU LAID

JENN SHAGGY'S GUIDE TO COOKING AND SHAGGING

I tend to be a very blunt, honest individual . . . unless I'm kissing someone's ass for selfish reasons. I firmly believe and boldly put forth the following three statements:

1. Everyone likes food. Don't let anyone try to tell you otherwise. They are probably lying to you due to ulterior motives, like denying they stole your missing leftovers from the fridge.
2. Everyone likes sex.
3. Walking in the front door after a long day at work to find my beloved preparing me a special meal is enough to make both my jaw and panties drop to the floor.

The correlations between food and sex are present in many areas of world culture, the exhibition of which varies from the sweet and innocent to the downright

Everyone deserves to be spoiled once in a while, whether you're treating yourself or someone special in your life. This chapter contains veganized versions of recipes you might find at fine dining establishments, sure to intrigue the adventurous home chef without being overwhelming.

pornographic. When we were children, such films as *Lady and the Tramp* with the classic spaghetti slurp kiss gently introduced us to the seductive elements of food and dining.

As we grew older, we learned the aphrodisiacal qualities of such delicacies as chocolate-covered strawberries. Or perhaps you saw the episode of *Seinfeld* where George decided that eating beneath the bedsheets during a coital interlude was exactly what he needed to *spice* up his sex life.

Regardless of our unique personal experiences, I think we can all blush a little and admit to ourselves that garlic breath isn't necessarily a turnoff after a fantastic meal à deux. Whether you're a carnivore trying to seduce that cute vegan coed in your Women's Studies lecture, or you're an omnivore who needs to get back in her husband's good graces after accidently throwing away his PETA newsletter, the recipes in this chapter are guaranteed to get you laid.

HEIRLOOM CANNELLINI BEANS WITH SAGE, CRISPY VEGAN PROSCIUTTO, AND FAVA BEAN PESTO RAGOUT

> Makes 4 large or 6 small servings

I come from a small town in northeastern Ohio called Youngstown. When I tell most people where I was raised, they usually have no clue where Youngstown is located. On the off chance that someone has heard of it, it's usually because they "drove through Youngstown once" or caught a CNN broadcast of an escape from one of the many maximum security prisons there.

Of course they just drove through it—nobody in their right mind stops to smell the roses there. You might get shot. Seriously—Youngstown was Murder City USA per capita for several years back in the '90s. At least now y'all know why I'm so gangsta.

Nonetheless, Y-Town is my town. Terrible place to be a vegan, but a great place for Italian food. You see, Youngstown was a steel town. Its economic heyday was back in the early part of the last century, when the steel mills were booming and vaudeville acts made it a regular destination. As a result of the burgeoning steel industry, many immigrants migrated there hoping to have an easier time finding work—bringing with them the cuisine of their native country.

Today, downtown Youngstown is not the most beautiful sight. Abandoned steel mills litter the landscape, and it was recently rated number 2 on Forbes's America's Fastest Dying Cities list. But! The great food never left. That's right—I was fortunate enough to grow up with a taste for amazing Tuscan and Sicilian cuisine right in the heart of the Midwest. Stay alive (if garlicky), Youngstown—XOXO.

Prepare the pesto: First, have ready a large bowl of ice water. If you're luckier than I am and have ice-cold tap water, this will also do the trick. Blanch the beans in salted boiling water for 1 minute, then shock them in the ice bath. Peel off the second skin (the tough gray/brown coating).

(continues)

Heirloom Cannellini Beans with Sage . . . (continued)

FAVA BEAN PESTO

1 cup fresh fava beans, first layer of skins removed (see tip)

4 teaspoons freshly squeezed lemon juice

1 tablespoon pumpkin seeds, toasted

1 tablespoon slivered almonds, toasted

¾ cup extra-virgin olive oil

12 leaves fresh basil

3 to 4 leaves fresh mint

1 to 2 cloves garlic (depending on how much you like garlic)

Salt and freshly ground black pepper

CANNELLINI BEANS WITH RAGOUT

2 cups fresh heirloom cannellini beans, or 2 (15-ounce) cans, rinsed and drained

3 bay leaves

4 cloves garlic: 3 whole and 1 minced

3 tablespoons extra-virgin olive oil

2 tablespoons fresh sage, chopped

1 tablespoon fresh thyme leaves, chopped

¾ cup Fava Bean Pesto

1 (15-ounce) can diced tomatoes with juices (fire roasted are my favorite!)

Juice of 1 lemon

Salt and freshly ground black pepper

1 pound pasta of your choice, cooked al dente

8 ounces Crispy Vegan Prosciutto (page 14), diced

Throw all the pesto ingredients in a blender or food processor, then show them who's the boss. Once pureed to a smooth texture, season with salt and pepper to taste. Store in the fridge until ready to use.

SHAGGY KITCHEN TIP You'll notice the terms *blanch* and *shock* in many recipe instructions. *Blanching*, also referred to as *parboiling*, is a fancy-shmancy chef's word meaning "to immerse uncooked vegetables in boiling water for a short length of time."

Shocking, also snazzy kitchen lingo, simply means plunging cooked veggies or pasta into ice water to halt the cooking process. An ice bath (a.k.a. a bowl of ice water) is prepared in advance to perform the shocking process.

WARNING: SOME INDIVIDUALS HAVE A RARE BUT DANGEROUS REACTION TO FAVA BEANS.

Prepare the cannellini beans: Allow the beans to soak in a copious amount of water overnight. Then drain them well, and place in a large pot and cover with water by about 3 inches. Bring the water to a boil, then add the bay leaves and 3 whole garlic cloves. Lower the heat to a simmer and cook for about 2 hours, or until the desired tenderness is achieved.

Once the beans are finished cooking, drain well and remove the bay leaves. I leave the garlic cloves in, but you can remove them, if you desire.

Heat the olive oil in a large, deep skillet over medium heat. Add the minced garlic, sage, and thyme, and sauté for about 30 seconds. Add the Fava Bean Pesto and canned tomatoes, mix well, and allow to simmer for 3 to 4 minutes, stirring once or twice. Add the beans and lemon juice, and allow to simmer for another 3 to 4 minutes. Season with salt and pepper to taste.

Serve over the pasta and top with the prosciutto.

Voilà!

PINEAPPLE FIVE-SPICE BUN WITH PINEAPPLE-ORANGE SHERRY-GLAZED TOFU

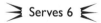 Serves 6

Sometimes the heat in Los Angeles has me shvitzing like a bubbe in menopause. I'll be the one sweating my tuchas off for no reason while all my friends lounge about in tube tops and hot pants. Okay, maybe my friends really aren't that scantily clad, but you get the point.

Anyway, we all need a recipe that helps us take the heat so we don't have to "get out tha kitchen."

I absolutely love Vietnamese food. Their use of fresh herbs and satisfying yet mild flavors really tickles my taste buds. This is a snazzy version of the traditional Vietnamese dish bun thit nuong, *which is a yummy chilled rice noodle dish.*

And in case you were wondering, I've yet to break a sweat after devouring a bowl.

(continues)

Pineapple Five-Spice Bun with Pineapple-Orange Sherry-Glazed Tofu (continued)

SAUCE

½ cup vegan brown sugar

¼ cup mirin

½ cup freshly squeezed lime juice

½ cup low-sodium soy sauce

2 teaspoons Chinese five-spice powder

GLAZED TOFU

⅛ cup sugar

¼ cup fresh pineapple juice

⅛ cup freshly squeezed orange juice

Zest of 1 orange (see tip)

1½ tablespoons sherry vinegar

⅙ cup plus 1½ tablespoons grape seed or canola oil

½ cup fresh pineapple, diced

8 ounces extra-firm tofu, sliced

NOODLES

1 carrot, sliced thinly

1½ cups kale, chopped

8 ounces vermicelli rice noodles

½ cup fresh basil, chopped

½ cup fresh mint, chopped

1 cup bean sprouts

½ cucumber, julienned

⅓ cup fresh cilantro, for garnish

3 tablespoons chopped peanuts, for garnish (optional)

Prepare the sauce: Place all the ingredients in a medium-size saucepan, and heat over medium-high heat until the sugar is completely dissolved. Set aside to cool.

Prepare the tofu: In a saucepan, heat the sugar and 1 tablespoon of water over medium-high heat. Boil for 1 to 2 minutes, stirring constantly, then remove the pan from the heat. Mix in the pineapple juice, orange juice, and orange zest, return to the heat and bring to a boil, then boil for 1 minute, still continually stirring. Remove from the heat again, add the vinegar and the ⅙ cup of oil, mix well to combine, and set aside.

In a large skillet over high heat, heat an additional tablespoon of oil. Grill the pineapple until golden brown, then remove from the pan and set aside until you're ready to toss it with the noodles.

Add the last ½ tablespoon of oil to the pan, heat completely, then add the tofu. Heat the tofu for 3 to 4 minutes on each side, until golden brown. Carefully add the glaze to the pan and, flipping after 2 to 3 minutes, and simmer the tofu in the sauce until all the liquid has completely reduced.

SHAGGY KITCHEN TIP The *zest* of a citrus fruit refers to the outer peel (colored flesh). Just underneath the zest is the pith (the bitter white part). When a recipe calls for the zest of a citrus fruit, it indicates that you should remove only the outer peel, and not the pith, by carefully using a knife or citrus zester. In my opinion, the Microplane company manufactures an effective, well-priced zester that every home chef should own.

Prepare the noodles: Start two pots of water boiling—one for blanching the veggies, the other for the noodles. Prepare another bowl of ice water (or again, if your tap water is cool enough, this will work for shocking).

Using a strainer, dip the carrots into one pot of the boiling water for 1 minute; leaving the pot still boiling on the stove, transfer the carrots to the ice bath. At this point, if you find you've begun to shvitz as well, plunge your face into the ice bath with the carrots. Depending on how strict you are, though, this may destroy the "veganness" of your recipe.

Using the strainer, dip the kale into boiling water for 10 seconds, then transfer to the ice bath. Drain both the carrots and kale well, and set aside. Cook the noodles in the other pot of boiling water for $1\frac{1}{2}$ to 2 minutes, then drain well and rinse with ice-cold water. Drain again, then set aside.

Once drained, mix well with the grilled pineapple, carrots, kale, basil, mint, bean sprouts, and sauce. Top with the glazed tofu and garnish with cucumber, cilantro, and crushed peanuts. Serve.

VEGAN GOAT CHEESE, SPINACH, AND SUN-DRIED TOMATO–STUFFED PORK CHOPS WITH ROASTED GARLIC FINGERLING POTATOES AND PEARL ONIONS

⇒ Serves 6 ⇐

STUFFED PORK CHOPS

2 tablespoons olive oil

2 cloves garlic, minced

6 sun-dried tomatoes, diced

1 (10-ounce) bag frozen spinach, thawed and moisture squeezed out, or 6 cups fresh spinach leaves, washed well

½ teaspoon salt

½ teaspoon freshly ground black pepper

¼ teaspoon dried thyme

¼ cup Vegan Goat Cheese (page 23)

1 batch Pork Chop–Style Seitan (page 7)

1½ cups prepared Better Than Bouillon No Chicken Base (see page xvi for how to prepare)

Zest of ½ lemon (see page 37 for how to zest a lemon)

2 tablespoons freshly squeezed lemon juice

2 teaspoons Dijon mustard

Prepare the stuffed pork chops: Warm 1 tablespoon of the olive oil in a medium-size sauté pan over medium heat. Add the garlic and cook until fragrant, about 1 minute. Add the sun-dried tomatoes, spinach, salt, pepper, and thyme. Cook for about 2 more minutes. Transfer the mixture to a medium-size bowl. Add the goat cheese and stir well. Set aside.

Using a sharp knife, carefully cut a pocket into the thickest portion of each pork chop. Stuff each pocket with one-quarter of the spinach mixture. Season the outside of the pork with salt and pepper.

In a small bowl combine the No Chicken broth, lemon zest, lemon juice, and mustard.

Warm the remaining 1 tablespoon of olive oil in a large, heavy skillet over medium-high heat. When the pan is hot, add the pork. Cook until golden and cooked through, about 4 minutes per side.

POTATOES AND ONIONS
15 pearl onions
5 cloves garlic, chopped
⅓ cup olive oil
⅓ cup fresh chervil, chopped
1½ tablespoons fresh sage, chopped
Salt and freshly ground black pepper
1 pound fingerling potatoes, washed
    and scrubbed, skin on

Transfer the pork to a dish and tent with foil to keep warm. Add the chicken broth mixture to the skillet and cook over medium-high heat. Scrape up the brown bits from the bottom of the pan as the broth simmers. Allow the broth to simmer until it has reduced by half, which takes 8 to 10 minutes. Spoon some broth over the pork before serving.

Prepare the potatoes and onions: Preheat the oven to 375°F.

Bring a medium-size pot of water to a boil, and blanch onions for 1 minute. Drain, then allow to cool. Using a paring knife, remove the root end of the pearl onions, and peel off the skins. Set aside.

Take an oven-safe heavy metal baking dish, place the pearl onions, garlic, olive oil, chervil, and sage in the baking dish, then toss together with salt and pepper to taste. Place the dish in the oven and allow to heat. When the baking dish is hot, add the potatoes. They should sizzle if the pan is hot enough. Roast until they turn brown, then lower the oven temperature to 350°F. Bake for about 30 minutes, or until a knife easily pierces the skins of the potatoes and their insides are softened.

ORZO WITH VEGAN CHICKEN-APPLE SAUSAGE, ASPARAGUS, BABY TOMATOES, AND VEGAN RICOTTA SALATA IN A WHITE TOMATO SAUCE

⋛ Serves 6 ⋜

WHITE TOMATO SAUCE
¼ cup olive oil
¼ cup white onion, diced finely
3 large or 4 small white or yellow heirloom tomatoes, chopped roughly, juices reserved
¼ cup white wine
3 cloves garlic, minced
I bay leaf
½ teaspoon red pepper flakes
Salt and freshly ground black pepper

SHAGGY KITCHEN TIP Depending on the type of vegan sausage casing you use, the cooking methods the casing will allow may vary. Check the casing instructions first to be sure they can endure high heat. If not, *or* if you're using premade sausages, slide the uncooked sausage out of the casing, slice and fry as the recipe indicates.

Prepare the sauce: Heat the oil in a large saucepan over medium heat, then add the onions and sauté for 30 seconds. Add the tomatoes and their juices, and stir/mash the tomatoes as you go along. If you have an immersion blender, use it now to puree almost all the tomatoes. If you don't, just smash with a potato masher or good wooden spatula.

Once the tomatoes are warmed through and smashed, add the white wine, garlic, bay leaf, red pepper flakes, and a touch of salt and pepper. Bring the sauce to a boil, then lower the heat to a fast simmer.

Allow the sauce to simmer until it has reduced by half, about an hour.

Taste for salt and pepper. The sauce shouldn't be overly salty, as White Tomatoes tend to have a sweeter taste.

ORZO WITH SAUSAGE

2 links Vegan Chicken-Apple Sausage
  (page 12) or packaged vegan
  sausage (see tip)

1 bunch asparagus

2 tablespoons olive oil, plus more for
  roasting the asparagus

Salt and freshly ground black pepper

3 cups prepared Better Than Bouillon
  No Chicken or Vegetable Base
  (see page xvi for how to prepare)

3 cups water

1 tablespoon kosher salt, plus more for
  sprinkling on asparagus

1 pound orzo

2 cloves garlic, minced

1 cup baby cherry tomatoes

1 batch White Tomato Sauce (page 40)

2 tablespoons chervil, chopped finely

1 tablespoon fresh flat-leaf parsley,
  chopped

1/4 batch Vegan Ricotta (page 22)

Prepare the orzo with sausage: Preheat the oven to 250°F.

Bake the sausages for 30 minutes, then raise the oven temperature to 350°F and bake for an additional 30 minutes, until firm. Remove the sausages from the oven, leaving the oven on, and set aside to cool. Once cool, slice into bite-size pieces.

Line a roasting pan with aluminum foil, then lay out the asparagus evenly. Brush each spear lightly with oil, then sprinkle with salt and pepper to taste.

Roast for 10 to 15 minutes, until soft, shaking the roasting pan once or twice throughout the roasting process. Once the stalks begin to brown, remove from the oven and set aside to cool.

In a medium-size saucepan, bring the No Chicken broth, water, and kosher salt to a boil. Add the orzo, and cool until al dente.

While the pasta is cooking, heat the 2 tablespoons of oil in a large skillet over medium-high heat. Add and sauté the sausage until cooked through and browning, about 4 minutes. Add the garlic and asparagus, and cook for 2 to 3 minutes until all heated through.

Drain the orzo well. Place in a large bowl, then toss with cherry tomatoes, sausage mixture, White Tomato Sauce, chervil, and parsley. Taste for salt and pepper. Crumble and top with the ricotta salata and serve.

COCONUT VINEGAR–CURED TOFU SCALLOPS WITH LEMONGRASS-BASIL CREAM SAUCE AND CILANTRO-GARLIC COCONUT RICE

> Makes 4 large or 6 small servings ≼

SCALLOPS

1 batch Tofu Scallops (page 17)
1/2 cup tightly packed cilantro sprigs, chopped finely
1/3 cup fresh mint leaves, finely chopped
1 cup coconut vinegar (substitute brown rice vinegar if you can't find it)
1/4 cup freshly squeezed lime juice
Small handful of brown mustard seeds
1/2 teaspoon sea salt
A few grinds of mixed peppercorns
2 to 3 tablespoons vegan margarine
Freshly cracked black pepper

COCONUT RICE

1/8 cup fresh cilantro leaves, chopped finely
2 cloves garlic, sliced
1/2 teaspoon salt
2 cups long-grain white rice
1 1/2 cups coconut milk
2 cups filtered water

Prepare the scallops: Place the scallops in a long, shallow container or plastic bag, and set aside.

In a medium-size bowl, combine the cilantro, mint, coconut vinegar, lime juice, brown mustard seeds, salt, and pepper. Whisk well to combine.

Pour the mixture over the scallops and place tightly covered in refrigerator for 3 to 4 hours, flipping the scallops after 1 1/2 hours.

Carefully drain the scallops.

In a large, heavy skillet over medium-high heat, heat the margarine until fully melted. Place the scallops in the skillet and season with salt and pepper. Carefully sear the scallops on each side until golden brown, making sure to roll them around a bit on the curved sides as well.

Remove the scallops from the pan and set aside, lowering the heat under the skillet to low.

Prepare the rice: Place the rice, cilantro sprigs, garlic, and salt in your rice cooker. Add the coconut milk and water, and stir well with a wooden or plastic spoon.

SAUCE

½ tablespoon vegan margarine

1 shallot, minced

1 clove fresh garlic, minced

⅓ cup vermouth

⅓ cup lemongrass stalks, chopped finely and outer layers discarded

1 cup fresh chiffonaded basil leaves (see tip)

¾ cup MimicCreme or soy creamer

½ cup prepared Better Than Bouillon No Chicken Base (see page xvi for how to prepare)

1 tablespoon freshly squeezed lemon juice

About ¼ teaspoon salt

Coarsely ground peppercorns

SHAGGY KITCHEN TIP To "chiffonade" an herb or leafy green means to slice it into long, thin ribbons. This can be done simply by stacking the fresh leaves on top of each other, then rolling them up like a scroll (or joint, if that makes more sense). Once rolled up, use either a knife or pair of kitchen shears to slice the leaves into ribbons.

Place the lid on the rice cooker and set the device to "Cook" mode. Most rice cookers will take 20 to 30 minutes to finish the cooking process.

After the "Cook" mode switches off, leave the rice cooker on "Warm" mode for about 10 minutes to finish the cooking process and obtain that great sticky quality.

Alternatively, if you do not own a rice cooker, cook the rice on your stove top as directed by the package instructions, substituting the coconut milk for some of the recommended amount of water. Make sure you add the cilantro, garlic, and salt when you add the liquid prior to cooking.

Prepare the sauce: Add the ½ tablespoon of margarine to the pan and let it melt—it'll happen quickly, so keep your eye on it. Add the shallots and garlic to the skillet and sauté for 5 minutes, stirring frequently.

Raise the heat to medium, add the vermouth, and allow it to deglaze the pan. Add the lemongrass, basil, MimicCreme, broth, lemon juice, salt, and pepper. Cook over medium heat until reduced by about half. Taste for salt and pepper.

Serve over the scallops and rice.

MAKING FRESH PASTA:
BECAUSE EVERYONE LOOKS SEXIER
COVERED IN FLOUR

FRESH PASTA

Back in the day, when I was just a little Shaglet, someone in my house was always in the kitchen. My mother and father are both great cooks and bakers. Most kids gain the freshman fifteen when they move away from home. I lost the Shagrin fifteen when I moved away.

My father loved to make homemade fresh pasta and sauce. Many a Sunday morning began with the smell of simmering tomatoes and olive oil seeping into my bedroom. That smell was the *only* smell that would rouse me out of bed before noon.

I knew that smell meant Dad was making fresh pasta, and I always loved to help. He had one of those nifty pasta machines that would flatten and slice the dough into whatever shape he wanted. Even ravioli! Sometimes I wish I had one of those machines when I make this recipe, but I always feel like a little Italian Mama doing it myself, and now you can, too!

So thank you, dear Father, for inspiring me to make fresh pasta. I now know how great it must have felt to see our joyful little sauce-covered faces slurping up dinner!

VEGANIZE THIS! HOMEMADE PASTA GUIDE

Now, let's get down to business. If you have a pasta maker, you're one step ahead of many of us. Technically, *pasta* is Italian for "dough." The dough can be made from the simplest of ingredients (flour and water), but many restaurants offering fresh pasta add eggs to their recipes. Some even add weird things like squid ink to produce black pasta noodles.

As a vegan, we often have to pass on fresh pasta noodles at Italian joints. But with a little elbow grease and Janis Joplin blasting in the background, making pasta can be a great, rewarding experience. And it's a darn cheap way to impress your dinner guests.

BASIC PASTA DOUGH

≥ Makes 6 servings ≤

1 ⅛ cups semolina flour (if you can't find semolina or bread flour, use 2 ⅛ cups all-purpose flour)

1 cup bread flour

½ teaspoon salt (optional)

½ cup lukewarm water, plus an extra ⅛ to ¼ cup for kneading the dough

1 tablespoon olive oil (optional)

In a large bowl, mix both of the flours and salt well. Using your fist, make a well in the center.

Combine the water and the olive oil. Then use one hand to slowly pour into the well, while using the other hand to slowly incorporate the wet into the dry. Once all the liquid has been poured into the well, get dirty, using both hands to knead a tough dough, adding more water if needed. You'll know the dough is done when it's firm and holding together, not flaking apart, when you knead it.

Place on a large, lightly floured surface and knead for about 5 minutes until the dough is smooth. If it's tearing or breaking apart, add a touch more water and keep your hands wet, then knead again for 5 minutes. Separate the dough into two balls and wrap each ball in a slightly damp cloth. Set aside for 20 minutes and give yourself, and the dough, a much needed rest.

Now flour your work surface well. Using a rolling pin (or any solid, cylindrical object like a wine bottle or baseball bat—just please clean them first), roll out the pasta into sheets, flipping the dough over occasionally during the process. At this point, the dough can be used to make:

- Lasagna
- Ravioli (page 47)
- Fettuccine (cut into strips)
- Spaghetti (cut thin strips and roll them gently)
- Tortellini

(continues)

Basic Pasta Dough (continued)

For more difficult or shaped pastas, a pasta maker will be your best friend. Let's just keep it simple for now.

Bring a large pot of salted water to a boil, then carefully drop in your noodles and allow to cook until al dente. Serve with your sauce of choice.

Be sure to lower the heat to a fast simmer if cooking filled pasta.

VEGAN EGGPLANT PARMESAN RAVIOLI WITH HEIRLOOM TOMATO, STRAWBERRY, AND CHOCOLATE MARINARA

Makes 4 large or 6 small servings

MARINARA
6 pounds heirloom tomatoes, peeled and chopped
30 small, fresh strawberries, hulled
1½ tablespoons olive oil
1½ tablespoons minced garlic
2 teaspoons salt
½ teaspoon cracked black pepper
3 (1-ounce) squares 100% cacao dark chocolate
3 tablespoons tomato paste
½ cup fresh basil, chopped
¼ cup fresh parsley, chopped

Strawberry Chocolate Marinara?! What? Trust me. The strawberry and chocolate provide unique subtle, aromatic undertones. This sauce kills two PMS cravings with one stone: comfort food and chocolate!

Prepare the marinara: First, dip each tomato in a pot of boiling water for 1 minute, then gently remove the skins. Chop them up, put them in a bowl, and set aside.

Puree the strawberries in a food processor with 1½ tablespoons of water. Set aside.

Heat the oil in a large saucepan over medium heat. Add the garlic, then cook for 2 minutes, stirring frequently.

RAVIOLI

I pound eggplant, roasted, peeled, and halved (see tip)

10 ounces extra-firm tofu

I teaspoon dried oregano

I teaspoon dried sweet basil

I to 2 cloves garlic

I tablespoon olive oil

I to 2 teaspoons salt

Freshly ground black pepper

I batch Basic Pasta Dough (page 45)

¼ cup vegan bread crumbs

Soy milk, enough for sealing the ravioli

Add the chopped tomatoes, strawberry puree, salt, and pepper, then bring to a boil.

Once boiling, lower the heat to a simmer and stir in the chocolate.

Simmer for 25 minutes, then add the tomato paste. Once the tomato paste is fully integrated, add the basil and parsley.

Let the sauce simmer over low heat while you do the rest of the work for the recipe. If it takes you more than an hour to do the rest, turn off the heat and rewarm before serving.

Prepare the ravioli: To make the filling, place all the ingredients except the pasta dough, bread crumbs, and soy milk, in a food processor. Blend well. Place in a bowl and refrigerate until ready to use.

Roll the dough out into long rectangular sheets, then cut the sheets into an even amount of squares, using a knife or square cookie cutter. Stir the bread crumbs into the filling, then use a teaspoon to measure and drop a dollop of the filling into the center of half of the cut pasta squares.

Dip your index finger into the soy milk, then brush around the dollop of filling to provide a gluelike sealant. Place the remaining squares on top of the filled pasta squares and press down firmly around the filling to seal well and push out any air bubbles.

Bring a large pot of salted water to a boil, then lower the heat to a fast simmer. Carefully drop in a few ravioli at a time, and let them cook until they rise to the top.

Drain the ravioli, top with marinara, and serve.

SHAGGY KITCHEN TIP Cooking eggplant intimidates some people. But I've never met an eggplant I couldn't wrestle to the ground. Here's an easy way to roast eggplant:

Preheat the oven to 350°F. Using a fork, pierce the eggplant in several places. Drizzle on and rub with a healthy coat of olive oil, then roast it whole and un-peeled on a baking sheet until it's soft and starting to collapse, about an hour.

Allow it to cool, then scoop out the flesh and place in a bowl. Set aside until ready to use.

PAN-ROASTED TEMPEH WITH WHITE BEAN BROTH, CILANTRO PESTO, AND ROASTED SHALLOTS WITH SAUTÉED KALE

> Serves 6 <

I have a big enough Jewish nose, so I'm not going to lie. I stole parts of this recipe from Bobby Flay. Call me crazy, but there's something sweetly satisfying about veganizing the creation of a man that prides himself on his animal-grilling abilities. Bring it, Mr. Flay. I'm ready for a cruelty-free throw-down.

Make sure you prepare the tempeh before making the broth. Some of the cooking of the tempeh is incorporated into the bean broth preparation.

PESTO
2 cups tightly packed fresh cilantro leaves
2 tablespoons pumpkin seeds
2 cloves garlic
3 tablespoons freshly squeezed lime juice
½ cup olive oil
¼ cup Dr-Cow Aged Tree Nut Cheese, grated, or Vegan Parmesan Blend (page 22)
Salt and freshly ground black pepper

Prepare the pesto: Get this one out of the way first, and stick it in the fridge until ready to plate.

Combine all the ingredients, except the salt and pepper, in a food processor, and blend until smooth. Add salt and pepper to taste.

Prepare the tempeh: Take drained tempeh and rub with rosemary, salt, and pepper. In a large sauté pan, heat the oil over medium heat, add the tempeh, and cook for 3 to 5 minutes on each side, until golden brown.

TEMPEH

6 (6-ounce) blocks tempeh, sliced

2 teaspoons dried rosemary

Salt and freshly ground black pepper

1 to 2 tablespoons olive oil

WHITE BEAN BROTH

5 cups water

1¼ cup low-sodium vegetable broth

¼ plus ⅛ cup mirin

3 tablespoons Au Lac Vegetarian Fish Sauce, or 1½ tablespoons soy sauce plus 1½ tablespoons Bragg Liquid Aminos

2 tablespoons rice wine vinegar

2 tablespoons tamari

Handful of dried shiitake mushrooms (8 to 10)

3 shallots, peeled, and sliced

Olive oil, enough for roasting the shallots

1 tablespoon mellow white miso paste

1 cup cooked white beans

2 ancho chiles, soaked, seeded and julienned (optional)

1 tablespoon agave nectar

Salt (optional)

Freshly ground black pepper

SAUTÉED KALE

3 tablespoons olive oil

2 to 3 cloves garlic, sliced thinly

½ cup low-sodium vegetable broth

2 tablespoons red wine vinegar

1½ pounds young fresh kale, chopped coarsely

Salt and freshly ground black pepper

Prepare the bean broth: Preheat the oven or a toaster oven to 375°F.

Place the water, vegetable broth, mirin, fish sauce, vinegar, tamari, and shiitakes in a large saucepot. Bring to a boil, uncovered.

While you're waiting for the broth to boil, roast the shallots by drizzling with olive oil (I also like to add a little fresh or dried rosemary), and placing in the preheated oven for 5 to 10 minutes, until softened.

Once the broth comes to a boil, add the miso paste, stir until dissolved, then cover with a lid. When the broth has reduced by one-third, add the sliced tempeh to the broth. Cover, and let the tempeh boil for 10 to 12 minutes.

Using tongs, transfer the tempeh to a colander. Set the colander in the sink or over a towel and let drain. Allow the broth to continue boiling, covered, until it has reduced by half.

Add the beans, shallots, and chiles (if using), and cook for 5 minutes.

Add the agave, and season with salt (if desired) and pepper to taste. Keep covered over low heat until ready to serve.

Prepare the kale: Heat the olive oil in a large saucepan over medium-high heat. Add the garlic and cook until soft but not yet browning. Raise the heat to high, add the vegetable broth and kale, then toss well. Cover and cook for 5 minutes. Remove the

(continues)

Pan-Roasted Tempeh . . . (continued)

lid, and continue to cook and stir until all the liquid has evaporated. Add the vinegar, and salt and pepper to taste. To serve, place a mound of the kale in the bottom of a bowl. Top with the tempeh, ladle with broth, then top with a dollop of pesto.

VEGAN JUMBO LUMP JACKFRUIT CRAB CAKES WITH SPANISH GARLIC MAYONNAISE AND WARM SAFFRON NAGE

> Makes 8 crab cakes <

My parents had high expectations for my undergraduate educational path. When I was fifteen, Mom and Dad decided that instead of taking a summer vacation, the Shagrin clan should pile into our trusty green Toyota Previa and tour some of America's finest colleges. I, of course, saw this as a divine opportunity to tour the social life available to the lucky bastards that had finally escaped parental rule.

First, we hit the University of Wisconsin in Madison. Mom wanted me to find a solid backup option to my (her?) first choice, Brown University, which would also provide a great four-year experience. What I found in Madison was my very first fake ID, which provided, I believe, an equally rewarding four-year experience. It would have been a much longer one, but a policeman in South Carolina decided that five foot five and 150 pounds didn't exactly fit my physical description.

Following a few more college visits when I wasn't exactly on my best behavior, we finally departed for Baltimore, Maryland. By then, I was on a pretty tight leash. I had to go everywhere glued to my parents' sides. In retrospect, I probably shouldn't have been angry. It gave me a chance to try real crab cakes for the first (and only) time—delicious.

Sans punishment, there's a 90 percent chance I would have skipped out on dinner for some happy hour carousing with the local youth, courtesy of my new fake ID, of course, and I would have missed the inspiring crab cakes.

SPANISH GARLIC MAYO

½ cup Vegenaise

¼ cup MimicCreme or alternative (page 3)

3 tablespoons Vegan Egg Mix (page 28)

¼ cup olive oil

5 cloves garlic, minced or mashed

2 tablespoons white wine vinegar

Freshly cracked black pepper

CRAB CAKES

4 to 5 tablespoons vegan margarine

3 tablespoons shallots, minced

2 (16-ounce) cans young green jackfruit in water, completely drained and patted dry (see page 19)

Salt and freshly ground pepper

¼ cup MimicCreme or alternative (page 3)

1 teaspoon mustard powder

Pinch of cayenne

½ cup Spanish Garlic Mayo

2 tablespoons unbleached all-purpose flour

¼ cup vegan bread crumbs

2 tablespoons vegan panko-style bread crumbs

2 tablespoons fresh baby dill

2 tablespoons fresh flat-leaf parsley leaves, chopped finely

Olive oil, for the pan

Although they were delicious, I cut crab and anything else that crawls, walks, flies, or swims out of my diet shortly thereafter. I hoped that making a vegan version of those crab cakes might rekindle some of my youthful guile, but instead I fell asleep on the couch during a Golden Girls rerun. Believe me though, someone will "thank you for being a friend," if you know what I mean, once they try these cakes. Oh, and if you're wondering just what nage is, it's fancy-shmancy chef talk for a broth in which crustaceans are cooked. Clearly not the case here, but it does sound spiffy!

Prepare the mayo: In a large bowl, whisk the mayo, MimicCreme and egg mix. Slowly drizzle in the olive oil, whisking constantly and vigorously until fully emulsified. Add the garlic and vinegar, then season with salt and pepper to taste. Keep in the refrigerator until ready to use.

Prepare the crab cakes: In a large skillet, melt the margarine over medium heat. Sauté the shallots in the skillet until they become translucent and begin to give off liquid (this is a technique called "sweating"). Add the jackfruit and stir, then season with salt and pepper. Continue to sauté until the jackfruit is considerably browned, then add the MimicCreme. Once the MimicCreme is fully incorporated, remove from the heat and place in a bowl. Set aside to let cool.

(continues)

Vegan Jumbo Lump Jackfruit Crab Cakes . . . (continued)

Preheat the oven to 375°F.

NAGE

6 cloves garlic, peeled

2 shallots, peeled and minced

2 tablespoons olive oil

1 pinch saffron threads

½ cup white wine (I used Sauvignon Blanc)

1 cup prepared Better Than Bouillon No Chicken Base (see page xvi for how to prepare)

1 teaspoon freshly squeezed lemon juice

6 tablespoons (¾ stick) vegan margarine

Kosher salt and freshly cracked black pepper

Once fully cooled to room temperature, combine jackfruit mixture, mustard powder, cayenne, garlic mayo, flour, bread crumbs, dill, and parsley in a bowl. Lightly grease a baking pan with olive oil, form the mixture into eight equal cakes, then dust the cakes lightly in the crumb mixture. Bake for 15 to 20 minutes, until nicely golden brown.

Prepare the nage: In small saucepan, combine the garlic and cold water to cover by 2 inches. Bring to a boil, then drain, add fresh cold water, and bring to a boil again. Drain again, and set aside.

In another saucepan, sauté the shallots in the oil over medium heat until they're translucent and begin to give off liquid (again, the sweating thing). Add the saffron, white wine, No Chicken broth, and garlic. Bring to a boil. Lower the heat to a simmer and reduce the liquid by half.

Carefully transfer the mixture to a blender, add the lemon juice and margarine, and blend at medium speed until smooth. Season with salt and pepper to taste. Pour through a fine-mesh strainer into a small saucepan, cover, and keep warm over very low heat until ready to use. Whisk before serving.

If you're serving the crab cakes immediately, pour a few tablespoons of the nage over the top of each cake. If you're not serving immediately, you can serve the sauce on the side so that the cakes don't get too soggy. If you're feeling extra fancy, you can serve the cakes atop a small bed of mixed greens, spinach, or watercress.

EGGS BENEDICT FLORENTINE OMELETS WITH SAGE HOLLANDAISE SAUCE

> Makes 2 large or 4 small omelets ⇐

I uncooked batch Vegan Scrambled
Eggs (page 27) prepared with
I whole pound of silken soft tofu
(omit the silken extra-firm tofu)

5 teaspoons agar powder

HOLLANDAISE SAUCE

¾ cup MimicCreme or alternative
(page 3)

½ teaspoon salt

Freshly ground black pepper

1¾ tablespoons cornstarch mixed with
1½ tablespoons cold water

Pinch of turmeric

2 tablespoons vegan margarine, melted

I tablespoon freshly squeezed lemon
juice

⅛ cup fresh sage leaves

Grease two medium-size (9- to 10-inch) or four small (6-inch) skillets very well with canola oil or non-stick spray, and set aside.

Blend all the Vegan Scrambled Egg ingredients (not the agar powder) in a food processor as directed on page 27, then pour into a medium-size saucepan. Sprinkle the agar powder over the top, quickly mix it in, and then allow the mixture to sit for 5 minutes.

Bring the mixture to a boil over medium-high heat while stirring constantly.

Boil for about a minute, then pour into the greased skillets and smooth out evenly with a spatula or spoon. Chill them in the refrigerator for a few hours until completely set.

When you're ready to make your omelets, place the skillets over low heat until each omelet is completely warmed through. Then gently remove from the pans, keeping the set mixture in one piece, by either turning the pan upside down over a plate, or gently pushing the omelet out of the skillet onto a plate.

From this point on, of course, you can make whatever type of omelet you want. I'm just a fancy pants sometimes.

Prepare the hollandaise sauce: Heat ½ cup of the MimicCreme in a saucepan over medium-high heat until it just begins to boil. Pour into a blender, add salt and pepper to taste, and cover with the lid to trap in heat.

(continues)

53

Eggs Benedict Florentine Omelets . . . (continued)

In the same saucepan, whisk together the rest of the MimicCreme, the cornstarch mixture, and the turmeric, and heat over medium-high heat, stirring constantly, until thickened and reduced by almost half. Scrape into the blender with the rest of the MimicCreme, add the melted margarine, lemon juice, and sage, and blend until smooth.

Reheat over low heat or microwave before serving.

ABOUT THE NEW MEXICAN HATCH CHILE PEPPER

Some like it hot . . . especially if you're my father. He took great pride in the fact that he owned a bottle of hot sauce called "Fire out the Ass." He's always been a unique flower.

Spicy foods did not used to be my cup of tea, but I was genetically predisposed to appreciate them. Now, I can't have my food hot enough. When I first discovered the New Mexican hatch chile pepper, I was enthused for two main reasons:

1. It is one of the most flavorful hot peppers I have ever tasted.
2. It comes in both smokin' hot and a milder variety, so I can prepare dishes with them for my guests that may not be as "fire-tongue inclined."

Unfortunately, the Hatch chile peppers, grown near the town of Hatch, New Mexico, are available fresh only once a year. Here is a step-by-step instructional guide as to how you can roast them, then either store them in the freezer or use in a recipe.

HOW TO ROAST A HATCH CHILE PEPPER

Step 1: Put on a pair of rubber gloves!

Step 2: Cut off the top of each pepper, then slit them open down the middle and scoop out *all* the seeds with a spoon.

Step 3: Line a baking sheet or roasting pan with foil, then preheat your broiler to its highest setting.

Step 4: Rinse the peppers with water, then dry them with a towel. Drizzle and rub them with cooking oil (I use olive oil), then set them on the baking sheet or roasting pan.

Step 5: Place the pan or baking sheet under the broiler and broil for between 5 and 10 minutes, or until the pepper skin blisters and blackens completely.

Step 6: Immediately place the peppers in an airtight bag and seal it completely. You can also place them in a glass bowl and cover it tightly with plastic wrap. Let the peppers sit in the bag or bowl until completely cool to the touch. Once cool (make sure your gloves are on!), use your hands to peel off the skin of each pepper. Discard the skin.

At this point, you can either use the peppers immediately, refrigerate for up to one week, or store in the freezer in an airtight container.

Here are two of my favorite recipes utilizing the New Mexican gem, and they'll hopefully inspire you to come up with some of your own!

HATCH CHILE CHICKEN CACCIATORE WITH BLACK GARLIC-TOMATO SAUCE

⋝ Serves 6 ⋜

BLACK GARLIC-TOMATO SAUCE

1/4 cup olive oil

2 cloves black garlic, minced

2 cloves regular fresh garlic, sliced thinly

1 yellow onion, diced small (about 1/4 inch)

1/2 medium-size carrot, finely grated

1 teaspoon dried thyme

1/4 cup fresh flat-leaf parsley, chopped

1 tablespoon fresh oregano

2 (28-ounce) cans whole tomatoes, with their juices (San Marzano is my favorite)

Salt and freshly cracked black pepper

Make the sauce: Heat the olive oil in a large saucepan over medium-low heat, then add the garlic and onions. Sauté for 5 to 8 minutes, until the onions are soft and translucent.

Add the grated carrots, thyme, parsley, and oregano, and sauté for 2 to 3 more minutes.

Pour in the tomatoes and their juices, and bring to a boil. Lower the heat to a simmer, and simmer until the sauce reduces and thickens, 30 to 45 minutes depending on how thick you like your tomato sauce. Taste for salt and pepper.

Prepare the chicken cacciatore: Mix the garlic, rosemary, salt, and pepper together in a shallow bowl, then add a few tablespoons of olive oil to create a wet rub for the chicken. Coat the chicken well in the mixture, then chill in an airtight container in the refrigerator for about 2 hours.

Take a Dutch oven or large, heavy stockpot, and heat the remaining olive oil over high heat. Add the chicken to the heated oil and cook until browned on all sides. Transfer the chicken to a paper towel–lined plate.

CHICKEN CACCIATORE

2 cloves garlic, minced

I sprig of fresh rosemary leaves, chopped finely

Salt and freshly ground black pepper

¼ to ⅓ cup olive oil

I batch Chicken-Style Seitan (page 5), cut into chicken-shaped pieces (see photo)

2 Hatch chile peppers (I red, I green), roasted, skinned, and diced (see page 55 for how to roast a pepper)

2 large yellow onions, chopped

I pound cremini mushrooms, quartered

4 ounces Vegan Pancetta (page 14), cut into ½-inch cubes

4 ribs celery, sliced into I-inch pieces

2 cups Black Garlic–Tomato Sauce

I cup dry white wine

I cup prepared Better Than Bouillon's No Chicken or Vegetable Base (see page xvi for how to prepare)

Pinch of vegan cane sugar (about ⅛ teaspoon)

Pinch of red pepper flakes

Add the chiles, onions, mushrooms, pancetta, and celery to the pan. Cook until the onions are browned and translucent, about 6 minutes.

Drain out the excess oil, then add the sauce and white wine. Stir well so that the bottom of the pan deglazes.

Next, add the No Chicken broth, sugar, and red pepper flakes, and bring to a boil.

Return the chicken to the pot, cover with a lid, and cook for 20 minutes. Uncover and cook the cacciatore for another 15 to 20 minutes.

Serve.

CRAB AND OYSTER MUSHROOM MEZZELUNE IN A ROASTED HATCH CHILE AND WALNUT CREAM SAUCE

≥ Serves 6 ≤

For my non-Italian-speaking friends, mezzelune *means "half-moons," which is the shape of the pasta you'll be making.*

FILLING

1 (16-ounce) can young green jackfruit packed in water (see page 19)
1 teaspoon freshly squeezed lemon juice, plus a little extra
1½ cups cold water
1 large stalk kombu, cut into 1-inch pieces
1 teaspoon mellow white miso paste
1 tablespoon dulse
½ teaspoon sea salt
1 tablespoon olive oil
2 cloves garlic, minced
1½ cups oyster mushrooms, diced
1 tablespoon vegan margarine
Sea salt and freshly cracked black pepper
¼ cup fresh flat-leaf parsley, chopped
1 tablespoon fresh dill, chopped
¾ cup Vegan Ricotta (page 22)
2 tablespoons chopped fresh chives, plus more for garnish, minced

Prepare the filling: Drain the jackfruit as well as possible in a colander over your sink. After all the water has drained out, use your hands to break up the jackfruit into lump crab–size pieces, squeezing out more water as you go along. Place in an airtight container (leave the lid off at this point), and set aside.

Place the teaspoon of lemon juice, cold water, and kombu stalk in a small saucepan, and bring to a boil. Boil for a minute, then remove the saucepan from the heat.

Stir in the miso paste until fully dissolved, then add the dulse and salt. Allow the mixture to sit until it reaches room temperature.

Once cooled, pour the kombu broth over the jackfruit. Make sure the jackfruit is fully submerged. Place in the refrigerator and allow to marinate for as long as possible. Overnight is ideal—2 hours should be the minimum.

Once you're ready to use, drain the fruit well and discard the kombu and dulse.

MEZZELUNE DOUGH

2 cups semolina flour

2 cups all-purpose flour, plus more for working surface/kneading

$\frac{1}{2}$ cup Vegan Egg Yolk Mix (page 28)

$\frac{3}{4}$ to 1 cup water, at room temperature

$\frac{1}{4}$ cup soy creamer, for sealing the mezzelune

SAUCE

6 tablespoons ($\frac{3}{4}$ stick) vegan margarine

4 cloves garlic, minced

$\frac{1}{2}$ cup vegan sour cream

2 cups MimicCreme or Vegan Buttermilk (page 4)

2 Hatch chile peppers, roasted, peeled and sliced finely (see page 55 for how to roast a pepper)

About 1 teaspoon freshly squeezed lemon juice

$\frac{1}{2}$ cup roughly chopped walnuts, plus more for garnish

$\frac{3}{4}$ cup Dr-Cow Aged Cashew Cheese, grated finely, or Vegan Parmesan Blend (page 22)

Salt and freshly cracked black pepper

Heat the olive oil in a large skillet over medium heat, then add the garlic and sauté for thirty seconds. Add the mushrooms, drained jackfruit, margarine, salt, and pepper to the pan, and sauté over medium heat for 6 to 8 minutes. Add a splash of lemon juice to the pan about halfway through the sautéing process. The oyster mushrooms should be tender and beginning to sweat (a.k.a. give off liquid).

Add the parsley and dill, then taste for additional salt and pepper. Set aside to cool.

Once cooled to room temperature, add the ricotta and chives, and stir well.

Prepare the mezzelune dough: Place the flours in a mountain on top of a large, wooden cooking surface or table. Make a well in the top of the mountain, then slowly pour in the egg yolk mix. Start adding the water in small amounts, stirring the flour, eggs, and water with your hands until a dough just begins to form. Push the flour up the "mountain" into the well as you go along.

Once about all the flour is incorporated, bring the dough together into a ball. Flour your work surface, and continue kneading the dough for 10 minutes until the dough is elastic and sticky.

Wrap the dough ball in plastic wrap and allow it to rest for 30 minutes.

(continues)

Crab and Oyster Mushroom Mezzelune . . . (continued)

When you're ready to make your mezzelune, divide the ball into four pieces. Roll out each piece as flat as possible using either a pasta maker or a rolling pin.

Use a 2½- or 3-inch round cookie cutter to slice circles out of the dough sheets.

Bring 6 quarts of water to a boil in a large pot, then add 2 tablespoons of sea salt to the boiling water.

Place 1 teaspoon of filling into the center of each pasta circle, then dip your index finger into the soy creamer. Rub a tiny bit of soy creamer around the edge of half of the pasta circle, then fold over the other half to form a semicircle. Press down firmly around the edge to seal well while making sure to push out any air bubbles.

Drop into the boiling water, and cook until tender, about 3 minutes. Drain well.

Prepare the sauce: Melt the margarine in a saucepan over medium-low heat.

Once melted, add the garlic and sauté for 30 seconds, then add the sour cream and MimicCreme. Cook over medium heat while whisking occasionally, until the sauce just begins to boil and has thickened slightly.

Add the chiles, lemon juice, walnuts, and cheese to the sauce, and continue to cook while whisking constantly until all the Parmesan is fully blended in (about 3 minutes).

Taste for salt, pepper, and lemon juice.

Top the mezzalune with the sauce, garnish with minced chives and more walnuts, then serve.

SAFFRON, OREGANO, AND GARLIC CHIVE–INFUSED VEGAN SEA BASS, CLAMS, BACON, AND BEECH MUSHROOMS IN WHITE WINE

⋟ Serves 6 ⋞

1 batch Vegan Bacon (page 15)

1 teaspoon olive oil

3 cloves garlic, sliced thinly

3.5 ounces whole beech mushrooms (Bunashimejis) or quartered creminis

2 leeks, white part only, halved lengthwise, cleaned well, and sliced thinly

2½ teaspoons kosher salt

1 batch Vegan Sea Bass (page 20)

Leaves from 3 sprigs of fresh oregano, chopped finely

2 garlic chives, minced

1 batch Vegan Clams (page 18)

½ teaspoon red pepper flakes

Pinch of saffron threads

1½ cups dry white wine

1 batch Vegan Clamshells (page 18 (optional), for garnish, or 1 French baguette, sliced ½ inch thick

2 tablespoons vegan margarine

2 lemons, sliced into wedges, for serving

I know what you're thinking. "This is some serious food, dude." You are absolutely correct. You see, there are these two hot young chefs that go under the label "the Food Dudes." Their real names are Jon Shook and Vinny Dotolo. Not only have they had their own show on the Food Network, but they just opened a very popular restaurant in Los Angeles. It's called Animal, and serves only exactly as the name indicates. They don't allow modifications to their menu items, so there's not a chance in hell I'm ever going to eat there.

Regardless, I bought their cookbook and decided to veganize one of their recipes with my own little twist. This recipe is perfect if you want to impress your dinner party guests. Do the prep work for the vegan sea bass, clams, and bacon a day in advance, and it throws together very quickly.

Preheat the oven to 350°F.

Place the bacon in a roasting pan, drizzle with the olive oil, then bake until it's crispy, 10 to 15 minutes, stirring often. Add the garlic, then roast until it's smelling good and beginning to brown, 1 to 2 minutes. Add the mushrooms and leeks, sprinkle

(continues)

Saffron, Oregano, and Garlic Chive–Infused Sea Bass . . . (continued)

with 1 teaspoon of the kosher salt, and continue to roast until the leeks soften. This should take 4 to 5 minutes.

Season the sea bass with half of the oregano, garlic chives, and remaining 1½ teaspoons of salt. Set aside.

Stir the remaining oregano and garlic chives into the mushroom mixture, then add the clams and red pepper flakes. Mix the saffron threads into the white wine. Place the sea bass on top of the clams, then pour the white wine mixture around the edges of the roasting pan.

Place the pan back in the oven and bake until the sea bass is firm, 8 to 10 minutes. Turn on the broiler and let the tops of the sea bass brown for about 5 minutes.

To serve: Place four clamshells (or slices of bread) in a large, shallow bowl. Place an equal amount of clams on each shell with a piece of sea bass in the center, then top with the mushroom mixture, bacon, and a dollop of the margarine. Serve with lemon wedges.

ROASTED WHITE EGGPLANT FETTUCCINE ALFREDO WITH FRESH FENNEL AND SPINACH

⋛ Makes 4 large or 6 small servings ⋞

I love the Wednesday farmers' market in Santa Monica. If you go before the market opens, you'll see all the chefs, or more likely their assistants, buying ingredients for their culinary masterpieces. I've taken quite a liking to following them around in stealth-mode so I can see what the best of the best is in seasonal produce.

I think they're on to me.

Perhaps one of the more interesting veggies I've seen there is the white eggplant. When I asked the nice lady behind the stand if there was any difference between the white and purple varieties besides coloration, she informed me that the white eggplant actually has a nuttier flavor. DING!

My little V.A.S. went off. I believe my train of thought went something like this: "Hmm. Nutty. Cashews. Cheeselike. Puree. Alfredo Sauce!"*

So I headed home with my bevy of veggies. After about an hour or two of tinkering around in my kitchen laboratory, I was very pleased with the results.

2 large white or purple eggplants
1/3 cup extra-virgin olive oil, plus extra to toss with the pasta
1 cup MimicCreme or alternative (page 3), or 1 cup soy milk plus
    1 tablespoon apple cider vinegar
1 pound fettuccine noodles (or use the Pasta Guide on page 47 to make your own!)
1 bulb fennel, sliced thinly
1/2 large yellow onion, sliced thinly
1 teaspoon dried thyme
1 teaspoon dried sweet basil
1 1/2 cups dry white wine
1 tablespoon freshly squeezed lemon juice
3 cloves garlic, quartered
Sea salt and freshly ground black pepper
2 cups fresh spinach leaves, washed well
Fennel fronds, for garnish

Preheat the oven to 350°F. Take the eggplants, prick all over with a fork, and brush lightly with olive oil. Roast them in the oven for 30 for 45 minutes, or until soft, turning them over after 20 minutes. Set aside to cool.

If you're not using MimicCreme, mix the soy milk and apple cider vinegar together and set aside to coagulate.

Cook the pasta until al dente, drain well, and toss with a little extra-virgin olive oil to prevent sticking.

Heat the 1/3 cup of oil in a large sauté pan over medium heat and sauté the fennel, onion, and herbs for 5 to 10 minutes, stirring occasionally. Add white wine and lemon juice, then simmer until the liquid reduces and the veggies are tender.

Once the eggplants are cooled, slice in half lengthwise and scoop the innards into a blender or food processor. Add the MimicCreme and garlic and blend until smooth and saucelike. Pour the mixture into the skillet with the fennel mixture,

Vegan Alert System

(continues)

Roasted White Eggplant Fettuccine . . . (continued)

and mix in well. Add salt and pepper to taste. Add the spinach to the sauce, and lower the heat to low.

Simmer over low heat for 5 minutes, then serve over pasta and garnish with fresh fennel fronds.

VEGAN TURKISH POMEGRANATE MEATBALL SOUP

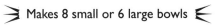 Makes 8 small or 6 large bowls

If the meatball recipe is familiar, it's an adaptation of the Meatballs recipe on page 11. The alterations make for a great Middle Eastern flavor. Make sure you rehydrate your dried shiitakes 30 minutes prior to making the meatball dough. Don't discard the water once they're hydrated.

MEATBALL SEITAN DOUGH

- 1 1/2 cups vital wheat gluten
- 1 1/2 cups water mixed with 1 1/2 teaspoons Better Than Bouillon No Beef Base
- 1/3 cup plus 2 tablespoons MimicCreme or alternative (page 3)
- 1 tablespoon vegan margarine
- 3 cloves garlic, minced
- 2 tablespoons fresh mint, minced
- 1/2 teaspoon ground cumin
- 3 flaxseed eggs (3 tablespoons ground flaxseed mixed with 3 tablespoons water; see page 29 for how to prepare)
- 1/3 cup vegan bread crumbs
- 1/2 cup wheat germ
- 1/2 cup pomegranate seeds

Prepare the meatball seitan: Using a stand mixer (if you have one—by hand, if not), mix together vital wheat gluten, No Beef broth, and 2 tablespoons of the MimicCreme. Set aside.

Prepare the meatball broth: In a large pot, bring all the meatball broth ingredients to a boil. Take the meatball seitan and break off little pieces, dropping them into the boiling broth until all the dough has been used.

Cover, lower the heat to a simmer, and cook for 1 hour. Stir every 10 minutes or so.

Remove from the heat. Place a strainer or colander in the sink and pour the contents of the pot into the strainer. Remove the bay leaves, then let the seitan mixture cool to room temperature. Once cool

MEATBALL BROTH

6 dried shiitake mushrooms rehydrated in 1 cup water

7 cups prepared Better Than Bouillon No Beef Base (see page xvi for how to prepare)

2 tablespoons tamari

1 portobello mushroom cap, chopped

1 tablespoon garlic powder

2 teaspoons onion powder

2 bay leaves

POMEGRANATE BROTH

6 tablespoons (¾ stick) vegan margarine

3 large leeks, white part only, halved lengthwise, cleaned well, and sliced thinly

12 cups prepared Better Than Bouillon No Chicken Base (see page xvi for how to prepare)

½ cup dried red lentils, rinsed

1½ cups pomegranate juice

1 cup parsley, minced

2 cups sliced carrots

½ cup uncooked rice

2 cups fresh spinach leaves, washed well

1 tablespoon fresh mint leaves, chopped, for garnish

1 tablespoon fresh cilantro leaves, chopped, for garnish

Salt and freshly ground black pepper

enough to touch, use a food processor to grind up the seitan mixture until it has a very fine texture.

In a small skillet over medium-high heat, melt 1 tablespoon of the margarine and sauté the minced garlic for about 30 seconds. Add the garlic, mint, and cumin to the ground seitan, and mix in well. Sauté for 2 to 3 minutes, then remove from heat and set aside to cool.

Once cool enough to touch, transfer the ground seitan mixture to a large bowl, then add the flaxseed egg, remaining MimicCreme, bread crumbs, and wheat germ. Use your hands to mix well.

Preheat the oven to 350°F and grease a baking sheet.

Gently add the pomegranate seeds to the meatball mixture. Form the mixture into ½-inch balls, then bake until browned and warmed through, 15 to 20 minutes.

Prepare the pomegranate broth: Melt the margarine in a large soup pot over medium-low heat, then add the leeks. Cook for 10 minutes, until soft and golden, then add the No Chicken broth and lentils.

Simmer, covered, for 45 minutes. Add the pomegranate juice, parsley, carrots, and rice, and continue to simmer, covered, for 20 more minutes.

Add the spinach leaves to the soup during the last 5 minutes of simmering. Place the meatballs in a bowl, ladle the soup over them, and garnish with mint and cilantro. Season with salt and pepper.

VEGAN VEAL CHOPS WITH SUNCHOKE CAPONATA

> Serves 4 ≶

CHOPS
4 Vegan Veal Chops (page 10)
Salt and freshly ground black pepper
Olive oil, enough for frying
2 bulbs garlic, halved, plus a few extra
    peeled cloves
2 sprigs fresh rosemary
1 tablespoon vegan margarine
1 lemon, halved

CAPONATA
2 sunchokes (Jerusalem artichokes),
    peeled and diced
1 small eggplant, diced
Sugar, for caramelizing the sunchokes
    and eggplant
Pinch of salt
1/2 yellow onion, diced
2 ribs celery, diced
Handful of grape tomatoes, halved and
    seeded
10 caper berries
2 tablespoons capers, rinsed and
    drained
Handful of green olives, halved
Handful of fresh basil leaves
Handful of pine nuts, toasted

Prepare the veal chops: Season the veal chops well with salt and pepper.

Take a large skillet and add enough olive oil to coat the bottom of the pan well. Heat the oil over medium-high heat, then add the garlic bulbs, rosemary, and chops.

Cook the chops for 2 to 3 minutes on one side, then add the vegan margarine to the pan. Once it melts, use a spoon or brush to baste the chops.

Cook for another 2 to 3 minutes on the other side, then transfer to a plate. Squeeze half a lemon over the chops, then cover loosely with foil.

Prepare the caponata: Wipe out the skillet, discarding the garlic bulbs and rosemary, and drizzle in more olive oil. Heat the oil over medium-high heat.

Fry the sunchokes and extra garlic cloves for 3 to 4 minutes, add the eggplant and cook for 2 minutes, then sprinkle with sugar and a pinch of salt. Cook for an additional 2 to 3 minutes, until the eggplant is browned.

Add the onions and cook for 2 to 3 minutes, then add the celery and cook for an additional 2 to 3 minutes. Add the tomatoes, caper berries, capers, and olives. Toss and cook for 1 minute.

Zest and juice the other lemon half (see page 37 for how to zest a lemon), add the zest and juice to the pan, and remove from the heat. Season with salt and pepper to taste.

Add the basil, and allow the leaves to wilt.

Serve the chops over the caponata, garnished with toasted pine nuts.

I have a deep, insatiable love for mushrooms. (Go ahead. Crack your hallucination jokes now and get them out of your system. Done? Okay.) True, I've taken my fair share of trips on the Magical Mystery Tour Bus, but I'm talking about the non-psilocybin-riddled variety. Button, cremini, portabella, porcini, wood ear, and, of course, morels. You name it, I love it.

My love for mushrooms started out as a young'un. My mother used to make these amazing mushroom turnovers for synagogue potlucks, family parties, funerals, and the like. They were something like a tiny mushroom-filled pie/calzone. Unfortunately for Mom, when I was eight, my petty larceny skills were about as refined as my taste buds. She eventually learned to make more than one batch.

As I grew older, I learned the different types of mushrooms, their best uses and different seasons. I think they have an amazing depth of flavor when sautéed with only a little vegan margarine, white wine, lemon juice, salt, pepper, and garlic. No rice or pasta needed. Just hand me a fork.

Yet I have a number of friends who can't stand mushrooms. When I traveled to Amsterdam, I paid a visit to the vegan café at the Unlimited Health Yoga Centre. After a long, informative (cough *excruciating* cough) lecture, I learned that the café's menu is based around the Sattvic diet, which is rooted in the practices of Ayurveda and Yoga. The Sattvic diet, which encourages foods that foster mental and physical clarity and balance, classifies mushrooms as a Tamasic (energy-draining) food. Well, I don't know about all you mushroom haters out there, but I can say that I've had some experiences with mushrooms that have induced quite the natural high. They are delicious, nutritious, and I've found that the nonpsilocybin varieties are far from energy draining when cooked to perfection.

FREE-FORM WILD MUSHROOM LASAGNE WITH CHAMPAGNE-LEMON CREAM SAUCE AND SUN-DRIED TOMATO AND ROASTED RED PEPPER SALSA

≩ Serves 4 ≨

This lasagne is termed "free-form" because instead of assembling it casserole style in a large dish, you individually stack and plate the servings. Warning: Be careful popping the cork on the champagne—I almost broke my face.

Prepare the salsa: Heat $\frac{1}{2}$ tablespoon of the olive oil in a skillet over medium heat. Add the pine nuts and cook until lightly golden brown. Remove from the pan and place on a cutting board, allow to cool, then chop roughly.

Add the rest of the olive oil to the pan, and once heated through, add the tomatoes, peppers, parsley, basil, and champagne. Stir until well mixed and cooked through, then season with salt and pepper. Add the pine nuts, and set aside.

SALSA

3½ tablespoons olive oil

½ cup pine nuts

5½ ounces jarred marinated sun-dried tomatoes, sliced thinly

1 (9-ounce) jar roasted red and yellow peppers, drained and sliced thinly

2 tablespoons flat-leaf parsley, chopped

2 to 3 tablespoons fresh basil, chopped

1½ tablespoons dry champagne

Salt and freshly ground black pepper

LASAGNE

¼ ounce dried porcini mushrooms

2 tablespoons vegan margarine

1 small onion, halved and sliced thinly

1 teaspoon fresh thyme, chopped

12 ounces mixed wild mushrooms (I used cremini, shiitake, and oyster)

8 (10 by 4-inch) sheets fresh lasagna (you can also use packaged)

SAUCE

1 tablespoon olive oil

½ cup dry champagne

1 cup MimicCreme or alternative (page 3)

¼ cup freshly squeezed lemon juice

Salt and freshly ground black pepper

Prepare the lasagne and sauce: Next, start some salted pasta water boiling in a large pot. Then begin readying the mushroom filling by soaking the dried porcinis in ¼ cup of boiling water for 15 minutes. Strain the porcinis through a wire-mesh strainer, and reserve the soaking liquid.

Heat the margarine in a large skillet over medium-high heat, then cook the onion for 1 to 2 minutes, until softened. Add the thyme and all mushrooms to the pan, and cook another 2 minutes. Add the reserved porcini soaking liquid to the skillet, and cook until all the water has evaporated. Set aside, but reheat before plating the lasagne. While you're waiting for the water to come to a boil, make the sauce.

In a medium-size saucepan, heat the olive oil, then add the champagne. Cook for 2 to 3 minutes, until slightly reduced. Add the MimicCreme and cook for another 3 to 4 minutes, until slightly thickened. Add the lemon juice, then season with salt and pepper. Keep warm over very low heat, stirring every few minutes.

Now the pasta water should be at a boil. Boil the fresh lasagna sheets as directed. Once al dente, drain well, and toss carefully with olive oil to prevent sticking. To plate, dip a sheet of lasagna into the sauce, top with the mushroom mixture, then another layer or two of sauced pasta sheets and mushrooms, then garnish with a spoonful of salsa.

WHITE LASAGNE WITH BASIL RICOTTA, SPINACH, YOUNG ROCKET, AND DICED VEGAN PANCETTA

⋙ Makes 6 large or 8 small servings ⋘

BASIL TOFU RICOTTA
12 ounces extra-firm tofu

12 ounces soft silken tofu

Big handful of fresh basil leaves

1 teaspoon dried oregano

4 teaspoons freshly squeezed lemon juice

1 teaspoon garlic powder

1 teaspoon kosher salt

$\frac{1}{4}$ cup Vegan Egg Mix (page 28)

SAUCE
5 tablespoons vegan margarine

$1\frac{1}{2}$ cups Dr-Cow Aged Cashew Cheese or any Vegan Parmesan (page 22), grated finely

$\frac{1}{4}$ cup plain soy creamer

$1\frac{1}{2}$ cups MimicCreme or alternative (page 3)

Salt and freshly cracked black pepper

TO ASSEMBLE
1 tablespoon olive oil

1 batch diced Vegan Pancetta (page 14)

1 batch Alfredo Sauce

1 pound no-boil lasagna noodles

1 batch Basil Tofu Ricotta

About 3 cups fresh spinach leaves

About $1\frac{1}{2}$ cups fresh young rocket (arugula)

1 cup Vegan Mozzarella (page 21), grated finely

Prepare the ricotta: Place the extra-firm tofu in your food processor and pulse until broken up and crumbled. Add the rest of the ingredients, and blend until the mixture just comes together. Be careful not to overmix into a paste.

Prepare the sauce: Melt the margarine in a saucepan over low heat. Add the cheese, soy creamer, and MimicCreme, then bring to a boil while stirring frequently.

Lower the heat to low and simmer for 2 minutes, stirring constantly, until the sauce has thickened slightly. Add salt and pepper to taste.

Use immediately, or reheat if the sauce thickens too much while sitting.

Prepare the lasagne: Preheat the oven to 375°F. Grease a 9 by 12-inch casserole dish and set aside.

Heat the olive oil in a skillet over medium-high heat. Sauté the pancetta until golden brown on both sides. Set aside to cool.

Take the greased casserole dish, and assemble the lasagne as follows:

1. Layer of sauce
2. Layer of lasagna noodles
3. Layer of basil ricotta
4. Layer of spinach and arugula
5. Layer of pancetta
6. 2nd layer of sauce
7. 2nd layer of lasagna noodles
8. 2nd layer of basil ricotta
9. 2nd layer of spinach and arugula
10. 2nd layer of pancetta
11. 3rd layer of sauce
12. 3rd layer of lasagna noodles
13. 3rd layer of basil ricotta
14. 3rd layer of pancetta
15. Final layer of vegan mozzarella

Cover the lasagne with a sheet of aluminum foil and bake on the middle rack of the preheated oven for 45 to 50 minutes, or until warmed through completely.

Once the lasagne is fully heated, remove the sheet of aluminum foil. Place under the broiler until all the mozzarella has melted and is beginning to brown.

Let cool slightly before serving.

VEGAN CHICKEN MARSALA MASALA WITH FRESH MORELS

⇒ Serves 6 ⇐

This dish tastes great served over mashed potatoes, rice, or pasta.

1½ cups Better Than Bouillon No Chicken Base (see page xvi for how to prepare)

½ teaspoon garam masala

Pinch of turmeric powder

A few threads of saffron

1 batch Chicken-Style Seitan (page 5), halved crosswise into thin patties

Salt and freshly ground black pepper

Unbleached all-purpose flour, enough for dredging the chicken

4 tablespoons (½ stick) vegan margarine

2 tablespoons finely diced shallots

2 cloves garlic, pressed or minced

3 cups morel mushrooms or portobellos, cleaned and halved

2 teaspoons olive oil

1 cup Marsala wine

2 tablespoons freshly squeezed lemon juice

½ cup MimicCreme or alternative (page 3)

1 sprig of fresh flat-leaf parsley, chopped

In a small saucepan, combine and heat the No Chicken broth, garam masala, turmeric powder, and saffron until just warm and all the spices are infused. Remove from the heat and set aside.

Sprinkle the chicken breast slices with salt and pepper, then lightly dredge each slice with flour.

In a large heavy skillet, melt 2 tablespoons of the margarine over medium heat. Brown the chicken in batches on both sides, adding ½ tablespoon more margarine before each new batch, then remove from the pan and set aside. In the same skillet, add the final tablespoon of margarine. Add the shallots, garlic, morels, and olive oil. Sauté until the shallots are translucent and the morels are softened. Pour the wine and lemon juice into the skillet, and cook until the wine is reduced by half.

Whisk in the spiced broth. Cook, partially covered, over medium-low heat until slightly reduced, 10 to 15 minutes. Stir in the MimicCreme and parsley, and stir well, scraping up any bits from the bottom of the pan. Taste for salt and pepper.

Arrange a few slices of chicken on each plate, pour the sauce and morels over the top, and serve.

VEGAN ESCARGOTS À LA BOURGUIGNONNE EN CROÛTE VEGAN BRIOCHE WITH CAFÉ DE PARIS BUTTER

⋗ Makes about 25 appetizers ⋖

ESCARGOTS

1 batch Vegan Brioche (page 210)
2 teaspoons vegan margarine
18 fresh morel or halved shiitake mushrooms, cleaned
1 medium-size carrot, chopped roughly
1 small onion, chopped roughly
1 rib celery, chopped roughly
4 cups low-sodium vegetable broth
6 black peppercorns
1 bay leaf
Fresh thyme
Salt

CAFÉ DE PARIS BUTTER

12 tablespoons (1½ sticks) vegan margarine
1 tablespoon shallots, minced
1 clove garlic, minced or pressed
1 tablespoon fresh parsley, chopped
1 teaspoon prepared mustard
⅛ cup MimicCreme or alternative (page 3) mixed with 2 tablespoons Vegan Egg Mix (page 28)
Dash of vegan Worcestershire sauce
¼ cup Burgundy wine
Salt and freshly ground black pepper

Prepare the escargots: Preheat the oven to 425°F.

Slice the brioche into 1-inch-thick slices, then use a cookie cutter or the rim of a glass to cut 2-inch round disks from the slices. Press down in the center of each round to create a well where the escargot will sit. Place the disks on a baking pan, put into the oven, and toast until light brown. Set aside.

Melt the margarine in a medium-size saucepan over medium heat, then sauté the morels for 2 minutes. Add the vegetables, vegetable broth, pepper, and herbs, then bring to a simmer. Simmer for 10 minutes.

Prepare the butter: Cream all the butter ingredients together. Place in the refrigerator to chill.

Preheat the broiler.

Place one escargot (a morel) in the well of each brioche disk. Top with a dollop of the butter mixture and broil for 1 to 2 minutes, until the butter has browned.

PAN-SEARED WHITE PEPPER TOFU SCALLOPS WITH BASIL CREAM SAUCE SERVED OVER LINGUINE

> Makes 4 large or 6 small servings ≤

LINGUINE AND SAUCE
1 tablespoon vegan margarine
2 shallots, peeled and minced
1 clove garlic, minced (use one from the garlic olive oil—yum!)
1½ cups fresh basil, chopped
¼ cup fresh parsley, chopped
¼ cup white wine
¼ cup plain soy creamer (I use Wildwood Organics)
¼ cup canned coconut milk
1 tablespoon garlic olive oil (a.k.a. GOO; see tip) or regular olive oil
1 teaspoon arrowroot powder or cornstarch
1 tablespoon freshly squeezed lemon juice
Salt and freshly ground black pepper
1 pound linguine noodles

SCALLOPS
1½ tablespoons vegan margarine
1 batch Tofu Scallops (page 17)
1 tablespoon GOO
1 teaspoon salt
1 teaspoon freshly cracked white pepper
2 teaspoons dry white wine (I use a Sauvignon Blanc)

SHAGGY KITCHEN TIP No garlic olive oil on hand? It's super easy to make: soak 8 to 10 peeled whole garlic cloves overnight in ¾ cup of extra-virgin olive oil. You can either leave the cloves of garlic in the oil, or strain them out and use them in any recipe that calls for fresh garlic. Keeps in a dark, airtight container in the refrigerator for up to two weeks. Mad props to vegan home-girl Leigh C. for this one.

Prepare the linguine and sauce: Begin boiling a large pot of salted water for your linguine.

Melt the margarine in a large skillet over medium-high heat. Lower the heat to low, then add the shallots and garlic. Sauté for 5 minutes, stirring frequently. Add the basil, parsley, wine, soy creamer, coconut milk, GOO, arrowroot powder, lemon juice, salt, and pepper.

Cook over medium heat, stirring frequently, until reduced by almost half. Taste for seasoning. Lower the heat to low, stirring occasionally, then turn off the heat and cover. Reheat over low heat 3 to 4 minutes just before serving.

Cook the pasta in the salted water until al dente. Strain, then rinse in cold water. Drizzle and toss the noodles with a bit of olive oil to prevent sticking. Set aside.

SHAGGY KITCHEN TIP Prepare the scallops: The scallop-searing process is done in two parts because it's important not to overcrowd your sauté pan. You will need lots of space to roll the scallops around to brown them on all sides. This also allows you to have enough time to ensure that all the scallops are cooked evenly and none end up burned or undercooked.

You'll be making this in two batches (see tip). Melt all the margarine over medium heat in a skillet. Place half of the Tofu Scallops in the pan, drizzle half of the GOO over the tops of the scallops, then sprinkle the scallops with half of the salt and half of the white pepper. Allow to brown on the bottom for 3 minutes, sliding them around occasionally to make sure they're not sticking to the pan. Once golden brown (see photo), flip over the scallops, add half the white wine, and allow that sizzle to make you feel like a master chef!

Sauté for another 3 minutes, still sliding them around occasionally. Flip them on their sides and roll them around until the entire thing looks perfectly golden brown. Place on a paper towel–lined plate. (Great time to start reheating your basil sauce.) Repeat the process with the remaining scallops/ ingredients. There should still be enough margarine in the skillet, but it's okay to add more if it's totally dry.

Serve the scallops atop the linguine, cover with the sauce, and enjoy!

RED CHARD, ROASTED GARLIC, AND RICOTTA-STUFFED PEPPERS WITH SUN-DRIED TOMATO AND TOASTED PINE NUT MARINARA

⇒ Serves 6 ⇐

For most, bell peppers are either a "love 'em or leave 'em" vegetable. As a Shaglet, my grandmother would bring over a batch of her infamous stuffed peppers at least once a month.

I would turn up my nose, stick out my tongue, then make myself SpaghettiO's. With my voracious preteen appetite, I'm pretty sure my parents didn't mind because it meant there was more for them to eat.

Then all of a sudden, I grew an intense love for peppers. I'll eat roasted red peppers out of the jar like they're potato chips.

I first made this recipe in the very unvegan Flagstaff, Arizona, for a dinner party attended by 80 percent omnivores. Aside from the fact that vegan groceries are difficult to procure in the small mountain town, I whipped the dish together in an hour or two, then watched it disappear in less than twenty minutes.

Try wooing your bell-pepper-hating compadres away from the dark side with this hot number.

Prepare the garlic for the stuffed peppers: Preheat the oven to 400°F. Take the head of garlic, and slice off the top ¼ inch of it so that all the cloves are revealed. Place the head of garlic on a sheet of aluminum foil, and drizzle liberally with olive oil. Wrap the head in the foil, leaving a small hole at the top. Roast on a baking sheet in the preheated oven for 30 minutes, until softened and browned.

While you're waiting for the garlic to roast, prepare the sauce: Blend all sauce ingredients in a food processor until combined well. Taste for salt and pepper and set aside.

Remove the garlic from the oven and lower the oven temperature to 350°F.

Slice off the top of the peppers about ¾ inch from the stem end, and scoop out the

STUFFED PEPPERS

1 head garlic

Olive oil, enough for coating the peppers and garlic

6 large red or yellow bell peppers

3 tablespoons vegan margarine, plus more for greasing baking dish (you can also use nonstick spray to grease the pan)

4 cups diced eggplant

2 cups yellow onions, diced

1 pound red chard, chopped roughly

1 cup Vegan Ricotta (page 22)

Salt and freshly ground black pepper

$\frac{1}{2}$ cup vegan bread crumbs

MARINARA SAUCE

1 (14-ounce) can fire-roasted or regular diced tomatoes

1 (8-ounce) can sun-dried tomatoes packed in oil (reserve one-quarter of the oil)

Juice of $\frac{1}{2}$ lemon

4 cloves garlic

Handful of fresh basil leaves, or 1 teaspoon dried

$\frac{1}{2}$ cup pine nuts, toasted

Salt and freshly ground black pepper

seeds and as much of the white part as possible. Grease a baking sheet, then rub each bell pepper well with some olive oil. Place the peppers stem side down on the baking sheet, and bake for 30 minutes, until the skin wrinkles and chars a little.

Get some plastic wrap ready. Remove the peppers from the oven and immediately place in a large bowl and cover with a sheet of plastic wrap to trap in the heat. Let them steam until they're cool enough to handle, about 10 minutes. Gently peel the skins off the peppers, and set aside.

In a large skillet over medium heat, melt 2 tablespoons of the margarine. Cook the diced eggplant until it begins to soften, about 5 minutes. Add the onion and cook until translucent and beginning to brown. Transfer the eggplant mixture to a cutting board, let it cool for a few moments, then chop finely with a knife. This can also be done in a food processor with a few short pulses.

In the same large skillet, add the remaining 1 tablespoon of margarine and melt over medium-high heat, then add the chard, toss with the margarine, and allow it to wilt for 1 minute.

Transfer the chard to a large bowl, add the eggplant mixture, ricotta, and $\frac{3}{4}$ cup of the marinara sauce. Then squeeze out the cloves of roasted garlic into the bowl as well. Mix well, then season with salt and pepper to taste.

(continues)

Red Chard, Roasted Garlic, and Ricotta-Stuffed Peppers . . . (continued)

Grease a 9 by 13-inch baking dish well with margarine. Stuff each pepper equally with the filling and place the peppers on their side in the baking dish. Pour the remaining sauce over the peppers, and sprinkle each pepper evenly with bread crumbs.

Bake until the tops are browned and the peppers are heated through, 25 to 35 minutes.

LEMON-ARTICHOKE CAVATELLI IN AN HEIRLOOM TOMATO–CREAM VINAIGRETTE WITH ENGLISH PEAS AND VEGAN PROSCIUTTO

 Serves 6

Cavatelli and I have a very interesting history. Growing up, my little sister (a.k.a. Queen of the Childhood Picky Eaters) would eat only cavatelli (shell-shaped pasta). Not spaghetti, not linguine, not even rigatoni. To make matters even sillier, she demanded that the tomato sauce be served on the side so that she could dip each individual cavatelli into the appropriate amount of sauce. I pity the waiters who wrote down the order wrong and served her a plate of sauce-covered pasta. Temper tantrum doesn't even begin to describe what would ensue. I still tease her about it to this day.

For whatever reason, cavatelli is almost nonexistent in the state of California. In Ohio, they serve it at nearly every Italian restaurant. I missed the wonderful texture of these noodles so much, I decided to make my own.

Prepare the puree: Place all the puree ingredients in a food processor and blend until the mixture achieves a pastelike texture. Set aside.

VEGAN RICOTTA AND ARTICHOKE PUREE

12 ounces extra-firm tofu

1 (14-ounce) can artichoke hearts, drained well

½ teaspoon dried basil

½ teaspoon dried oregano

2½ tablespoons freshly squeezed lemon juice

½ teaspoon garlic powder

1 teaspoon salt

1 tablespoon nutritional yeast

1 teaspoon sesame seeds

5 or 6 walnuts, chopped

78

CAVATELLI

2 cups semolina flour

1½ cups all-purpose flour

½ cup MimicCreme or alternative (page 3)

2 tablespoons nutritional yeast

Pinch of turmeric powder

1 teaspoon lemon zest (see page 37 for how to zest a lemon)

1¼ cups Vegan Ricotta and Artichoke Puree

2 cups shelled English peas

1 batch Vegan Prosciutto (page 14), diced

Vegan Parmesan Blend (page 22) (optional)

VINAIGRETTE

4 tablespoons extra-virgin olive oil

3 tablespoons white wine vinegar

3 cloves garlic, peeled

5 heirloom tomatoes, peeled

¼ cup MimicCreme or soy creamer

½ to 1 tablespoon freshly squeezed lemon juice

Salt and freshly ground black pepper

Prepare the pasta: In a large bowl, mix the flours together well. Place three-quarters of the flour mixture in a separate large bowl. Make a well in the center of the flour. In a small bowl, combine the MimicCreme with the nutritional yeast and turmeric, and whisk together until fully blended. Pour 1¼ cups of the puree, the MimicCreme mixture, and the lemon zest into the well in the flour. Gradually work the mixture together, adding more flour if necessary, making a soft but not sticky dough.

On a lightly floured surface, knead the dough until it's smooth. Cover with plastic wrap and let the dough rest at room temperature for about 30 minutes.

Form the dough into one large round ball, then cut the ball into quarters. Take one quarter at a time (keeping the rest covered), and on a lightly floured surface, roll it out into a ¼-inch-thick rope. Cut the rope into ½-inch lengths. Gently press down on and flatten each piece, then roll the top downward so that it makes a tiny shell–like shape. Transfer to a lightly floured baking sheet and let dry at room temperature for 30 minutes.

Prepare the vinaigrette: Blend all the vinaigrette ingredients together in a food processor until fully pureed. Taste for salt and pepper. Set aside.

Boil a large pot of salted water, add the pasta and peas, and cook for 6 to 8 minutes. The cavatelli will float to the surface when they're done. Drain well, then toss with a touch of olive oil. Combine with the vinaigrette and prosciutto, then garnish with Parmesan, if desired.

VEGAN SURF AND TURF

These recipes are a good mouthful in two ways: To say and to eat! Think you'd never be able to enjoy surf and turf after going vegan? Think again. Impress the misses or mister with one of these dishes after they've had a long day at work, and you will earn yourself a long night in bed *wink*.

LEMON-THYME-AGAVE–BRAISED VEGAN SHORT RIBS AND SEARED TOFU SCALLOPS IN A MINEOLA TANGELO–SAFFRON SAUCE

 Serves 6

SHAGGY KITCHEN TIP If you're making both parts of this recipe, it's a good idea to prep the scallops and allow them to marinate in seafood marinade (page 16) while you make the short ribs. Then they're ready to go when it's time to begin the Surf.

Prepare the short ribs: Preheat the oven to 350°F.

Rub your seitan "ribs" well with some sea salt and pepper.

In a large, oven-safe cast-iron pot, heat the olive oil over medium-high heat. Add the ribs to the pot, and cook until browned on all sides. Using tongs, remove the ribs from the pot and set aside.

Add the onion, carrot, paprika, caraway, and lemon thyme to the pot and cook until the vegetables are softened, about 10 minutes. Pour in the agave, wine, and No

SHORT RIBS

1 batch Beef-Style Seitan, sliced into rib-shaped pieces (page 6)

Sea salt and freshly cracked black pepper

2 tablespoons extra-virgin olive oil

1 medium-size sweet Maui onion, chopped

2 carrots, chopped

$\frac{1}{2}$ tablespoon sweet paprika

$\frac{1}{2}$ teaspoon caraway seeds

3 sprigs of fresh lemon thyme

$\frac{1}{3}$ cup agave nectar

1 cup dry red wine

2 cups prepared Better Than Bouillon No Beef Base (see page xvi for how to prepare)

SCALLOPS

1 cup prepared Better Than Bouillon No Chicken Base (see page xvi for how to prepare)

$\frac{1}{2}$ cup MimicCreme or alternative (page 3)

Zest of 1 Mineola tangelo, regular tangelo, or orange (see page 37 for how to zest a tangelo)

Pinch of saffron

1 batch Tofu Scallops (page 17; see tip)

Sea salt and freshly cracked black pepper

3 tablespoons extra-virgin olive oil

Thinly sliced green onions, for garnish

Beef broth, then bring to a boil. Return the ribs to the pan, making sure they're fully covered with the liquid, then turn off the heat and place a lid loosely on top so that steam can escape.

Place the pot on the center rack in the preheated oven. Cook until the sauce has thickened, $1\frac{1}{2}$ to 2 hours. Remove the pot from the oven and place on a cooling rack while you make the scallops.

Prepare the scallops: Combine the No Chicken broth, MimicCreme, tangelo zest, and saffron in a saucepan, and place over high heat. Cook until the liquid is reduced and thickened, about 10 minutes.

Season the scallops well with salt and pepper.

Heat the olive oil in a large skillet over medium-high heat, then sear the scallops for 1 to 2 minutes on each side until both sides are browned. Remove the scallops from the pan and set aside.

Carefully pour any excess oil out of the pan, then add the broth mixture. Allow it to cook over high heat for about 2 minutes, until reduced. Return the scallops to the pan and cook until they are heated through, about 1 more minute.

Top with the green onions and serve alongside the short ribs.

VEGAN CARNITAS, CARAMELIZED SHALLOT, AND MUSHROOM ENCHILADAS WITH TOMATILLO, GREEN APPLE, AND AVOCADO SAUCE AND LIME CRÈME FRAÎCHE

> Serves 6 ⫷

CRÈME FRAÎCHE
1 batch Vegan Crème Fraîche (Page 25)
½ teaspoon lime zest (see page 37 for how to zest a lime)
1 teaspoon freshly squeezed lime juice

CARNITAS
1 batch Pork Chop–Style Seitan (page 7), 3 cups broth reserved and cooled
3 tablespoons extra-virgin olive oil
1 tablespoon ground coriander
1 tablespoon ground cumin
Juice of ½ lemon
2 teaspoons kosher salt

SAUCE
6 to 7 tomatillos, husked and rinsed
1 Granny Smith apple, cored and diced
2 small avocados, pitted and peeled
½ cup fresh cilantro sprigs
1 to 2 cloves garlic
1 teaspoon ground cumin
¼ cup apple juice
1 tablespoon freshly squeezed lime juice
1 tablespoon light agave nectar
Salt and freshly ground black pepper

Prepare the crème fraîche: After the 12-hour resting time for the refrigerated crème fraîche, whip in the lime zest and lime juice. Refrigerate until ready to serve.

Prepare the carnitas: Mix all carnitas ingredients together, except for the seitan. Place the seitan in an airtight container, and pour the marinade over it. Marinate in the refrigerator for at least 2 hours.

Once the seitan has marinated, make the carnitas by taking a nicely sharpened knife, holding it almost parallel to the seitan, and cutting very thin slices. Once it's all sliced into strips, chop into even smaller pieces.

Prepare the sauce: Place the tomatillos and 3 to 4 cups of water in a small saucepan. Simmer uncovered for 8 to 10 minutes, stirring occasionally, until soft. Remove the tomatillos with a slotted spoon, and place in a colander to drain and cool for 15 minutes.

Once cooled, place all the sauce ingredients in a food processor and beat them into submission (a.k.a. fully puree).

ENCHILADAS

2 tablespoons vegan margarine

1 clove garlic, minced

1 shallot, minced

2 cups cremini or button mushrooms, chopped coarsely

1 bell pepper, seeded and chopped coarsely

2 cups carnitas

1 teaspoon ground cumin

$\frac{1}{2}$ teaspoon cayenne

Salt and freshly ground black pepper

8 to 10 tortillas

Prepare the enchiladas: Preheat the oven to 350°F. Using a large skillet or saucepot, melt the margarine over medium-high heat. Once melted, add the garlic to the pan, and sauté for 15 to 20 seconds.

Add the shallots, and sauté until translucent and starting to brown. Add the mushrooms and bell pepper, and cook until they start to sweat. Then add the shredded seitan, cumin, cayenne, salt and pepper, and cook until the seitan is well done.

It's not necessary, but I like to stick the tortillas in the oven for a few minutes and toast them a bit on each side.

Roll the filling up inside of each tortilla, place in a greased baking dish, and smother with the sauce. Bake for 20 to 30 minutes, until warmed through (crisping around the edges of the tortillas is a good indicator).

Top with the crème fraîche and serve!

QUINOALENTA AND ROSEMARY SQUASH CHIPS WITH WILD MUSHROOMS AND VEGAN MASCARPONE

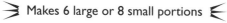 Makes 6 large or 8 small portions

I created this recipe around the time a hotly debated issue was placed on the ballot in California: Proposition 8. For those of you not residing in the land of the Governator, Proposition 8, when it passed, revoked homosexuals' state-recognized marriage rights. It was very important to me and many of my friends that Californians voted NO on this initiative. Unfortunately, Proposition 8 passed. I was so pissed when I had to return my wedding dress.

(continues)

Quinoalenta and Rosemary Squash Chips . . . (continued)

QUINOALENTA
1 cup uncooked red quinoa
8 cups water
2 teaspoons salt
1¾ cups yellow cornmeal
3 tablespoons vegan margarine

MUSHROOMS
1 pound mixed exotic mushrooms
(porcini, shiitake, oyster,
chanterelle, cremini, etc.), cleaned
3 tablespoon extra-virgin olive oil
2 cloves garlic, smashed
½ teaspoon salt
¼ teaspoon freshly ground black
pepper
¼ cup water
3 tablespoons vegan margarine
1½ tablespoons freshly squeezed
lemon juice
2 tablespoons fresh parsley, chopped

SQUASH CHIPS
One winter squash (I find butternut or
pattypan work best), sliced thinly
1 tablespoon extra-virgin olive oil
2 teaspoons fresh rosemary
Salt and freshly ground black pepper

TO ASSEMBLE
1 batch Vegan Mascarpone (page 23)
Fresh parsley sprigs, for garnish

How does this relate to the recipe, you ask? The marriage of two things that society would see as preposterous, but actually come together quite harmoniously and even make the world a better place: Quinoa and polenta (a.k.a. quinoalenta). The marriage of these two ingredients actually creates one very nourishing meal. Quinoalenta not only packs all those great body-building proteins and amino acids, but also carbohydrates and fats to help round out a really well-balanced meal. It's simple, yet looks and sounds fancy, and tastes delicious. I used red quinoa to get a fun polka-dot effect (I had to go for flair to pay homage to all my stylish gay guy friends).

You can also use regular quinoa if you can't locate the heirloom red variety.

Now go register to vote!

Note: Read this recipe entirely before making. Timing is everything with this one.

Prepare the quinoalenta: Rinse the quinoa, then place in a medium-size saucepan with 2 cups of the water. Cover and bring to a boil, then lower the heat to a simmer. Cook until the liquid is absorbed, about 15 minutes. Set aside. Line a 9 by 13-inch baking pan with parchment paper. Set that aside as well.

In a large saucepot, bring the remaining 6 cups of water to a boil over medium-high heat. Add the salt, then slowly start whisking in the cornmeal until all is mixed in well. Lower the heat to low and cook, stirring often, until the mixture thickens and the cornmeal is tender, 10 to 15 minutes.

Turn off the heat and add the vegan margarine. Once it has melted, add the quinoa, and stir until all the quinoa is mixed in well. Pour the mixture into the prepared baking pan and leave in the fridge for a few hours to set and cool.

Prepare the mushrooms: Thinly slice the small-capped mushrooms and cube large-capped mushrooms. Heat the olive oil in a large, heavy skillet over medium-high heat. Add the mushrooms, garlic, salt, and pepper, and sauté, stirring occasionally.

Once the mushrooms are golden brown and all natural moisture has evaporated from the pan, add the water, margarine, lemon juice, and parsley, and heat until the margarine melts. Lower the heat to as low as possible, cover, and allow to simmer while you make your squash chips and crisp up your quinoalenta.

Prepare the squash chips: Preheat the oven to 375°F. Arrange the squash slices on a rimmed baking sheet and brush both sides of each slice with olive oil. Sprinkle each slice with rosemary, salt, and pepper, and bake for 5 to 7 minutes, or until crispy and beginning to brown.

Once the wild mushrooms are simmering on the stove, slice the quinoalenta into serving-size portions. Coat a skillet with a teaspoon or two of olive oil, and brown each slice of quinoalenta for a few minutes on each side.

Place a squash chip on each plate and top with one serving of quinoalenta and wild mushrooms. Add a dollop of mascarpone, and garnish with fresh parsley.

DIJONAISE-CRUSTED BEEF TENDERLOIN MEDALLIONS WITH VEGAN BÉARNAISE SAUCE OVER ROASTED EGGPLANT AND GARLIC SMASHED POTATOES

⇥ Serves 6 to 8 ⇤

I come from meat-and-potatoes country. When I return to visit, I find myself growing overly friendly with the local salad bar options and grocery store produce aisles. My point is, I know how to thrown down a hearty feast.

I spent last year's Christmas holidays with my parents. I not only wanted to prove that I have yet to abandon my true Ohio roots, but also to cook them up something super snazzy. I felt the need to impress my parents with my culinary flare to assure them that, when I call them at the end of the month begging for a little extra cash because I spent all my money on ingredients, I'm really not using the money to buy weed. It's in my past. Unless I'm baking special brownies. Then it's an ingredient.

Prepare the medallions: Preheat the oven to 350°F.

Cut each piece of seitan into 2- to 3-inch medallions, and season them with a bit of salt and pepper.

Heat the olive oil in a large sauté pan over medium-high heat and sear the medallions well on each side, about 3 minutes, until browned. Place on a plate to cool.

Once the medallions are cool enough to touch, mix together the toasted bread crumbs, rosemary, thyme, melted margarine, and touch of salt and pepper.

Coat the largest sides of the medallions generously with Dijon mustard, then press the mustard-covered sides of the medallions firmly into the bread-crumb mixture.

Prepare the sauce: Heat the margarine in a medium-size saucepan over low heat until it browns, 20 to 25 minutes. Set aside.

TENDERLOIN MEDALLIONS

1 batch Beef-Style Seitan (page 6)
Salt and freshly ground black pepper
Olive oil, for searing
1 cup vegan bread crumbs, toasted
$\frac{1}{2}$ teaspoon fresh rosemary, chopped
1 teaspoon fresh thyme, chopped
3 tablespoons vegan margarine, melted
Dijon mustard, for coating

VEGAN BÉARNAISE SAUCE

1 cup vegan margarine
$\frac{1}{2}$ cup white wine
2 tablespoons tarragon or white wine vinegar
2 teaspoons chopped shallots
4 white peppercorns
1 sprig of fresh tarragon, plus 2 tablespoons chopped
1 cup Vegan Egg Mix (page 28)
2 tablespoons unbleached all-purpose flour

ROASTED EGGPLANT AND POTATOES

1 large eggplant
Olive oil, for coating
1 head garlic
$\frac{1}{4}$ teaspoon freshly ground black pepper
5 medium-size baking potatoes, peeled and cut into eighths
$\frac{1}{2}$ cup MimicCreme or alternative (page 3)
4 tablespoons ($\frac{1}{2}$ stick) vegan margarine
1 teaspoon salt

In a separate saucepan, place the white wine, tarragon vinegar, shallots, white peppercorns, and tarragon sprig. Bring to a boil, then cook until reduced by half.

Place the egg mix in a bowl and strain the reduced mixture into the bowl while whisking continuously. Slowly whisk the mixture into the saucepan with the browned margarine, add the chopped tarragon, and cook over medium heat. Add the flour, and cook while whisking vigorously until the sauce has the consistency of mayo. (If the sauce isn't thickening well, try adding 1 tablespoon of cornstarch mixed with 1 tablespoon of cold water. You will have to whisk extra hard to incorporate it.) Keep warm until ready to use.

Prepare the eggplant and potatoes: Preheat the oven to 350°F. Pierce the eggplant in several places, drizzle and rub with olive oil, then roast it whole and unpeeled on a baking sheet until it's soft and starting to collapse, about an hour. Allow it to cool, then scoop out the flesh and place in a bowl. Set aside.

Increase the oven temperature to 400°F. Peel away the outer layers of the garlic bulb skin, making sure to leave the skins of the individual cloves intact. Cut off one-quarter of the top of the cloves to reveal the individual cloves of garlic. Place the

(continues)

Dijonaise-Crusted Beef Tenderloin . . . (continued)

garlic head on a sheet of aluminum foil, drizzle and rub well with olive oil, then wrap the foil around the garlic head.

Bake on a baking sheet at 400°F for 30 to 35 minutes, or until the cloves feel soft when pressed. Allow the garlic to cool, then squeeze the roasted cloves into the bowl with the roasted eggplant. Season the mixture with a touch of salt and pepper, and set aside.

Cook the potatoes in enough boiling water to cover, about 15 minutes or until tender. Drain well and mash. Stir in the eggplant mixture, MimicCreme, and remaining ingredients. To serve, place the medallions atop a portion of the smashed potatoes, then drizzle with béarnaise sauce.

3

SATISFYING THE VEGAN MUNCHIES: WHETHER IT'S PMS OR VMS*, THESE RECIPES WILL CURE WHAT AILS YOU

I've decided to eliminate all shame related to my childhood dietary choices, following a conversation with a close vegan friend of mine. We somehow broached the topic of our fat kid indulgences, and it went a little something like this:

> Me: "I was such a ramen noodle whore. I knew how to make it alone by the time I was six."
>
> Her: "Oh! Me, too. And SpaghettiO's with the little meatballs!"
>
> Me: "Holy shit, yes. Thank god, my parents had an automatic can opener so my fat little hands didn't try prying through aluminum. I used to eat a ton of fast food, too, like McDonald's cheeseburgers [insert obnoxious gagging noise here]."
>
> Her: "I know. I would never admit that to anybody else. But I can top you one. KFC fanatic."
>
> Me: "Dude. Chicken potpies. The most craptastic meal ever. I could eat a whole one myself. They have something like 100 grams of fat. I'm really surprised I didn't have a coronary playing dodge ball in ninth grade."

* *Vegan munchies syndrome*

Let's face it: We all need to satisfy our inner fat kid now and then. Why not do it with style? With recipes ranging from Vegan Quattro Formaggio White Truffle Macaroni and Cheese to Home-made Vegan Doritos, no craving will be left unsatisfied.

Her: "No way. You're so small. You'd have to give birth after eating one of those. You should start veganizing all those junky childhood comfort foods."

Me: "Game on. I'll sit in my meditation corner and channel my inner fat kid tonight!"

After some serious "Om-ing" and deep reflection, I decided perhaps it was best if I didn't become the Paula Deen of the vegan community. True, the main reason I decided to go vegan stemmed from my love for animals, not for kale smoothies. But I still didn't want to start posting a slew of deep-fried vegan recipes. This chapter gives you some munchies that will satisfy the KFC lover in you without clogging your arteries . . . enjoy!

VEGAN QUATTRO FORMAGGIO WHITE TRUFFLE MACARONI AND CHEESE

⇒ Serves 8 ⇐

You can simplify (or cheapify) this recipe by using just one cheese, or any combination of cheese you'd like, and omitting the truffle oil. See the last part of the recipe for baked mac and cheese instructions.

I pound macaroni

¾ cup vegan bread crumbs

6 tablespoons (¾ stick) vegan margarine

6 tablespoons all-purpose flour

Salt and freshly ground black pepper

½ tablespoon white miso paste

1¾ cups soy milk

1½ cups MimicCreme or alternative (page 3)

½ teaspoon yellow mustard powder

⅓ pound Teese cheddar-style cheese, grated

⅓ pound Teese mozzarella-style cheese, grated

½ (190 g) package Cheezly Gouda or Edam-style cheese, grated

½ (2.5-ounce) package Dr-Cow Aged Tree Nut Cheese (any flavor), grated finely

2 drops white truffle oil

Cook the macaroni until al dente, drain well, toss with a touch of canola oil to prevent sticking, and set aside.

If you want to bake your macaroni and cheese, preheat the oven to 400°F and grease a large baking dish. If you will enjoy it unbaked, toast the bread crumbs now by preheating the oven to 350°F, then spreading out the bread crumbs on a cookie sheet. Bake in the preheated oven for 5 to 10 minutes, until golden brown, watching carefully so that they don't burn. Set aside.

In a large saucepan, melt the margarine over medium-high heat. Add the flour, and salt and pepper to taste, and whisk together. Add the miso paste and blend in well. Pour in the soy milk and MimicCreme gradually while stirring constantly. Continue stirring until the mixture begins to boil. The sauce should have thickened up quite a bit at this point.

(continues)

91

Vegan Quattro Formaggio White Truffle Macaroni and Cheese (continued)

Add the mustard powder and stir it in well. Lower the heat to medium and add one-third of the cheeses, stirring constantly, until the cheese has almost completely melted. Repeat the process twice more until all the cheese has melted and is fully incorporated. It should take about 10 minutes. Add the drops of truffle oil, then taste to see if more salt is needed.

Turn off the heat and stir in the cooked macaroni. You can serve now, sprinkled with the toasted bread crumbs, or, if you're baking it . . .

Transfer the mac and cheese to the prepared baking dish and top with untoasted bread crumbs. Bake for 20 minutes, then let cool for 5 minutes before serving.

MOREL MUSHROOM AND BACON WHITE MACARONI AND CHEESE

 Serves 6

Even as a wee one, I had serious issues with hearing the word no. At the age of two, my mother had me in the toddler prison seat of a shopping cart at our local Sparkle Market. As she was making her way to the checkout aisle, we passed the dangerous, tantrum-inducing impulse snack rack. I snatched a bag of Doritos off the only shelf my stubby little arm could reach and looked up at her with my irresistible eyes.

"No!" she stated firmly. "You've had enough junk today." According to my mother, I responded with my now-signature devious, defiant, eyebrow-raising glare, and tore the bag open with one triumphant rip. I was pretty ballsy for a toddler . . . truly believing that once the bag was open, she'd have to purchase the chips, and then they would be my sweet yet salty victory.

Wrong.

She pulled that bag out of my hands faster than I could blink, handed them to the checkout lady, and said, "I'll pay for these, but throw them away."

Even into adulthood, no is still not a word I enjoy having to hear. As vegans, we all know how many times the ingredient list for dishes at a restaurant can feel like just one giant no.

Butter? No! You cannot have those delicious garlic rolls. The butternut squash bisque? No! There's crème fraîche in there, sister. And mac and cheese? Forget about it. All the high-end gastronomic establishments would never consider adapting their Burrata with Basil and Prosciutto for a vegan. So unless you want to get stuck with a sprig of basil on a plate, take matters into your own hands instead and play by your own damn rules!

Here you are, ladies and gents. A fancy mac and cheese, all the meat you can shake a stick at. Oh yes, we can.

I pound macaroni

¾ cup vegan bread crumbs

8 tablespoons (1 stick) vegan margarine

½ cup fresh morel, shiitake, or chanterelle mushrooms, cleaned and diced

6 tablespoons all-purpose flour

Salt and freshly ground black pepper

1¾ cups soy milk

1½ cups MimicCreme or vegan buttermilk (page 4)

½ teaspoon yellow mustard powder

⅓ pound vegan mozzarella cheese, grated

½ (190 g) package Cheezly white cheddar cheese, grated

½ (190 g) package Cheezly cheddar cheese with bacon (see tip)

½ (2.5-ounce) package Dr-Cow Macadamia Nut Cheese, grated finely, or ½ cup Vegan Parmesan Blend (page 22)

SHAGGY KITCHEN TIP If you can't find the Cheezly with bacon bits, use an entire package of white cheddar Cheezly and add 1 tablespoon of vegan bacon bits (see page xvi) when you add the cheeses.

Cook the macaroni until just al dente, drain well, toss with a touch of canola oil to prevent sticking, and set aside.

If you want to bake your macaroni, preheat the oven to 400°F and grease a large baking dish. If you will enjoy it unbaked, toast the bread crumbs and set aside.

(continues)

Morel Mushroom and Bacon White Macaroni and Cheese (continued)

In a large saucepan, melt the margarine over medium-high heat. Add the morels and sauté for 2 to 3 minutes, until beginning to soften. Add the flour, and salt and pepper to taste, and whisk together.

Pour in the soy milk and MimicCreme gradually while stirring constantly. Continue stirring until the mixture begins to boil. The sauce should have thickened up quite a bit at this point.

Add the mustard powder and stir in well. Lower the heat to medium and add one-third of the cheeses, stirring constantly, until the cheese has almost completely melted. Repeat the process twice more until all the cheese has melted and is incorporated. It should take about 10 minutes. Taste to see if more salt is needed.

Turn off the heat and stir in the cooked macaroni. You can serve now, sprinkled with the toasted bread crumbs, or, if you're baking it . . .

Transfer the mac and cheese to the prepared baking dish and top with untoasted bread crumbs. Bake for 20 minutes, then let cool for 5 minutes before serving.

SPANISH PURPLE PEPPER VEGAN BEEF STEW

Serves 8

STOCKPOT
- 6 tablespoons (¾ stick) vegan margarine
- 6 tablespoons unbleached all-purpose white flour
- 10 cups prepared Better Than Bouillon No Beef Base (see page xvi for how to prepare)

SHAGGY KITCHEN TIP You'll need two large stockpots for this recipe. You're going to be multitasking both pots simultaneously, but it's much easier than it sounds. Just be mindful when reading the directions to note when you're working with the "beef and vegetable pot" or the "stock-

BEEF AND VEGETABLE POT

3 tablespoons extra-virgin olive oil

1 batch Beef-Style Seitan (page 6), cut into $\frac{1}{2}$-inch cubes

2 cloves garlic, minced or pressed

$\frac{1}{2}$ teaspoon ground cumin

$\frac{1}{4}$ teaspoon ground coriander

$\frac{1}{2}$ teaspoon smoked Spanish paprika

Pinch of freshly grated nutmeg

Salt and freshly cracked black pepper

1 medium-size yellow onion, chopped roughly

2 purple bell peppers, seeded and chopped roughly

2 small russet potatoes, unpeeled but cleaned and cubed

2 carrots, cleaned and sliced

2 large ribs celery, sliced

$\frac{1}{4}$ cup red Bordeaux wine or cooking sherry

1 tablespoon sherry vinegar

2 tomatoes, seeded and roughly chopped

2 bay leaves

2 sprigs fresh thyme

Cayenne (optional)

3 tablespoons cornstarch mixed with 3 tablespoons cold water (optional, for further thickening)

6 sprigs fresh flat-leaf parsley, stems removed

pot." Also, it can be helpful to mix all of the spices together prior to beginning the cooking process, to save time and chaos.

In the "beef and vegetable pot," warm the olive oil over medium-high heat. Add the cubed seitan, garlic, cumin, coriander, paprika, nutmeg, and a pinch of salt and pepper. Stir well to mix in all the spices. Sauté until the beef just begins to brown, 2 to 3 minutes.

While the beef cubes are sautéing, start melting the margarine in the other, designated "stockpot" over medium-low heat. Keep an eye on it to make sure it doesn't burn.

Add the onions, purple peppers, potatoes, carrots, and celery to the "beef and vegetable pot," then add the red wine and sherry vinegar to deglaze. Sauté, stirring occasionally, until the onions are translucent.

While the vegetables are sautéing, return to the "stockpot." Once the margarine has melted, stir in the flour until fully combined. Pour in the beef broth and whisk the pot's contents well. Raise the heat to medium-high and cook, whisking occasionally, until the broth begins to thicken, about 15 minutes.

Back to the "beef and vegetable pot." Once the onions are translucent and the other veggies are softening,

(continues)

95

Spanish Purple Pepper Vegan Beef Stew (continued)

> pour the thickened contents of the "stockpot" into the "beef and vegetable pot." Stir well to mix everything together.

Stir in the chopped fresh tomatoes, bay leaves, and thyme. Add salt, pepper and cayenne to taste.

Lower the heat to medium-low and allow to simmer until all the vegetables are soft and the stew has thickened, about 35 minutes. If the stew is not thickened to your liking, you can thicken more by adding the cornstarch mixture; stir well and allow it to simmer for about 5 minutes longer.

Discard the thyme sprigs and bay leaves, mix in the flat-leaf parsley, then taste again for salt and pepper.

Serve.

VEGAN SAUSAGE AND BEER GRAVY OVER CHEDDAR, GREEN ONION, AND CILANTRO BUTTERMILK BISCUITS WITH FRIED DILL AND DANDELION GREENS

Serves 8

If you're from the right part of the good ole US of A, you know of a place called Bob Evans. I'd call it a restaurant, but people in the know understand that it's more like kitschy, inter-active dinner theater. Let me first paint a pretty picture . . .

Red-and-white checkered tablecloths; waitresses named Fran and Ethel who ask, "What'll it be, sweet pea?" in a raspy, twangy voice; biscuits that melt in your mouth like the butter smeared all over them; good pie; and last, a smoking section. As their slogan indicates, Bob Evans truly is a "Home of Homestyle" establishment.

BISCUITS

$2\frac{1}{3}$ cups full-fat (4 to 5 g per serving) soy milk

$\frac{3}{4}$ cup vegan sour cream

3 tablespoons white vinegar

$\frac{1}{3}$ cup green onions, finely diced

$\frac{1}{2}$ cup fresh cilantro leaves, chopped finely

$\frac{1}{2}$ (8-ounce) package Daiya Vegan Cheese Shreds or other vegan cheddar, grated finely)

$4\frac{3}{4}$ cups all-purpose flour

Heaping $\frac{1}{2}$ tablespoon salt

$\frac{1}{3}$ cup baking powder

$\frac{1}{3}$ cup sugar

SAUSAGE

6 tablespoons olive oil

1 (16-ounce) Original Field Roast Classic Meatloaf, cut into 12 slices, or 2 (10-ounce) packages Garden-Burger Meatless Breakfast Sausage, well thawed

$\frac{1}{2}$ cup fresh dill

2 cups dandelion greens, halved crosswise and stems removed

Salt and pepper

2 cloves garlic, minced

1 leek, trimmed, halved lengthwise, cleaned well, and sliced thinly

$\frac{1}{2}$ cup all-purpose flour

1 cup prepared Better Than Bouillon No Beef Base (see page xvi for how to prepare)

$\frac{1}{2}$ cup vegan dark ale of your choosing

$1\frac{1}{2}$ tablespoons cornstarch mixed with $1\frac{1}{2}$ tablespoons cold water (optional, for further thickening)

But I had and heard my share of weird experiences that slightly taint my nostalgia. For example, my best friend, a vegetarian, ordered scrambled eggs and hash browns. As she's mid-chow, she looks up. Her face turns cracker-ass white.

"What?!" I ask, thinking she's about to start waving her hands in the air and I'm going to have to do Heimlich.

"There's a piece of chicken in my hash browns!" she screams.

Don't get me wrong—unintentional poultry aside, I still have a special place in my heart for Bob's place. I can't really eat there anymore—haven't in a long time, really. But damn, do I miss my childhood feastings on their sausage, biscuits, and gravy. Hell, I just miss the damn biscuits.

I decided my own version was in order.

To make the biscuits: Preheat the oven to 375°F. Lightly flour a work surface or large cutting board. Grease a baking sheet or line it with parchment paper.

Make the buttermilk by whisking the soy milk and sour cream together until fully combined. Stir in the white vinegar and set aside for at least 5 minutes until thickened. Once thickened, mix the green onions, cilantro, and cheddar into the buttermilk.

In the bowl of a stand mixer or large mixing bowl, completely combine the flour, salt, baking powder, and sugar on a low speed or by hand. Raise

(continues)

Vegan Sausage and Beer Gravy . . . (continued)

the mixer speed to medium, then slowly pour in the buttermilk mixture and beat until the batter just comes together.

Quickly turn the dough out onto the prepared work surface, then roll out to a $\frac{1}{4}$-inch thickness. Using a 3-inch round cookie cutter or the rim of a drinking glass, cut circles out of the dough and place on the prepared baking sheet.

Bake for 8 to 10 minutes, then transfer to a cooling rack until ready to serve.

To make the sausages and gravy: In a large saucepan, heat 4 tablespoons of the olive oil over medium-high heat. Cook the sliced meatloaf in batches until browned and thoroughly cooked through, then transfer from the pan to a plate. Cover with aluminum foil to keep warm and set aside.

Add the remaining 2 tablespoons of olive oil to the saucepan and raise the heat to high. Once the oil is hot, carefully add the dill, dandelion greens, and a sprinkle of salt and pepper, then fry for 1 minute. Remove the dandelion greens and as much of the fried dill as possible from the pan. Lower the heat to medium, add the garlic and leek, and cook until soft.

Sprinkle the cooked leek with the flour and stir well to combine. Then slow pour in the No Beef broth and ale, stirring until all the lumps of flour are completely eliminated.

Bring the gravy to a boil, then lower the heat to a simmer and cook until thickened to your liking. If you like your gravy very thick, whisk in the cornstarch mixture and simmer for a few minutes longer. Add salt and pepper to taste.

To serve: Split each biscuit in half lengthwise, then serve topped with browned sausage and gravy.

Looking for killer (but not killed) vegan sausages? Check out Isa Moskowitz's *Vegan Brunch* for cherry sage, chorizo, and Italian flavors— pages 137–140.

VEGAN BRACIOLE

≥ Serves 6 ⋹

I batch Beef-Style Seitan (page 6; see tip)

I tablespoon vegan margarine or olive oil

$\frac{1}{2}$ teaspoon garlic powder

$\frac{1}{2}$ yellow onion, diced finely

$\frac{1}{2}$ cup Vegan Ricotta (page 22)

$\frac{1}{2}$ cup Italian-flavored or plain vegan bread crumbs

$\frac{1}{4}$ cup fresh parsley leaves, chopped

3 tablespoons fresh basil leaves, chopped

Kitchen twine or string, enough for tying up braciole

About I cup marinara sauce (Try the San Marzano and Port Wine Marinara Sauce on page 112!)

In traditional American Italian cuisine, braciole is a flat-pounded meat (usually steak) rolled up with bread crumbs and cheese, then baked. My grandfather on my mother's side, who I affectionately referred to as "Oo-Oo," made a version of braciole that never ceased to amaze me. It's one of the first dishes that pops into my mind when someone mentions "comfort food." Oo-Oo, this is for you. You will always have a very special place in my heart . . . and stomach.

SHAGGY KITCHEN TIP When making the Beef-Style Seitan, do not cut into small pieces. Instead, use your hands or a mallet to pound out the dough as flat as you can, and drop the flattened disk into the boiling broth. Allow the seitan to drain and cool completely before topping, rolling, and baking.

Preheat the oven to 325°F.

Heat the margarine in a skillet over medium-high heat, and sauté the onion until browned. Remove from the heat and set aside.

Once the seitan is cooled and drained, place it on a cutting board. Top pizza style in the following order:

1. Garlic powder
2. Ricotta

(continues)

Vegan Braciole (continued)

    3. Half the bread crumbs

    4. Onions

    5. Fresh herbs

Then, carefully roll up the seitan like a jelly roll, and fasten in the middle and at each end with twine. Place the braciole in a roasting pan, cover with marinara sauce, and sprinkle with the remaining bread crumbs. Bake for 35 to 45 minutes, until completely cooked through.

HERBES DE PROVENCE AND ROASTED GARLIC PIZZA DOUGH WITH MELTING VEGAN CHEESE BLEND

Makes 2 medium-size or 3 small deep-dish pizzas, or 3 regular-size (12-inch) pizzas

This recipe is great for a deep-dish pizza. Following the basic crust recipe, I've included one of my favorite ways to make a vegan deep dish. If you're not making a deep-dish, you may want to half the recipe, or make more pizza! Top with Melting Vegan Cheese Blend (recipe follows) or Homemade Vegan Mozzarella (page 21), and Port Wine Marinara Sauce.

GARLIC PIZZA DOUGH

2 cups warm water

2 ($\frac{1}{2}$-ounce) envelopes rapid-rise yeast

$\frac{1}{2}$ cup vegetable oil

$\frac{1}{4}$ cup olive oil

$\frac{1}{2}$ cup cornmeal

3 cups bread flour

$2\frac{1}{2}$ cups white whole wheat flour

I head garlic, roasted (see page 87 for how to roast)

I tablespoon herbes de Provence

Vegan margarine, for greasing the pan (optional)

Prepare the pizza dough: This can be done by hand, but using a stand mixer really helps. Pour the water into a large bowl, then pour the yeast into the water and stir to dissolve. Add the oils, cornmeal, and $1\frac{1}{2}$ cups of the bread flour, and $1\frac{1}{4}$ cups of the whole wheat flour. Beat by hand for 10 minutes. Slowly mix in the remaining bread flour and whole wheat flour, roasted garlic, and herbs. Knead for several minutes.

If you're using a stand mixer, in the bowl of the mixer, combine the yeast, water, oils, cornmeal, $1\frac{1}{2}$ cups of the bread flour, and $1\frac{1}{4}$ cups of the whole wheat flour as above, using the regular beaters. Then attach the dough hook and slowly mix in the remaining bread flour and whole wheat flour, roasted garlic, and herbs. Knead for several minutes with the mixer on a lower setting.

Place the dough in a large greased or floured metal bowl. Cover the dough with a clean dish towel, and allow it to rise until it doubles in size (about 90 minutes, depending on your climate). Show the dough who's boss by punching it down to size, then allow it to rise again.

Punch down again, and you're good to go!

To bake, either follow the recipes below, or . . .

Preheat the oven to 425°F.

(continues)

Herbes de Provence and Roasted Garlic Pizza . . . (continued)

MELTING VEGAN CHEESE BLEND

1 (20-ounce) package vegan mozzarella-style cheese

4 ounces soft tofu

2 cloves garlic

½ teaspoon dried basil

½ teaspoon dried oregano

2 teaspoons freshly squeezed lemon juice

2 tablespoons Vegan Parmesan Blend (page 22)

1 to 2 tablespoons MimicCreme or high-fat (4 to 5 g per serving) soy milk (page 3)

TOPPING

1 batch Port Wine Marinara Sauce (page 112)

Any veggies/fake meats of your choosing

Grease your pizza pan with a touch of margarine. Take a ball of the dough (portion per pans recommended in the serving suggestions), then stretch it out to fit your pizza pan. It may take a little elbow grease, but stretch it all the way out to the edge of the pan. Continue with the remaining dough, or refrigerate the extra dough as directed below.

Prepare the cheese: Blend all the cheese ingredients well in a food processor. Bam! Heap on top of your favorite pizza. Top with the sauce and other toppings of your choosing.

Bake until the crust is brown underneath, 10 to 15 minutes.

Store extra dough by wrapping in plastic wrap, then placing in the fridge. Just be sure it's done rising or you may have a doughy surprise the next morning.

EGGPLANT LASAGNE–STYLE VEGAN DEEP-DISH PIZZA

Makes 1 (12-inch-wide) deep-dish pizza

Vegan margarine, for greasing the pan

1 batch Herbes de Provence and Roasted Garlic Pizza Dough (page 100)

1 eggplant, sliced into ⅛-inch-thick rounds

Olive oil, for brushing and sautéing

Salt and freshly ground black pepper

1 onion, diced finely

1 batch Vegan Mozzerella (page 21)

A few tablespoons fresh basil, chopped

A few teaspoons dried oregano

1 (15-ounce) jar Muir Glen Organic Pizza Sauce

3 to 4 cloves garlic, chopped

Preheat the oven to 350°F.

Grease a deep-dish pizza pan very well with margarine. Place enough of the dough in the pan that you can run the crust right up the side of the pan, about ⅛ inch thick throughout. Using a fork, prick the stretched-out dough in several places. Prebake the dough in your preheated oven for 7 minutes, then allow it to cool a bit prior to the final pizza assembly.

Brush the eggplant slices with olive oil and season with a touch of salt and pepper. Place on a baking pan and bake until the rounds are tender, about 15 minutes. Set aside to cool.

Heat a little olive oil in a skillet over medium-high heat. Sauté the onion until translucent. Let cool for a few moments.

Raise the oven temperature to 450°F.

When assembling the pizza, the "cheese" goes on the bottom for a deep dish. Traditionally, there's no more cheese added. I just happen to really enjoy my vegan cheese. This is my assembly method:

1. Vegan cheese blend
2. Layer of eggplant rounds

(continues)

103

Eggplant Lasagne-Style Vegan Deep-Dish Pizza (continued)

    3. Layer of finely diced onions

    4. Layer of herbs

    5. Layer of sauce and garlic

    6. 1 more thin layer of vegan cheese blend

    7. 1 more layer of eggplant rounds

    8. 1 last layer of sauce and garlic

Bake for 30 to 45 minutes. The center of the pizza should be completely cooked through, and the cheese should be melted. Let cool for 3 minutes prior to serving.

THE QUICK WAY

NO-YEAST PIZZA CRUST

⋗ Makes 1 regular-size (12-inch) pizza ⋖

2⅛ cups unbleached all-purpose flour
¼ cup extra-virgin olive oil, plus extra oil for greasing the pan
⅚ cup high-fat (4 to 5 g per serving) soy milk
¼ cup cold water
2 tablespoons baking powder
½ teaspoon salt
¼ teaspoon sugar

For the gal or guy on the go, this crust recipe really works in a pinch. I can't really say I'm "on the go"; I just didn't feel like "going" to the store to buy yeast.

Preheat the oven to 425°F.

Take all of the ingredients except ⅛ cup of the flour, and mix well in a bowl. It will be pretty sticky, but the dough should actually have an element of elasticity to it. Work in the remaining ⅛ cup of flour. You may need to add a little more or less based the humidity levels where you live.

Place the dough ball in the refrigerator for about 15 minutes.

Take your pizza pan and oil it lightly. Spread out the pizza dough to the edge of the pan, making sure that it's even in thickness. You'll notice that no-yeast dough may tear a little easier, but it's easy to patch together. Once it is spread out, brush it with olive oil, and poke holes all over it with a fork.

Bake the dough for 4 minutes, then remove from the oven. Add the toppings, bake for another 10 to 12 minutes, and then feast.

COFFEE-RUBBED VEGAN STEAK TACOS WITH GRILLED LOBSTER MUSHROOM, HEIRLOOM CHERRY TOMATO, AND CORN SALSA

 Serves 8

COFFEE-RUBBED STEAK
1 batch Beef-Style Seitan (page 6; see tip)
1 tablespoon ground organic coffee
2 teaspoons organic vegan brown sugar
2 teaspoons cracked black pepper
1/2 teaspoon ground coriander
Pinch of ground cinnamon
1/2 teaspoon kosher salt
Organic canola oil spray, for greasing grill pan or grill
About 8 tortillas, warmed before serving
Optional taco incidentals: vegan sour cream, fresh sliced avocado, or guacamole

Most of you probably don't know what I'm referring to when I say something "smells like L.A." It's kind of an aromatic blend of sweat, sewage, exhaust fumes, and Mexican food that permanently lingers in the air anywhere east of Hollywood. While this may not sound appetizing to you in the slightest, it smells like home . . . and somehow delicious.

I've never been a huge fan of the fourth meal, but my father gave me two solid bits of advice the first time he found me hungover on a Saturday morning:

(continues)

Coffee-Rubbed Vegan Steak Tacos . . . (continued)

SALSA

2 tablespoons canola oil

2 cloves garlic, minced or pressed

2 ears fresh corn kernels, or about 1 cup frozen, thawed

½ ounce dried lobster mushrooms (see tip), 1 cup fresh, or sub 1 cup white button mushrooms, diced

3 ounces shiitake mushrooms, sliced (about 1½ cups)

1 small sweet onion, halved and sliced thinly

5 teaspoons freshly squeezed lime juice

1 jalapeño pepper, seeded and diced

1 cup heirloom cherry tomatoes, quartered

3 tablespoons green onion, sliced thinly

⅛ cup fresh cilantro leaves, chopped

¼ teaspoon chili powder

Sea salt

1. You know you've had too much to drink when you try to brush something off your shoulder, and it's the floor.
2. If possible, drink a tall glass of water and eat something to soak up the booze before passing out.

These tacos will guzzle up the alcohol in your stomach ten times faster than you did. My face ends up covered in the salsa by the end of the meal, and usually stays there until I finally look in the mirror because I believe my friends find this humorous.

Jokes aside, these tacos are a really great homemade variation of the favorite Mexican street food. Viva tacos!

SHAGGY KITCHEN TIPS When you prepare the Beef-Style Seitan, make sure you cut the dough into steak-shaped pieces before dropping into the boiling broth. Make sure your steaks are drained well.

If you're using dried lobster mushrooms, soak them in water for about an hour. Drain the mushrooms well, then dice roughly on a cutting board.

Coconut Vinegar–Cured Tofu Scallops with Lemongrass-Basil Cream Sauce
and Cilantro-Garlic Coconut Rice, page 42

Lemon-Thyme-Agave–Braised Short Ribs and Seared Tofu Scallops
in a Mineola Tangelo–Saffron Sauce, page 80

Orecchiette and Wild Arugula Salad in Vegan Basil-Mint Aioli, page 180

Roasted White Eggplant Fettuccine Alfredo with Fresh Fennel and Spinach, page 62

Vegan Green Papaya Salad (Som Tum), page 192

Pan-Asian Black Sesame–Cabbage Slaw Tossed with Rose Water, Cilantro, and Mint Pesto, page 183

Vegan Tuna and Garlic Cannellini Bean Salad, page 188

White Pepper Vegan Turkey Shawarma with Chipotle-Tomato Relish and
Roasted Garlic, Sage, and Artichoke Tahini Paste, page 173

Basic Burgers, page 164

Coffee-Rubbed Vegan Steak Tacos with Grilled Lobster Mushroom,
Heirloom Cherry Tomato, and Corn Salsa, page 105

Vegan Butternut Squash, Apple, and Onion Galette with Blue Cheese, page 200

Oregano and Basil–Rubbed Marsala Flank Steak Stuffed with Saffron Wild Mushrooms, page 143

Pineapple Five-Spice Bun with Pineapple-Orange Sherry-Glazed Tofu, page 35

Bourbon Buffalo Mole Chicken Wings with Vegan Bleu Cheese–Avocado Oil Aioli, page 166, and Frisée, Carrot, and Celery Stick Salad with Toasted Garlic and Cumin Vinaigrette, page 168

Southern Sea Salt–Pecan Pralines, page 219

Vegan Twinkies, page 198

Satisfying the Vegan Munchies

. . . .

Prepare the steaks: In a small bowl, combine the coffee, brown sugar, black pepper, coriander, cinnamon, and salt well, to create a dry rub. Rub each steak liberally with the coffee rub, then place in an airtight container or plastic bag. Chill the rubbed steaks in the refrigerator for at least an hour. In the meantime . . .

Prepare the salsa: Heat 1 tablespoon of the canola oil in a large skillet over high heat. Add the garlic, corn, lobster mushrooms, and shiitakes to the pan, and cook for 3 to 5 minutes, until browned. Add the sliced sweet onion, plus 1 teaspoon of the lime juice to deglaze the pan. Sauté for about 1 minute, then add the another teaspoon of the lime juice, the corn kernels and the jalepeño. Sauté until the onions are translucent and beginning to brown.

Lower the heat to medium-low and add the quartered heirloom cherry tomatoes to the pan. Sauté for 30 seconds, remove the pan from the heat, and allow to cool to room temperature.

Once cooled, transfer the contents of the pan to a large bowl and toss with the remaining 1 tablespoon of lime juice, green onions, fresh cilantro, and chili powder. Add salt to taste.

Use a sharp knife or electric blade to thinly slice the steak.

Grease a grill pan or large skillet well. Heat the pan over medium-high heat, then grill the slices of steak for 3 to 4 minutes on each side until browned.

Assemble your tacos, adding your desired incidentals and topping with the salsa.

GLUTEN FREE

VEGAN CHICKEN-FRIED TOFU STEAKS WITH ROSEMARY-THYME CHICKEN GRAVY, TWO WAYS: GLUTEN FREE AND REGULAR

> Serves 6 ⋲

1 pound extra-firm tofu, drained well

1 batch Beef-Style Seitan broth (page 6), allowed to cool

2 teaspoons kosher salt

1 teaspoon freshly ground black pepper

½ cup white rice flour

⅓ cup corn flour (not to be confused with cornmeal)

¾ cup cornstarch

¾ teaspoon baking soda

¾ teaspoon paprika or chili powder

1 cup Vegan Egg Yolk Mix (page 28)

Vegetable oil, enough for frying

2 cups prepared Better Than Bouillon No Chicken Base (see page xvi for how to prepare)

½ cup soy milk

½ teaspoon dried rosemary

½ teaspoon dried thyme leaves

1 tablespoon cornstarch dissolved in 1 tablespoon cold water (optional, to thicken gravy)

The love of my life is not only a beautiful woman inside and out, but also gluten free. She also happens to be a Southern gal, and I wanted to make her some down-home comfort food for our first Valentine's Day together. She loved the dish; she asks me to make it about once every two weeks. I know when she calls me from work with that sing-songy, "Honey, are you busy today?" that I'm about to bust out my cast-iron skillet and get crackin'.

I made the non-gluten-free version for her whole family in Louisiana, and they loved it, too. Most of them didn't even know it was vegan! Now what y'all waitin' for. Get fryin'!

Take your block of extra-firm tofu and drain off all the liquid. Then, quarter the block of tofu into eight ¼-inch-thick rectangular slices. Place a sheet of paper towel below and another on top of the tofu, and rest heavy objects on top to press out the moisture. Let sit for 30 minutes, flip the tofu over, and place the objects on top. Let drain for another 30 minutes.

Place the drained tofu in an airtight container, cover with the cooled Beef-Style Seitan broth, and allow to sit in the fridge for at least 3 hours.

Preheat the oven to 250°F. Place a wire cooling rack on top of a baking sheet, and set aside.

Drain the tofu well and season each piece on both sides with the salt and pepper. Place the rice and corn flours, cornstarch, baking soda, and paprika in a pie pan and mix well. Place the Vegan Egg Yolk Mix in a separate pie pan. Dredge each piece of tofu on both sides with the flour mixture, followed by the egg yolk mixture, then finally coat in the flour mixture again. Place the tofu on a plate, and allow it to sit for 10 to 15 minutes before cooking. Reserve the remainder of the flour mixture.

Pour in enough vegetable oil to completely cover the bottom of a 12-inch slope-sided skillet, and set over medium-high heat. Once the oil begins to shimmer, add the tofu in batches, being careful not to overcrowd the pan. Cook each piece on both sides until golden brown, about 4 minutes per side. Place the fried steaks on the cooling rack on top of the baking sheet, then place the sheet into the oven once all of the tofu is fried. Keep warm in the oven until the gravy is ready.

Add more vegetable oil, at least 1 tablespoon, to the pan. Whisk in 3 tablespoons of the flour mixture left over from the dredging. Add the No Chicken broth and deglaze the pan. Whisk until the gravy comes to a boil and begins to thicken. Add the soy milk, rosemary, and thyme, and whisk until the gravy coats the back of a spoon, 5 to 10 minutes. Season to taste, with more salt and pepper, if needed. Thicken with the cornstarch mixture if desired. Serve the gravy over the steaks with Louisiana-Style Yellow Rice (see page 111).

REGULAR

⇒ Serves 6 ⇐

SHAGGY KITCHEN TIP Once your six steak-shaped pieces of seitan have drained and are cool enough to touch, lay each steak on its large, flat side on a cutting board. Holding the knife parallel to the cutting surface, carefully slice the "steaks" in half so that you now have two thinner pieces of steak.

I batch Beef-Style Seitan (page 6), drained well and cut into steak-shaped pieces (see tip)

½ unbleached all-purpose flour

⅓ cup corn flour (not to be confused with cornmeal)

¾ cup cornstarch

¾ teaspoon baking soda

¾ teaspoon paprika

I cup Vegan Egg Yolk Mix (page 28)

Vegetable oil, enough for frying

2 tablespoons vegan margarine

2 sprigs of fresh rosemary

2 sprigs of fresh thyme

2 tablespoons of the flour mixture that you used to dredge the "steaks"

2 tablespoons cornstarch dissolved in 2 tablespoons of cold water (optional, for further thickening)

2 cups prepared Better Than Bouillon No Chicken Base (see page xvi for how to prepare)

Preheat the oven to 200°F or its "Keep Warm" setting. Place a wire cooling rack on top of a baking sheet, and set aside.

Place the all-purpose and corn flours, cornstarch, baking soda, and paprika in a pie pan or large bowl, and mix well. Place the Vegan Egg Yolk Mix in a separate pie pan or large bowl. Dredge each steak lightly on both sides with the flour mixture, followed by the egg yolk mixture, then finally coat in the flour mixture again. Reserve the remaining flour mixture.

Place the steaks on a clean plate, and allow them to sit for 10 to 15 minutes before cooking.

Pour in enough vegetable oil to completely cover the bottom of a 12-inch slope-sided skillet, and set over medium-high heat. Once the oil begins to shimmer, add the steaks in batches, being careful not to overcrowd the pan. Cook each steak on both sides until golden brown, about 5 minutes per side.

Place the fried steaks on the cooling rack on top of the baking sheet, then place the sheet in the oven once all of the steak is fried. Keep warm in the oven until the gravy is ready. If you're a multitasker, feel free to make the gravy while you're frying the steaks.

To make the gravy: Melt the margarine in a saucepan over medium-low heat. Add the sprigs of rosemary and thyme, and sauté for 15 seconds.

Add the 2 tablespoons of the flour mixture to the saucepan, and stir well to combine.

Slowly pour in the No Chicken broth, whisking constantly while pouring, until the flour, margarine, and broth have fully combined. Bring the gravy to a fast simmer, or until thickened to your liking. If you like your gravy extra thick, feel free to whisk in the cornstarch mixture and let it simmer for 2 to 3 minutes longer.

Serve the gravy over the steaks with Louisiana Style Yellow Rice (recipe follows).

LOUISIANA-STYLE YELLOW RICE

Serves 6

2 cups long-grain white rice

1 cup prepared Better Than Bouillon No Chicken Base (see page xvi for how to prepare)

Water

2 to 3 teaspoons salt

1 tablespoon vegan margarine, melted

½ cup chopped shallots or white onions

2 tablespoons olive oil

1 small pinch of saffron

Wash the rice until it is clean. Place the rice in a 2-quart pan. Add the No Chicken broth, then enough water to cover the rice 1 inch above rice line. Add the salt and margarine, and stir well.

Sauté the shallots in the oil until transparent. Add the saffron to the onions. Stir into the rice.

Cover the pan. Simmer for 30 minutes (keep it covered!) until the rice is tender. Remove from the heat, then allow to sit for 5 minutes. Fluff with a fork and serve hot.

SPAGHETTI AND MEATBALLS WITH SAN MARZANO AND PORT WINE MARINARA SAUCE

> Makes 4 large or 6 small servings

2 tablespoons olive oil

2 tablespoons garlic, chopped

1/4 cup fresh basil, chopped

1 teaspoon fresh oregano, chopped

1 teaspoon fresh mint, chopped

1 teaspoon fennel seeds

Salt and cracked black pepper

1/4 teaspoon red pepper flakes

1 (28-ounce) can whole San Marzano tomatoes

2 tablespoons port wine

1 teaspoon sugar

1 pound spaghetti noodles

1 batch Vegan Meatballs (page 11)

Heat the olive oil in a medium-size saucepan over high heat. Add the garlic and cook for 30 seconds. Add the herbs, fennel seeds, a little salt and pepper, and the red pepper flakes. Cook for an additional 30 seconds.

Add the tomatoes, port wine, and sugar. Crush the tomatoes with a potato masher or something sturdy, then bring the mixture to a boil. Lower the heat and simmer, stirring occasionally, until the sauce reaches your desired thickness. The cooking can take anywhere from 30 minutes to 1 hour and 15 minutes, depending on how thick you like your pasta sauce. Taste for salt and pepper.

Cook the spaghetti as directed on the package, until al dente. Drain, toss with a bit of olive oil to prevent sticking, then serve topped with the meatballs and sauce.

SHAGGY KITCHEN TIP This sauce tastes amazing on a pizza. Just make sure you let it thicken a lot before topping it on your favorite pie. It needs to reduce for at least an hour.

THAI TOFU, VEGETABLE, AND COCONUT SOUP

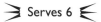 Serves 6 ⋶

1 $\frac{1}{2}$ tablespoons vegetable oil

3 cloves garlic, minced

12 ounces firm tofu, drained well and cut into $\frac{1}{2}$-inch cubes

$\frac{1}{2}$ teaspoon dried red chile pepper flakes

1 teaspoon salt

2 $\frac{1}{2}$ tablespoons sesame oil

1 shallot, minced

$\frac{1}{2}$ teaspoon fresh ginger, grated (jarred is also fine)

1 stalk lemongrass, sliced thinly (see tip)

1 medium-size yellow onion, diced

$\frac{1}{2}$ cup carrots, sliced thinly

$\frac{3}{4}$ cup red or yellow bell peppers, seeded and julienned

$\frac{1}{2}$ cup water chestnuts (optional)

$\frac{1}{2}$ cup black mushrooms (optional)

2 cups coconut milk

2 cups prepared Better Than Bouillon No Chicken Base (see page xvi for how to prepare) or vegan vegetable broth

1 tablespoon Au Lac Vegetarian Fish Sauce, Bragg Liquid Aminos, or light soy sauce)

1 teaspoon curry powder

1 teaspoon coriander seeds

$\frac{1}{4}$ teaspoon ground cumin

Pinch of turmeric

2 tablespoons freshly squeezed lemon juice

1 teaspoon freshly squeezed lime juice

1 cup tightly packed fresh Thai basil leaves

Freshly ground black pepper

$\frac{1}{4}$ cup tightly packed cilantro leaves

As hard as this may be to believe, this was one of my "what can I throw together with the contents of my kitchen?" recipes. Although I love going to the grocery store more than I love shoe shopping, sometimes even I cave to laziness. When the California weather turned cold (okay . . . it was 55 degrees out, but I've been spoiled), my cravings were hell bent on a nice bowl of soup. If you've got the soup-itis, I promise this will satisfy it.

SHAGGY KITCHEN TIP Chop all the vegetables in advance. Make sure you pound the lemongrass with a heavy object, then remove the tough outer layers before slicing.

Heat the vegetable oil in a large soup pot over high heat. Add 1 clove of the minced garlic and sauté 30 seconds, until fragrant. Add the tofu, chile pepper flakes, and $\frac{1}{2}$ teaspoon of the salt, and fry the tofu until golden brown on all sides. Lower the heat to medium-high and transfer the tofu to a paper towel–lined plate.

Heat the sesame oil in the same pot, then add the rest of the garlic, shallot, ginger, and lemongrass.

(continues)

113

Thai Tofu, Vegetable, and Coconut Soup (continued)

Sauté for 2 minutes. Add the onion, carrots, peppers, water chestnuts, and mushrooms, and sauté until all the onions are browned and translucent. Lower the heat to medium, add the coconut milk, broth, fish sauce, the spices, and the lemon and lime juice. Stir to combine, then allow the soup to come to a boil. Lower the heat to low. Add the Thai basil and tofu. Taste for salt and pepper. Let simmer another 15 minutes, then serve garnished with cilantro.

GREEN GARLIC GUMBO

 Serves 12

My personal experiences with the South are a bit limited, and, quite frankly, embarrassing.

The farthest South I've ever traveled is Boca Raton, Florida, to visit my Jewish grandparents. They welcomed me with open arms to their ostentatious housing development where I, at the ripe age of eighteen, had the unique opportunity to experience the Lifestyles of the Rich and Senile. I drank coffee at 6:00 A.M. and read the Wall Street Journal *with Papa. I played mah-jongg poolside with ladies named Dolores, Ruth, and Helen while noshing on tea sandwiches and absorbing every ounce of gossip about the scandalous elderly Boca Jewish women. And at promptly 4:15 P.M. every day, we piled into Papa's BMW and headed out to dine at one of his favorite Michelin-starred restaurants. The only, and I do mean only, thing that distracted me from their conversations about the stock market and beta-blockers were the amazing, complex flavors dancing on my palate. I feel like that brief point in my life spoiled my taste buds rotten, and I loved every minute of it.*

Why this long-winded story, you ask? Well, I don't want anyone to think I claim to know the true ways of grits, gravy, or gumbo. I did have some delicious veggie gumbo when I was living with my grandparents, but a waiter named Gustave served it to me on fine china. I don't believe it counts. You'll also have to forgive the fake meat madness in this

1 cup all-purpose flour

$\frac{2}{3}$ cup canola or vegetable oil

2 stalks green garlic, chopped

5 to 6 cloves garlic, chopped

2 large yellow onions, chopped

2 ribs celery, chopped

1 large carrot, chopped

1 large bell pepper, seeded and chopped

3 bay leaves

2 quarts water

Tabasco sauce

Vegan Worcestershire sauce

Salt and freshly ground black pepper

2 to 3 pounds okra, tops removed and sliced into $\frac{1}{2}$-inch-thick rounds

2 (8-ounce) cans tomato sauce

3 to 4 green onions, chopped

1/4 cup water mixed with 1$\frac{1}{2}$ tablespoons Better Than Bouillon No Chicken Base

1 small bunch flat-leaf parsley, chopped

Paprika

Cayenne

Onion powder

1 (10.5 ounce) package Vegetarian Plus Vegan Shrimp, thawed

$\frac{1}{2}$ batch Chicken-Style Seitan (page 5) or store-bought, cubed

1 (13-ounce) package Vegan Sausage (I used Field Roast Italian Flavor)

1 big-ass pot of fluffy white rice (just basic prepared white rice)

delicious Green Garlic Gumbo. It was go big, or go home. Use store-bought vegan meats to save a lot of prep time.

If it suits your fancy, precook your vegan meats in a large skillet with some Cajun seasonings. As Emeril would say, it'll give your gumbo some bam! Also, prep/cut everything in advance. Note that this recipe makes a lot of gumbo. You may want to halve the recipe.

Preheat a large skillet over medium-high heat. Make a roux by combining the flour and oil, and stirring it as it cooks until it reaches a chocolate brown color. Add both garlics, and sauté for 30 seconds, until fragrant. Add the onion, celery, carrot, bell pepper, and bay leaves. Transfer to a large non-reactive pot. Add the water and bring to a boil. Add the Tabasco, Worcestershire, salt, pepper, okra, and tomato sauce. Boil for about 1 hour. Add the green onions, bouillon mixture, and parsley, and boil for another 20 minutes. Lower the heat to a simmer, and season with paprika, cayenne, and onion powder. Add the shrimp, chicken, and sausage. Allow the gumbo to simmer until the meats are fully cooked through, about 20 minutes. Add the cooked rice, or serve over rice.

BELGIAN ALE AND ROASTED GARLIC-INFUSED WHITE CHICKEN CHILI GUMBO

 Serves 8

Olive oil, enough for sautéing ground vegan chicken

½ batch Chicken-Style Seitan (page 5), ground in a food processor or blender (about 8 ounces)

16 tablespoons (2 sticks) vegan margarine

1¼ cups self-rising flour

1 head garlic, roasted (see tip)

1 medium-size yellow onion, chopped finely

4 ribs celery, chopped finely

1 yellow bell pepper, seeded and chopped finely

2 bay leaves

4 cups prepared Better Than Bouillon No Chicken Base (see page xvi for how to prepare)

1 (12-ounce) bottle Belgium White Ale

1 tablespoon green Tabasco sauce

1 teaspoon vegan Worcestershire sauce

½ cup salsa verde

½ pound okra, sliced

½ pound white button mushrooms, sliced thinly

Salt and freshly cracked black pepper

1 bunch collard greens

1 (15-ounce) can cannellini beans, drained

5 green onions, sliced thinly

½ cup flat-leaf parsley leaves, chopped

½ cup fresh cilantro leaves, chopped

2 teaspoons ground cumin

SHAGGY KITCHEN TIP To roast garlic, preheat the oven to 400°F. Slice off the top of the head of garlic so that all the cloves are revealed. Place the head of garlic on a sheet of aluminum foil, drizzle with olive oil, then wrap the head in foil. Bake for 30 minutes, then set aside to cool. The roasted cloves should squeeze right out.

Drizzle some olive oil into a large skillet and heat over medium-high heat. Add the ground chicken to the skillet and sauté until browned, 6 to 8 minutes. Set aside.

Preheat a large stockpot over medium-high heat. Make a roux by melting the margarine, then combining with the flour and stirring until it just reaches the color of the margarine. Add the roasted garlic and sauté for 30 seconds, until fragrant.

Add onions, celery, bell pepper, and bay leaves. Stir to combine. Sauté until the mixture begins to soften, 6 to 7 minutes. Add the No Chicken broth and beer, then bring to a boil.

Add green Tabasco, Worcestershire, salsa verde, okra, mushrooms, and a pinch of salt and pepper. Boil for about 30 minutes.

1 teaspoon Creole seasoning

$\frac{1}{2}$ teaspoon dried oregano

Pinch of cayenne

Pinch of onion powder

$\frac{1}{4}$ teaspoon filé powder

$1\frac{1}{2}$ tablespoons yellow cornmeal

$1\frac{1}{2}$ tablespoons freshly squeezed lemon juice

Salt and freshly cracked black pepper

3 to 4 cups cooked white rice

Add collard greens, beans, green onions, parsley, and cilantro, and boil for another 20 minutes.

Lower the heat to a simmer, and season with cumin, Creole seasoning, oregano, cayenne, and onion powder. Add the chicken, and allow the gumbo to simmer until the vegan meats are fully cooked through, about 20 minutes. Stir in the filé, cornmeal, and lemon juice, then cook for an additional 4 minutes. Taste for salt and pepper.

Serve with rice.

HEIRLOOM BEAN, RED RUSSIAN KALE, AND WHEAT BERRY CHILI

⋙ Serves 6 to 8 ⋘

I love this recipe because it covers all the "taste bases." It's savory, sweet, a tad bit spicy, and completely satisfying. The lime juice and avocado added at the end really does this chili justice. If you can't find Red Russian kale, fear not. You can substitute one bunch of regular or purple kale instead.

In a large pot over medium-high heat, heat the olive oil until it's hot but not smoking. Add the garlic, and sauté 30 seconds until fragrant. Add the onion, bell pepper, Jamaican allspice, chili powder, cumin, salt, and pepper, and sauté for 5 to 7 minutes, until tender. Add the tomatoes, beans, No Chicken broth, and agave. Raise the heat to high and bring to a boil, then lower the heat to a simmer and cover. Allow the soup to simmer for 25 minutes.

(continues)

Heirloom Bean, Red Russian Kale, and Wheat Berry Chili (continued)

2½ tablespoons olive oil

6 cloves garlic, minced

I large onion, chopped

I yellow bell pepper, seeded and chopped

Pinch of Jamaican allspice

2 teaspoons chili powder

1½ teaspoons ground cumin

Salt and freshly ground black pepper

2 (14-ounce) cans fire-roasted diced tomatoes

2½ cups cooked fresh mixed heirloom beans (I used scarlet runner and cannellini)

2 cups prepared Better Than Bouillon No Chicken or Vegetable Base (see page xvi for how to prepare)

2 teaspoons blue or light agave nectar

I large bunch Red Russian kale, chopped roughly

2 cups wheat berries, cooked

Juice of I lime

I avocado, seeded and diced

½ cup fresh cilantro leaves, chopped

Add the kale and cooked wheat berries, and allow the kale to wilt and the wheat berries to heat through, 5 to 7 minutes. Remove from the heat, add the lime juice, and taste for salt and pepper. Serve garnished with diced avocado and cilantro.

CREAMY ROASTED PUMPKIN, SHERRY, AND TARRAGON SOUP

⇒ Serves 6 ⇐

1 (2-pound) sugar pie pumpkin, cored, seeded (seeds reserved), and quartered (see tip)

1 teaspoon canola oil, plus more for roasting the pumpkin

Salt

2 tablespoons vegan margarine, melted

1 medium-size onion, chopped

3½ cups prepared Better Than Bouillon No Chicken Base (see page xvi for how to prepare)

2 sprigs fresh tarragon

¾ cup MimicCreme or alternative (page 3)

⅛ teaspoon white pepper

¼ cup dry sherry

SHAGGY KITCHEN TIP If you can't find fresh pumpkin, you can substitute 2 cups of canned pumpkin instead. Just make sure you also buy about a cup of pumpkin seeds as well, for the garnish. If you are using prewashed seeds, there's no need to clean and dry them. Skip to tossing them with the melted margarine. If you are using canned pumpkin, begin with the "Heat the 1 teaspoon of canola oil" step below.

Preheat the oven to 400°F.

Place the pumpkin seeds in a colander, and give them a good rinse and drain. Set on a paper towel–lined baking sheet, blot dry, and set aside.

Brush a little canola oil on the pumpkin quarters, sprinkle them generously with salt, and then bake on a baking sheet until soft, about 1 hour. Lower the oven temperature to 300°F.

Once the pumpkin seeds are dry, place in an airtight container or plastic bag and toss with melted margarine and a few pinches of salt. Spread out on a baking sheet and bake for about 45 minutes, while you make the rest of the soup.

(continues)

119

Creamy Roasted Pumpkin, Sherry, and Tarragon Soup (continued)

Once the pumpkin is cool enough to handle, scoop the flesh away from the skin, place into a large bowl, and mash well with a potato masher or puree in a food processor.

Heat the 1 teaspoon of canola oil in a large stockpot over medium-high heat. Add the onion and sauté until translucent. Add the pumpkin, No Chicken broth, and tarragon, and stir well. Bring to a boil, cover, and lower the heat to a simmer. Allow to simmer for about 35 minutes.

Turn off the heat, then remove tarragon sprigs (don't discard) and puree the mixture with an immersion blender, or in batches in a regular blender.

Return to the stockpot and whisk in the MimicCreme, white pepper, sherry, and tarragon.

Heat over medium-high heat until fully warmed, taste for salt, then serve garnished with toasted pumpkin seeds.

CHEESY SWEET ONION AND HEIRLOOM TOMATO PIE*

> Makes 1 pie, 6 to 8 servings

SHAGGY KITCHEN TIP You can substitute 2 tablespoons of Vegan Egg Mix (see page 28) since you're already making it for the scrambled eggs. It tastes very similar to the Parmesan.

Preheat the oven to 375°F.

Bake the premade piecrust for 10 to 13 minutes, or until lightly golden around the edges. Remove from the oven, then transfer to a cooling rack to cool. Take 2 tablespoons of the scrambled eggs and ½ tablespoon of the olive oil, and whisk

* *Inspired by an original most unvegan recipe by Emeril Lagasse and Jessie Tirsch.*

2 tablespoons Vegan Parmesan Blend (page 22; see tip)

1 unbaked store-bought piecrust (make sure it's a vegan one!), or Piecrust (page 212)

½ cup plus 2 tablespoons Vegan Scrambled Eggs (page 27)

1½ tablespoons olive oil

2 pounds ripe heirloom tomatoes, peeled

Salt and freshly ground black pepper

⅓ cup plain vegan bread crumbs

¼ cup Vegenaise

¾ cup thinly sliced sweet onions, such as Vidalia

¼ teaspoon fresh thyme leaves

2 teaspoons fresh basil, chiffonaded (see instructions on page 43)

½ cup Vegan Fontina, (page 24)

½ cup grated vegan mozzarella cheese

together well. Brush the surface of the piecrust with a light coating of the mixture, and set the crust aside.

To peel the tomatoes, drop them in salted, boiling water for 1 minute. When they're cool enough to handle, cut an X on their bottoms, and peel off the skins. Cut off the stem and root ends of the tomatoes, the cut into ¼-inch slices and sprinkle with salt and pepper.

Sprinkle one-third of the bread crumbs on the bottom of the piecrust.

Mix the mayonnaise and the remaining ½ cup of the scrambled eggs in a small bowl until fully combined. Then place a layer of the sliced heirloom tomatoes (you should use about half of them) on top of the bread crumbs in the bottom of the piecrust. Top the tomato layer with half of the sliced onions.

Spoon half of the mayo mixture over the onions, and gently smooth out evenly with a spatula. Then layer on half of the thyme and fresh basil, half of the fontina, and half of the mozzarella. Top with half the remaining bread crumbs, remaining tomato slices, remaining onions, remaining fontina, and remaining mozzarella.

Once again, spoon the remaining mayo mixture on top, and gently smooth out evenly. Sprinkle with the remaining thyme and basil, top with the last of the bread crumbs, and drizzle with the remaining tablespoon of olive oil.

Cover the top with Parmesan, place in the oven, and bake until bubbly hot and golden brown, about 1 hour and 15 minutes. Remove from the oven and allow to cool for at least 30 minutes before slicing and serving. Serve warm or at room temperature.

CHICKEN PAPRIKASH

⋛ Serves 8 ⋚

1 pound dried eggless wide noodle ribbons (Garden Time Organic Pasta is my favorite)

1 to 2 tablespoons canola oil, for de-sticking noodles

½ cup sweet paprika

1 tablespoon smoked Spanish paprika

¼ cup unbleached all-purpose flour

2 tablespoons vegan margarine

2 batches Chicken-Style Seitan (page 5), cubed

Salt and freshly ground black pepper

5 cups yellow onion, chopped finely

1 leek, trimmed, halved lengthwise, cleaned well, and sliced thinly

3½ cups prepared Better Than Bouillon No Chicken Base (see page xvi for how to prepare)

3 tablespoons garlic, chopped or pressed with a garlic press (about 10 medium-size cloves)

2 bay leaves

Pinch of cayenne

Pinch of ground cumin

1½ to 2 teaspoons kosher salt

2 cups Vegan Crème Fraîche (page 25) or store-bought vegan sour cream

1 teaspoon white vinegar

1 to 2 tablespoons freshly squeezed lemon juice

Cook the noodles until al dente, drain well, and toss with the canola oil. Set aside.

In a small bowl, combine both paprikas and the flour.

Using a very large, heavy-bottomed, non-nonstick skillet (that's right, kids . . . Bubbe said the chicken must stick, for that golden glow!), melt the margarine over medium-high heat.

Once the pan is heated and the margarine is melted, sprinkle the chicken with some salt and pepper. Add the chicken to the pan, and fry until golden brown on each side. Once fully browned, leave the heat source on, but transfer the chicken to a paper towel–lined plate.

Add the onions and leek to the pan and sauté, stirring constantly, until they begin to brown. Add the paprika mixture and stir constantly for 1 minute, until a thick paste is formed. Stir in the No Chicken broth, garlic, bay leaves, cayenne, cumin, kosher salt, and 1 teaspoon of pepper, then bring to a boil. Cover and let simmer, stirring occasionally, for 15 to 20 minutes.

Leaving the burner on, remove the pan from the heat, add the crème fraîche, and mix well. Place the pan back over the heat and return to a boil. Taste for salt, add the vinegar and lemon juice, then serve over the noodles and enjoy!

VEGAN DORITOS

≩ Makes 1 large bag of Vegan Doritos ≩

1 (10-ounce) block vegan cheddar cheese
1½ teaspoons onion powder
1 teaspoon garlic powder
½ teaspoon yellow mustard powder
¼ teaspoon red paprika
¾ teaspoon salt*
Pinch of cayenne
1 (10- to 12-ounce) bag corn tortilla chips

* *The amount of salt you need may be more or less, based on the sodium levels of the corn chips you use.*

I woke up the other morning, took a shower, and then ran across the street to the drugstore to pick up some deodorant. As I was leaving the store, there was this guy sitting outside on his lunch break. He was eating . . . no . . . he was making love to a bag of Nacho Cheese Doritos. The wide, neon orange smile on his face unleashed my inner fat kid. My favorite lunch in second grade was a bagel with cream cheese, an apple, and a mini bag of Doritos. The craving took over me. I needed to figure out a way.

Following a trip to my favorite co-op, I set to work in my kitchen. It took up most of my afternoon, but it was completely worth it. These chips even leave that nacho-y, cheesy aftertaste in your mouth!

This recipe is not difficult, but it does require quite a bit of time and effort. If you have a deep fryer, I highly recommend you use it in place of the oven-baking step at the end of the recipe. Just fry for a minute or two, then allow to cool.

(continues)

Vegan Doritos (continued)

Preheat the oven to 325°F. Line a rimmed baking pan with parchment paper. Grate the cheddar cheese as finely as possible, then spread out onto the parchment paper. Bake for 5 minutes, or until it's fully melted but not burned. Remove the pan from the oven, leaving the oven on.

Allow the cheese to cool for a few moments, then use a paper towel to blot as much excess moisture off the top as possible. Place the cheese back in the oven and bake for another 4 minutes. Let the cheese cool again, and blot once more.

Scrape the cheese into a bowl and use a paper towel to gently pat as much moisture out as possible. Allow the cheese to sit for another 10 to 15 minutes.

Make your spice blend by mixing together the remainder of the ingredients in a small bowl.

Place the cheese in a food processor and blend until it becomes a creamy yet dry paste.

And now, the crazy part . . .

Raise the oven temperature to 350°F, and bust out another large baking pan.

Use your fingers to rub each chip with a very thin coat of the nacho cheese paste.

If you don't like a lot of spice, skip the next step and just sprinkle the seasoning blend on when the chips are on the baking pan. If you like a lot of spice, place each cheese-covered chip in a large, airtight container or paper bag, and gently toss with the spice blend.

Spread the chips out on a baking pan and bake for 3 to 5 minutes, or until starting to get crispy (just starting to brown.) Enjoy immediately!

VEGAN SPICY NO-TUNA SUSHI ROLL

⋛ Makes about 6 rolls ⋚

TEZU
1 1/8 cups water
2 tablespoons rice vinegar

SUSHI RICE
2 1/4 cups sushi rice
2 1/2 cups water

SUSHI VINEGAR
1/4 cup rice vinegar
2 tablespoons sugar
1 teaspoon salt

JACKFRUIT SPICY TUNA
1 (16-ounce) can young green jackfruit, packed in brine (see page 19)
1 tablespoon canola oil, plus more for cooking
1 1/2 teaspoons tamari
3 tablespoons Au Lac Vegetarian Fish Sauce or light soy sauce
2 to 3 tablespoons Vegenaise (depending on how creamy you like it)
As much chili sauce as you can handle (also adds the tuna-ish color)
A pinch of salt and freshly ground black pepper

OTHER SUSHI INCIDENTALS
6 to 8 sheets nori
Daikon sprouts
Shredded carrots
Sliced avocado
Whatever other veggies you'd like!

First things first, you are going to need some ass-kickin' sushi rice. Go to your local Asian grocer, and equip your fine self with some real sushi rice, nori sheets, and a sushi rolling mat. Use a rice cooker if possible—it really helps the process go more smoothly. If not, a heavy pot with a tight lid is necessary. Make sure to measure the ingredients carefully. You want the rice to be perfectly moist and sticky, and have a great mild flavor to boot.

Prepare the tezu, a basic water-and-vinegar mixture that prevents the sushi rice from sticking to your fingers: Combine the vinegar and water in a shallow bowl. Set aside.

Prepare the rice: Place the rice in a colander in your sink, and rinse and drain it several times until the water draining out of the bottom runs pretty clear. Then, let the rice sit to dry for 30 minutes.

Place the rice in your rice cooker, then add the water. Turn the cooker on, then let it work its magic. No peeking! Leave the lid on.

If you're doing this on the stove top, place the rice and water in a lidded, heavy-bottomed pot, heat until the water's boiling, then cover and lower the

(continues)

Vegan Spicy No-Tuna Sushi Roll (continued)

heat as low as it'll go. Let the rice steam for 18 minutes. Again, don't pick up the lid. After the 18 minutes, remove the pot from the heat source and let it stand, covered, for another 15 minutes.

While the rice is cooking, prepare the sushi vinegar: Combine the rice vinegar, sugar, and salt in the smallest saucepan you have. Heat over medium-low heat, stirring constantly, until all the sugar dissolves. Remove from the heat and allow the vinegar mixture to cool to room temperature.

Remove the lid from your cooked rice, and using a wooden spatula or spoon, gently fold the rice over itself. Do your darnedest not to smash the grains as you fold.

If you have a gigantic wooden bowl, great! If not, a gigantic glass bowl will also work. Using a cloth or paper towel, wipe down the bowl with some of the tezu mixture. Add the rice to the bowl, and pour one-quarter of the sushi vinegar over the rice. Fold the sushi vinegar into the rice, then repeat the process until all the sushi vinegar has been incorporated.

Next, either fan the rice or place it in front of an electric fan for 5 minutes. The rice should be sticky to the touch and a little bit chewy.

Prepare the jackfruit spicy tuna: Drain the can of jackfruit well by squeezing over a colander. Break up the fruit into smaller pieces as you squeeze out the liquid. Place in a bowl and drizzle with the tablespoon of canola oil, tamari, and fish sauce. Mix well.

Heat a little more canola oil in a large skillet over medium-high heat. Pan-fry the jackfruit until it's just beginning to brown, then set aside in a bowl to cool to room temperature.

Once cooled, mix in the mayo and chili sauce. Taste for salt and pepper. You can optionally puree the spicy tuna in a food processor.

Refrigerate until ready to use.

While the spicy tuna chills, it's a great idea to prep and lay out the incidental vegetables on a cutting board next to your sushi-rolling space, for ease and convenience.

To assemble: Bust out your spicy tuna, tezu, and rice, and set to work! I use about a handful of rice—I don't like gigantic sushi rolls, and I find that less is more when learning how to roll sushi. Place one nori sheet on the sushi rolling mat. Spread out the rice over about two-thirds of the nori sheet, and line up your fillings along the middle of the rice, parallel with the direction in which you are going to roll up the mat.

Brush a little tezu along the un-rice-covered end of the nori so that the sushi rolls will seal properly. Then use the rolling mat to slowly but firmly roll the nori up like a jelly roll.

Once all rolled, on a hard surface and using a good (a.k.a. sharp) serrated knife, slice the rolls into six pieces. Have self-confidence and slice quickly and firmly (trust me—I have to psych myself into it).

VEGAN PORK CHOPS AND CRANBERRIES IN OREGON PINOT NOIR REDUCTION WITH WILD MUSHROOM, KALE, BEET, AND HAZELNUT HASH

≥ Serves 6 ≤

And now, a poem written following the first bite of this creation:

Rachael Ray, you make my day.
Alas, everything you cook contains so much whey!
You love your meat,
Which I don't eat.

(continues)

Vegan Pork Chops and Cranberries . . . (continued)

1½ batches Pork Chop–Style Seitan
(page 7)

Salt and pepper

4 tablespoons extra-virgin olive oil—or
as Rachel would say, "Evoo."

1 cup chopped hazelnuts

2 leeks, trimmed, halved lengthwise,
cleaned well, and sliced

½ cup dried cranberries

1 cup Willamette Valley Pinot Noir
(2 Buck Chuck is also fine)

1 cup prepared Better Than Bouillon
No Chicken Base (see page xvi for
how to prepare)

3 tablespoons vegan margarine

2 shallots, sliced thinly

1 pound cremini mushrooms, sliced

½ pound shiitake caps, sliced

1 bunch kale, chopped

1 (15-ounce) can sliced beets, drained

6 ounces Sunergia Soyfoods Soy Bleu
Cheese Alternative, crumbled
(optional)

1 loaf crusty French bread, for dipping
in the sauce. Trust me.

I wish a little fairy
Would make you hate dairy!
You know your way around the kitchen,
So I decided to stop bitchin'.
And after veganizing your recipe,
I am totally smitten.

All right, all right. I'm just messin' around. I don't really think Rachael's that bad. In fact, this recipe was originally hers. It worked so well veganized. Try to get the Willamette Valley Pinot Noir, if you can. It really is delicious, and there will be plenty left over to drink with dinner.

Preheat a large skillet over medium-high heat. Sprinkle the pork chops with salt and pepper. Pour 2 tablespoons of the olive oil into the hot skillet, then add the chops. Allow the chops to brown, 4 to 5 minutes per side. Remove the chops from the pan and set them aside, leaving the pan on the stove.

Fully preheat a second very large skillet or wok over medium-high heat. Place the hazelnuts in the skillet and brown for 2 to 3 minutes. Remove from the pan and set aside.

To the pork chop skillet, add another tablespoon of olive oil, then add the sliced leeks. Cook until the leeks are soft, about 4 minutes. Add the cranberries and wine, then scrape the pan well and add the No Chicken broth. When the sauce comes to a boil, place the chops back in the pan, lower the heat to low, and simmer for about 10 minutes. Add 2 tablespoons of margarine to the sauce, and stir until fully melted and incorporated.

Take your second (hazelnut) skillet, and add the final tablespoon of olive oil and 1 tablespoon of the margarine. When the margarine melts, add the shallots, then the mushrooms, and cook 5 minutes. Add the kale, and allow it to wilt. Season with salt and pepper to taste. Once the kale has fully wilted, add the beets and gently stir.

Serve the chops and sauce over the vegetable hash, and garnish with hazelnuts and Soy Bleu crumbles.

Don't forget the bread! Spread remaining margarine on the bread prior to serving, if desired.

TAIWANESE MINCED PORK AND GARLIC CHIVE CHOW MEIN

⇉ Serves 6 ⇇

I love a good cooking challenge. I sent out invites to a dinner party, specifically wanting to impress a friend of mine who had recently moved to California from Taiwan.

"What's something from home you've been craving?" I asked her.

"Chow mein. Real chow mein," she replied.

Deal. Game on. With the help of Google Translator, I was able to decipher and adapt a real Taiwanese chow mein recipe for our vegan shindig. She loved it so much, I think she

(continues)

Taiwanese Minced Pork and Garlic Chive Chow Mein (continued)

¼ cup dried shiitake mushrooms
½ batch Pork Chop–Style Seitan (page 7)
1 pound thin rice noodles
Peanut or vegetable oil, for cooking
1 medium-size yellow onion, sliced
6 cloves garlic, minced
2 teaspoons Chinese five-spice powder
½ plus ⅓ cup light soy sauce
⅛ teaspoon sugar
About 2 cups water
1 small bunch green onions, cut into
    1-inch pieces
½ cup carrot, julienned
1 bunch garlic chives, chopped
2 cups bean sprouts
Small handful of cilantro leaves, for
    garnish

ate at least three bowls. She also hooked me up with some authentic cookbooks from her native land, so I'm pretty sure she was impressed and wanting more.

Soak the shiitake mushrooms in some warm water for about 30 minutes. Drain.

Break up the Pork Chop–Style seitan into very small pieces. Place them and shiitakes in your food processor or blender, then process until both are minced finely.

Bring a large pot of water to a boil, turn off the heat, and allow the rice noodles to soak as directed on the package (usually 1 to 3 minutes). Drain well, then rinse with ice-cold water. Toss with a touch of vegetable oil, then set aside.

In a large skillet, heat a few tablespoons of cooking oil over high heat. Add the sliced yellow onion, sauté until translucent, then transfer to a paper towel–lined plate.

Add a little more cooking oil to the same pan. Add the garlic and sauté for about 30 seconds. Add the pork, shiitakes, and five-spice powder, and stir-fry for 2 to 3 minutes. Pour ⅓ cup of the light soy sauce into the pan, then add the sugar and 1 cup of the water. There should be enough water in the pan to just fully cover the contents of the pan. Add more if needed.

Lower the heat to a simmer, cover the pan, and allow the mixture to cook for 50 minutes. Remove the lid, place the onions back in the pan, and stir well. Cover again, and let cook an additional 10 minutes.

Bring the additional cup of water to a boil in a small saucepan.

In a separate large skillet or wok, heat a few tablespoons of cooking oil over high heat, then lightly stir-fry the green onions and carrots for 3 to 4 minutes. Add the remaining ½ cup of light soy sauce and 1 cup of boiling water to the pan, then add the rice noodles and toss the mixture well.

Place the noodle mixture in a large bowl, then toss with garlic chives and bean sprouts. Pour the contents of the pork skillet over the noodles, toss well again, garnish with cilantro leaves, and serve.

4

VEGAN HOLIDAY SURVIVAL KIT: WHEN YOU'RE ⊰DREADING⊱ GOING HOME FOR THE HOLIDAYS

It's been said time and time again: Veg heads have it tough during the holiday seasons. True, places like Whole Foods Market now sell whole vegan turkeys and premade vegan mashed potatoes, but that takes all of the fun out of the game. There's something very special to me about sweating over a hot stove and mulling about the kitchen with the rest of the chefs in my family.

At first, they were skeptics. But when my vegan dishes disappeared long before my relative's omnivore competition, I knew I'd won my family's hearts.

Now I know that when Mom calls every October to ask, "Are you coming home for the holidays, dear?" and I answer, "Not this time," she's not sad because I'll be missing her cooking, she's sad because she was hoping I'd kick her out of the kitchen and take over.

In this chapter, you'll find not only a list of vegan recipes that will help you survive through just about any holiday season, but a way to show off with vegan food bling.

> Being a vegan during any holiday season often conjures up thoughts of dry, flavorless cardboard. Let that myth be dispelled! Whip up some Vegan Sautéed Shallot, Cremini, and Fennel Green Bean Casserole or Vegan Kugel with Broccoli Rabe and Chanterelles. After dinner, you may not be the only vegan in the family anymore.

VEGAN LEMONGRASS, GINGER, AND CORIANDER-INFUSED MATZO BALL SOUP

 Serves 6

MATZO BALLS

- ¾ cup MimicCreme or alternative (page 3)
- 6 tablespoons Vegan Egg Mix (page 28)
- 4 tablespoons (½ stick) vegan margarine, melted
- 6¼ cups prepared Better Than Bouillon No Chicken Base (see page xvi for how to prepare)
- 1 flaxseed egg (1 tablespoon ground flaxseed mixed with 1 tablespoon water; see page 29 for how to prepare)
- 2 tablespoons Ener-G Egg Replacer powder (do not add water to it)
- ½ cup matzo meal
- ¾ cup Arrowhead Mills vital wheat gluten
- 2 teaspoons salt

Passover tends to be a less-than-thrilling holiday for the vegan Jew. I suppose I wouldn't really use the adjective thrilling to describe any Shagrin family religious-oriented gathering. Well, maybe at my bat mitzvah when my grandma and Aunt J drank too much wine and ended up doing the Macarena on top of a table.

Anyway, I derailed for a minute. Back on track.

Passover is a difficult food holiday for vegans because many of the recipes are egg or meat laden. The absence of yeast in Passover products forces many recipes and packaged goods to rely on eggs for their rising effect. Great for Jews, bad for vegans. And just as my grandma could shake a mean tailfeather on the dance, um, table, she could also shimmy and shake her way through the kitchen like nobody else in the family. I would eat so much

134

SOUP BROTH

2 tablespoons canola oil

1 (1-inch-long) piece fresh ginger, grated

1 teaspoon shallot powder

1 teaspoon onion powder

1 teaspoon roasted garlic powder

2 bay leaves

Pinch of celery seeds

CHICKEN SEITAN

1 cup Arrowhead Mills Vital Wheat Gluten

1 teaspoon Better Than Bouillon No Chicken Base mixed with 1 cup water

2 tablespoons MimicCreme or alternative (page 3)

SOUP INGREDIENTS

1 stalk fresh lemongrass, cleaned, pressed, and sliced thinly

A few ribs of celery, sliced

A few carrots, sliced

1 to 2 parsnips, peeled and sliced

1 large yellow onions, diced large

1 leek, trimmed, halved lengthwise, cleaned well, and sliced

Handful of fresh cilantro, chopped

Salt and freshly ground black pepper

of her matzo ball soup that I barely had room for the rest of the meal. Don't worry, though. I'd sit for five minutes until letting out a burp large enough to rattle the fine china and everyone's nerves, then get down to business with the actual meal.

So, why couldn't I just go for it and veganize a basic matzo ball soup recipe? Well, as any good Jewish granddaughter knows, never try to beat Grandma at her own game. Even though she's not with us today, I'm sure my Meemaw would find some way to let me know she was displeased if I messed with perfection. Instead, I'll leave well enough alone and give you a fun East-Meets-Jew soup for your Passover pleasure.

SHAGGY KITCHEN TIP You can simplify this recipe by buying premade vegan chicken, and just cooking the soup until the vegetables are done to your liking.

To make the matzo balls: Combine the MimicCreme, egg mix, ¼ cup of No Chicken broth, margarine, and flaxseed egg, and margarine in medium-size bowl and beat until blended. In a separate bowl, combine the egg replacer, matzo meal, vital wheat gluten, and salt, then gradually add to the wet ingredients while mixing well. Cover with plastic wrap and refrigerate for at least one hour.

(continues)

Vegan Lemongrass, Ginger, and Coriander-Infused Matzo Ball Soup (continued)

Bring the remaining 6 cups of No Chicken broth to a boil in a large pot.

Remove the dough from the refrigerator and roll into walnut-size balls. Drop gently into the boiling broth. Cover the pot and cook for 45 minutes to 1 hour, or until tender and cooked through.

Use a slotted spoon to remove from the broth and serve in the soup.

Start the broth: Take a very large soup pot. Heat the canola oil over medium-high heat, then add the ginger and sauté for 30 seconds, until fragrant. Remove the pot from the heat.

Take all the rest of the soup ingredients and mix them together in the very large pot. Bring to a boil.

While the broth's starting to heat up, make your chicken seitan by mixing and kneading the vital wheat gluten, No Chicken mixture, and MimicCreme until it's completely mixed. It should be a moist seitan dough. Squeeze out the excess liquid and form the mixture into a ball. On a cutting board, flatten out the ball and use a sharp knife or kitchen shears to cut pie-wedge style into six chicken breast–shaped pieces.

Before putting into the boiling broth, flatten each piece of seitan by pressing it firmly between your hands, then drop into the pot along with the lemongrass, celery, carrots, parsnips, onion, and leek.

Cover the pot with a lid, lower the heat to a simmer, and allow to cook for about an hour. Stir every 10 to 15 minutes. Add the cilantro during the last 5 minutes of simmering. Taste the broth for salt and pepper.

Once the seitan is finished, use a slotted spoon to remove each piece from the pot, allow to cool for a moment, then dice as many as you want to serve and return them to the soup pot.

Serve over the matzo balls, garnishing with more cilantro if desired.

VEGAN KUGEL WITH BROCCOLI RABE AND CHANTERELLES

⇒ Serves 6 ⇐

---

1 (1-pound) package Garden Time Organic Egg-less Wide Noodles

½ pound broccoli rabe

6 tablespoons (¾ stick) vegan margarine

1 clove garlic, minced

1 large yellow onion, diced

1 cup chanterelle mushrooms, cleaned well

1 (12-ounce) package Mori-Nu Silken Extra Firm Tofu

1 cup Vegan Crème Fraîche (page 25) or vegan sour cream

1½ cups Vegan Scrambled Eggs (page 27)

2 teaspoons kosher salt

Freshly cracked black pepper

Kugel, by definition, is a traditional Jewish pudding made with noodles, rice, matzo, and potatoes or other vegetables. They can be savory or sweet, a side dish or dessert. My granny Fannie made hers savory, and was considered the family kugel master. There were only a few times I cried from "food mourning" after going vegan, and one of those moments was having to pass up Granny's kugel.

I couldn't just take her recipe and make it vegan. I would have spent way too much time repenting during the Jewish High Holidays. Instead, I decided to give savory kugel my own creative twist. I love the way chanterelles taste in "creamy" sauces, and find the flavor holds strong during extended cooking times. While chanterelles are my favorites, feel free to use any kind of mushrooms in this dish.

Preheat the oven to 350°F, and grease a 9 by 13-inch baking dish.

Cook the noodles in a large pot of salted water until just al dente, then rinse with cold water and toss with a touch of cooking oil to prevent sticking.

Prepare an ice bath (a large bowl of ice water), and set aside.

(continues)

137

Vegan Kugel with Broccoli Rabe and Chanterelles (continued)

Bring a medium-size pot of salted water to a boil, drop in the rabe, and allow to cook for 2 minutes. Drain the rabe, then plunge immediately into the ice bath. Drain well again and set aside.

Melt 2 tablespoons of the margarine in a large skillet over medium-high heat, then add the garlic. Sauté for 30 seconds, then add the onion and sauté until almost translucent. Add the rabe and chanterelles and sauté for another 4 to 5 minutes. Remove the pan from the heat and set aside to cool.

In a food processor, blend the tofu and crème fraîche until mixed well. Don't over-process; there should still be tiny pieces of whole tofu visible.

Using a spatula, transfer the sautéed vegetables to a cutting board. Use a sharp knife to chop roughly. In a large bowl, combine the vegetables, tofu mixture, and all the rest of the ingredients except for the cooked noodles. Once mixed well, stir in the noodles and transfer to the prepared pan. Bake for 50 to 60 minutes, until the top is browned and the center is firm.

VEGAN SAUTÉED SHALLOT, CREMINI, AND FENNEL GREEN BEAN CASSEROLE

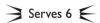 Serves 6

At eight years old, I should have already known I was destined for vegetarianism, at the very least. At Thanksgiving, it was never the turkey that motivated me to drag my behind over to Meemaw and Papa's to endure five long hours of cheek pinching, wine-induced sing-alongs and bad old people breath. It was the side dishes. Macaroni and Cheese and Sweet Potatoes put up a great fight, but Green Bean Casserole will always be at the top of my list.

1½ tablespoons kosher salt

1½ pounds green beans

2 tablespoons vegetable or canola oil

2 teaspoons minced fresh garlic

¼ cup shallot, diced

½ bulb fresh fennel, diced

1 cup cremini mushrooms, chopped

½ teaspoon dried sage

½ teaspoon dried marjoram

½ teaspoon dried thyme

6 tablespoons (¾ stick) vegan margarine

6 tablespoons all-purpose flour

½ teaspoon salt

Freshly cracked pepper

½ tablespoon white miso paste

1¼ cups Imagine Foods Creamy Portobello Soup

¼ cup MimicCreme or alternative (page 3)

1 cup store-bought vegan French-fried onions

2½ tablespoons cornstarch mixed with 3 tablespoons cold water

My mom's was the most ultimate food-coma-inducing, comfort-filled version ever. This stuff didn't just stick to your ribs, it stuck to your heart.

Okay . . . that's enough. Now go buy some green beans.

Preheat the oven to 350°F.

Place 3 quarts of water in a large saucepot, and bring to a boil.

Prepare an ice bath (a large bowl of ice water). Keep it in the freezer so it stays chilled. Add 1½ tablespoons of kosher salt and the green beans to the boiling water. Cover and cook for about 6 minutes, or until crisp-tender and still bright green. Keep an eye on the beans just in case they start to brown before the 6 minutes is up.

Drain the beans in a colander, then plunge into the ice bath. Drain well, then place them on a double layer of paper towels on top of a flat surface. Lay a second double layer of paper towels over the top, then pat down to help dry the beans.

Assemble the casserole: Heat the vegetable oil in a large skillet over medium high heat. Sauté the garlic and shallots for 30 seconds, then add the fennel, mushrooms, and herbs. Sauté until slightly softened. Remove the pan from the heat and set aside.

Using a whisk, in a very large saucepan, melt the vegan margarine over medium-high heat. And the flour, the salt, and ½ teaspoon of the cracked pepper, and whisk together. Add the miso paste and blend in well. Pour in the mushroom soup and

(continues)

Vegan Sautéed Shallot, Cremini, and Fennel Green Bean Casserole (continued)

MimicCreme gradually while stirring constantly. Add the cornstarch mixture, then continue to stir until the mixture begins to boil and thicken.

Add the green beans and about half of the French-fried onions. Stir well.

Pour that mixture into a casserole dish or pan and top with the remaining French-fried onions. Bake for 10 to 15 minutes, until the onions begin to brown. Remove from the oven. Let it cool if you're more patient than I am. Eat.

ROASTED CHESTNUT, MARBLE RYE, AND PANCETTA STUFFING WITH SHERRY, LEEKS, AND BLUE FOOT AND SHIITAKE MUSHROOMS

 Serves 8

Preheat the oven to 425°F.

Using a sharp paring knife, slice a large X along the flat side of the chestnuts. Place on a baking sheet with the X upward. Bake for 20 to 30 minutes, until the chestnuts open up and turn golden brown. Set aside to cool.

Once cool enough to handle, peel the chestnuts, slice into quarters (discard any moldy or black-spotted ones), and set aside.

Lower the oven temperature to 375°F. Grease a 9 by 13-inch casserole dish with either vegan margarine or nonstick spray, and set aside.

On a long, rimmed baking sheet, toast the bread cubes for 15 minutes, stirring halfway through the toasting process. Once the lighter pieces of bread are golden brown, transfer the cubes to a large bowl and set aside.

Melt the margarine in a large skillet over medium-high heat. Add the onion, leek, blue foots, and shiitakes, and cook until all are soft, about 10 minutes. Add the

1 pound whole chestnuts, unpeeled

1 loaf marble rye bread, cut into 1-inch cubes

4 tablespoons (½ stick) vegan margarine

1 yellow onion, halved and sliced thinly

1 leek, white part only, halved lengthwise, cleaned well, and sliced thinly

¼ pound bluefoot white button mushrooms, sliced

¼ pound shiitake mushrooms, stemmed and sliced

1 teaspoon fresh sage, chopped

1 teaspoon fresh thyme

1 teaspoon fresh rosemary, chopped finely

1 batch Vegan Pancetta (page 14)

2 cups prepared Better Than Bouillon No Chicken or Vegetable Base (see page xvi for how to prepare)

½ cup sherry wine

¼ cup Vegan Egg Yolk Mix (page 28)

1½ to 2 teaspoons kosher salt

Freshly cracked black pepper

herbs and sauté for an additional minute. Transfer the contents of the skillet, along with the chestnuts, to the bread bowl.

Add the diced pancetta to the same skillet, and cook over medium heat until browned. Transfer the pancetta to the bread bowl.

In a separate bowl, whisk the No Chicken broth, sherry, and Vegan Egg Yolk Mix together well, then pour over the bread mixture. Sprinkle on the salt and pepper, then toss well. Scrape into the prepared baking dish and cover with foil. Allow it to sit for 1 hour, or overnight in the refrigerator.

Bake for 30 minutes with the foil on top, then remove the foil and bake for an additional 30 minutes. Serve.

GARLICKY WHITE BEANS

⋛ Serves 6 as a side dish ⋚

1 pound dried cannellini beans
2 bay leaves
3 cloves garlic, sliced thinly
3 tablespoons extra-virgin olive oil
1½ teaspoons sea salt
Pinch of black pepper

I love these beans so much, sometimes I just eat them by themselves. I use them in several recipes throughout the book, so you'll see this recipe referenced a few times. If you don't have time to soak and cook fresh beans, see the Shaggy Kitchen Tip.

SHAGGY KITCHEN TIP
If you're under a time crunch, use two cans of cannellini beans. Combine with the remaining ingredients, but reduce the amount of salt to a few pinches (to taste). Allow the beans to sit, covered, in the refrigerator for a few hours. Discard the bay leaves, then use as directed in a recipe or warm on the stove and serve plain.

Soak the beans overnight in a deep bowl of water. Drain the beans well, then place in a large saucepan. Add enough water to the pan to cover the beans by about 3 inches, then bring to a boil. Allow the beans to boil for 20 minutes, then drain and rinse with cold water.

Return the beans to the saucepan, then add the bay leaves, garlic, olive oil, salt, pepper, and enough cold water to fully submerge and cover the beans by a few inches.

Bring to a boil, then let the beans cook for 1 to 2 hours, until softened to your liking.

Drain over a colander in the sink, then discard the bay leaves. Let cool to room temperature. Use as directed in the recipes in *Veganize This!* or eat plain as a side dish.

Keeps covered in the refrigerator for up to one week.

OREGANO AND BASIL-RUBBED MARSALA FLANK STEAK STUFFED WITH SAFFRON WILD MUSHROOMS

⇒ Serves 6 ⇐

1 ¼ batches Beef–Style Seitan (page 6; but see tip)

½ cup tamari

⅛ cup Marsala wine

1 ½ cups tightly packed fresh basil leaves

¼ cup fresh oregano leaves

1 tablespoon olive oil

Splash of freshly squeezed lemon juice

1 ½ teaspoons salt, plus a pinch

Freshly ground black pepper

2 tablespoons vegan margarine

Pinch of Spanish saffron threads

½ leek, white part only, halved, cleaned well, and sliced thinly

¼ cup shallots, diced finely

1 cup cremini mushrooms, sliced

1 cup shiitake mushrooms, sliced

1 cup oyster mushrooms, sliced

Kitchen twine or string

Place the beef in a large, shallow container. Combine the tamari and Marsala wine, then pour over the steak. Allow to marinate for 30 minutes on each side. When finished marinating, reserve the marinade to use as a dipping sauce. You can also reduce it in a saucepan, if desired.

In your food processor or blender, puree the basil, oregano, olive oil, lemon juice, 1½ teaspoons of the salt, and pepper to taste until it forms a uniform paste. Place in an airtight container in the refrigerator until ready to use.

Preheat the broiler.

In a medium-size saucepan, melt the margarine, then add the saffron, leek, and shallots. Sauté for 5 to 8 minutes, until soft. Add all the mushrooms to the pan, sprinkle with salt and pepper, and cook for about 5 minutes, until tender. Set aside.

SHAGGY KITCHEN TIP When making the vegan beef, instead of cutting into steak-size pieces before dropping into the broth, leave it all in one piece. Shape it into a long, flat rectangle 7 to 8 inches long and 4 to 5 inches wide. Drop into the broth and boil for 1 hour, turning every 15 minutes. Drain well, and you're ready to go.

(continues)

143

Oregano and Basil-Rubbed Marsala Flank Steak . . . (continued)

Butterfly-slice the beef so that it opens like a book, being careful not to cut all the way through into two separate pieces. Place the mushroom stuffing inside the steak, then roll it up lengthwise and tie up well with twine.

Rub all over with the herb paste, then broil for 5 to 10 minutes per side until browned but not drying out. Serve.

JUNIPER BERRY AND WHITE PEPPERCORN-RUBBED FIELD ROAST WITH SAGE-INFUSED VEGETABLES AND BALSAMIC ALE-CRANBERRY REDUCTION

 Serves 6

I made this for the first Thanksgiving dinner I ever spent without my parents, and it helped me realize something very profound: If your parents are not at your side enjoying a Thanksgiving feast, they are also not there to help you clean up the gigantic mess produced by said feast.

Was it worth every minute of recipe testing, sweat, and tears? Yes.

To prepare the roast: Using a mortar and pestle or coffee grinder, grind together the juniper berries, peppercorns, and mustard seeds until coarsely ground. Add the thyme, rosemary, and kosher salt, and stir in well.

Place the Celebration Roast on a large sheet of aluminum foil. The sheet of foil must be large enough that it will completely wrap the roast. Brush the roast with 1 tablespoon of the canola oil, then rub roast with a healthy coat of the spice blend. Wrap the foil gently around the roast, then refrigerate for 30 minutes.

1 teaspoon juniper berries

1 teaspoon white peppercorns

1 teaspoon brown mustard seeds

1 teaspoon dried thyme

1 teaspoon dried rosemary

1 to 2 pinches of kosher salt

1 Field Roast Celebration Roast

2 tablespoons canola oil

3 cups vegetable stock

1/3 cup apple juice

1/3 cup white wine

1/8 cup tamari

Big handful of fresh sage leaves

1 cup chopped fresh haricots verts

1 cup chopped heirloom carrots

1 cup well-cleaned and chopped leek

1 cup chopped fingerling potatoes

REDUCTION

1 pound fresh cranberries

1/8 cup balsamic vinegar

10 ounces Duchesse de Bourgogne Flemish Red Ale (trust me . . . best beer ever!), or other red or amber ale

1 teaspoon ground cinnamon

Juice of 1/2 lemon

2 to 3 teaspoons raw sugar

While the roast is in the refrigerator, preheat the oven to 325°F. Bring the stock to a slow boil over medium-high heat. Add the apple juice, white wine, tamari, and remaining tablespoon of canola oil, then lower heat to a simmer. Simmer 4 to 5 minutes, then remove from the heat and allow to cool for 15 to 20 minutes.

Place just the sage and veggies in the bottom of a roasting pan, and cover with the apple juice mixture. Roast for 40 to 50 minutes, until about halfway cooked.

Remove the roasting pan from the oven and place the foil-wrapped roast in the center of the pan, leaving a small opening at the top of the foil to vent. Use a baster or ladle to spoon some of the broth over the roast, then place the roasting pan, covered, back in the oven. Bake the roast for 20 to 25 minutes, or until tender, basting again with pan juices a few times during the cooking time.

To make the reduction: Bring all the reduction ingredients, except the sugar, to a boil, stirring well, and cook until reduced by about one-quarter. Stir in the sugar and remove from the heat. Enjoy hot, cold, or at room temperature.

SHAGGY KITCHEN TIP This also works amazingly well with a Tofurky Holiday Roast.

VEGAN RED WINE AND PEPPERCORN-BRAISED BRISKET

> Serves 6 to 8

- 1 batch Beef-Style Seitan (page 6, but see tip), 1 cup broth reserved
- Salt
- 1½ tablespoons mixed whole peppercorns, crushed
- 1½ tablespoons unbleached all-purpose flour
- ½ tablespoon garlic powder
- 1½ tablespoons olive oil
- 4 whole cloves garlic, peeled
- ½ cup sliced carrots
- 2 medium-size red potatoes, quartered
- 1 large shallot, chopped roughly
- 1 tablespoon chopped fresh rosemary leaves
- 1 cup kosher red wine
- ⅛ cup tomato paste
- ¾ teaspoon paprika
- 1 dried Turkish bay leaf
- ¾ teaspoon dried thyme

For my dear granny Fannie's ninetieth birthday, I thought it was only right to honor her by veganizing one of her signature Shabbos dinner meat recipes. My grandma Fannie is the cutest little old lady I've ever seen in my life, and she has a great sense of style, to boot. She was wearing knit cardigans, cat glasses, and skinny pants before it was the cool thing to do. I'm always getting caught trying to steal her sweaters, so her sassy little self told me that when she goes to the Great Kishka in the Sky, I get first dibs. I swear to Moses, I'm not being morbid. Any time I open my yap and say, "Wow, Grandma—this is so cute!" she lets out a hearty chuckle, throws her hand grandiosely into the air, and says, "I'll will it to ya!" I love her. I hope I have to wait another twenty years for those sweaters.

Season the drained seitan brisket all over with salt and crushed peppercorns. In a shallow dish, with a spoon, combine the flour and garlic powder. Roll the brisket in the flour mixture to coat.

Heat the oil in a large stockpot over medium-high heat. Add the brisket and cook for 5 minutes on each side, or until golden brown on all sides. Transfer to a plate or platter.

Lower the heat to medium and add the garlic, carrots, potatoes, shallots, and rosemary, stirring often, until golden, about 10 minutes. Pour in the wine and stir to deglaze the bottom of the pot. Stir in the tomato paste, paprika, bay leaf, and thyme. Raise the heat to high and bring to a boil.

Cook rapidly, stirring often, until almost all the liquid has evaporated. Pour in the reserved stock and bring back to a boil. Lower the heat to medium and add the brisket. Lower the heat to medium-low, cover, and cook for about an hour. Transfer to a shallow casserole dish, slice, and serve!

SHAGGY KITCHEN TIP Make the Beef-Style Seitan, but do not cut the seitan dough into small pieces. Instead, flatten the giant ball of dough into a roast shape and drop the whole thing into the boiling water. Let it simmer longer than directed—about 1 hour and 15 minutes.

Using tongs, remove the brisket from the broth, and place in a colander to drain. Do not discard the broth. You need at least 1 cup for the braising process. You can also make the brisket in advance and let it marinate in the broth overnight. I feel that's when it's at its finest.

VEGAN MATZO BREI

> Serves 4 <

2½ cups Vegan Scrambled Eggs (page 27)
4 large squares matzo
3 to 4 cups water
1 to 2 tablespoons vegan margarine
Salt and freshly ground black pepper

While I was growing up, I didn't really like matzo. I dreaded the arrival of Pesach, fully knowing that the Matzo Curse was about to rear its ugly head in the Shagrin household. "Curse?" you ask.

Yes.

When it was that time of the Jewish year when leavened bread products could not be consumed, all chaos broke loose. My mother, typically the sweetest, strongest woman I know, would be stricken with matzo-itis. It's a condition that affects the lower digestive organs, plugging her up in the worst way possible. She would try so hard to make it through the duration of the holiday without yeast-risen products. The matzo would continue to accumulate in her lower organs, forcing all of her tension and anxiety to explode from her top . . . and something not so nose-friendly to explode from elsewhere.

Okay. So perhaps I embellished slightly. But I still could rarely get into matzo. The only time I remember thinking, "Wow! Yum!" after taking a bite was when Nanny or Mom would cook matzo brei (a.k.a. fried matzo). Not to be confused with the cheese, brei is actually pronounced like "rye" with a "b" at the beginning. Traditionally, it's matzo scalded with hot water, dipped in beaten eggs, and pan-fried. Some like it savory, some like it sweet. If your sweet tooth is larger than mine, add a little sugar at the end.

Even if you're not Jewish, this makes one hell of a great breakfast, brunch, or even snack. Did I mention it's also great for nursing a hangover? I'll just let that be our little secret.

Make the scrambled eggs first, then set aside.

Break up the matzo into 2- to 3-inch pieces, then place in a colander.

Bring the water to a boil.

Melt the margarine in a large skillet over medium heat.

Once the margarine has melted, brei (scald) the matzo pieces by pouring the boiling water over them, then draining as quickly as possible to prevent sogginess. Quickly mix with the scrambled eggs, and cook over low to medium heat until golden brown on one side, then flip over and brown the other side.

Taste for salt and pepper, then serve immediately.

INDIVIDUAL BROCCOLI, CHEDDAR, AND RICE CASSEROLES IN A CHANTERELLE AND ROSEMARY CREAM SAUCE

 Serves 6

8 tablespoons (1 stick) vegan margarine

6 cloves garlic, minced

1 tablespoon fresh rosemary, minced finely

3 tablespoons all-purpose flour

1 pound chanterelle or cremini mushrooms, chopped roughly

2 to 3 tablespoons water

1¾ cups MimicCreme or vegan buttermilk (page 4)

½ teaspoon salt

Freshly cracked black pepper

1 (16-ounce) package frozen chopped broccoli, thawed, or 3½ cups fresh, chopped

3 cups cooked white rice

½ cups vegan cheddar cheese, grated finely (preferably Daiya brand)

¼ cup seasoned vegan bread crumbs

Preheat the oven to 350°F.

Melt the margarine in a large skillet over high heat, then add the garlic and rosemary. Sauté for about 30 seconds, then stir in the flour to create a roux.

Add the chopped chanterelles and stir well to fully combine.

Lower the heat to medium-high, stir in the water, and cook, stirring frequently, for 2 to 3 minutes, until the mushrooms begin to soften.

Slowly whisk in the MimicCreme, then lower the heat to medium and bring the sauce to a slow boil while stirring frequently. Add salt and pepper to taste.

(continues)

Individual Broccoli, Cheddar, and Rice Casseroles . . . (continued)

Combine the broccoli, rice, 1 cup of the cheddar, and the chanterelle sauce in a large bowl, then spoon the mixture into six individual ramekins. (You can also spoon all of the mixture into one large casserole dish, but see the different baking directions below.) Top casserole with equal amounts of the remaining ½ cup of cheddar and the bread crumbs.

Bake, covered with foil, for 15 minutes. Remove the foil, then bake for an additional 5 minutes, until the cheese is bubbly.

For one large casserole dish, bake in your preheated oven, covered with foil, for 20 minutes. Remove the foil, then bake for an additional 10 minutes until the top is brown and the cheese is bubbly.

Serve.

BUTTERNUT SQUASH AND VANILLA BEAN RISOTTO*

⇒ Serves 6 ⇐

I have this insane ability to never tire of Italian food. It has to be deeply rooted in my genetic lineage, not just my taste buds. It was our cuisine of choice in my household, and I especially love really rustic Italian cuisine that centers around fresh herbs, veggies, oils, lemon juice, and so on. When I'm not working on developing a recipe in another genre, Italian is pretty much all I cook.

I wanted to figure out a way to incorporate "Thanksgiving" and "Italian," and this seemed like a happy medium. It's amazing how the vanilla aroma almost tricks your senses into believing the dish has a sweet taste, when it's actually quite savory. It's the most unusual flavor balance, but it works quite well.

* *Original recipe by Giada De Laurentiis, adapted to suit your vegan fancy.*

4 cups vegan vegetable broth

1 large vanilla bean

12 ounces butternut squash, peeled and cubed

3 tablespoons vegan margarine

¾ cup onion, chopped finely

1½ cups arborio rice

½ cup dry white wine

½ cup Dr-Cow Aged Tree Nut Cheese (any flavor), grated finely, or ¼ cup Vegan Parmesan Blend (page 22) plus ¼ cup vegan mozzarella, grated finely

½ teaspoon salt

Cracked white peppercorns

2 tablespoons chives, chopped finely (for garnish)

Warm the vegetable broth in a saucepan over medium-high heat. Split the vanilla bean in half lengthwise, scrape out the seeds, and add, along with the empty bean pod, to the broth.

Bring to a simmer, then lower the heat to low. Add the squash to the simmering broth, and cook until desired tenderness, about 10 minutes. Remove the squash with a slotted spoon and set aside. Lower the heat to low and cover the pot.

While the broth is covered and simmering, take a large, heavy saucepan and melt 2 tablespoons of the margarine over medium heat. Add the onion and sauté until tender, about 3 minutes. Add the rice and stir well with the margarine.

Add the wine and simmer until it has almost completely evaporated, about 3 minutes. Add ½ cup of the simmering broth and stir until almost completely absorbed, about 2 minutes. Continue cooking the rice, adding the broth ½ cup at a time, stirring constantly. Allow each addition of the broth to absorb before adding the next, until the rice is tender but still firm to the bite and the mixture is creamy, about 20 minutes total.

Discard the vanilla bean pod. Turn off the heat. Gently stir in the butternut squash, cheese, the remaining tablespoon of margarine, and the salt.

Transfer the risotto to a serving bowl and sprinkle with chives. Serve!

QUATTRO GARLIC MASHED POTATOES AND WHITE BEANS

≳ Serves 6 ≲

6 large russet potatoes (I use 3 purple and 3 regular)

Olive oil

1 cup Garlicky White Beans (page 142)

2½ tablespoons garlic paste

½ teaspoon garlic powder

1 cup MimicCreme or alternative (page 3)

3 cloves black garlic, minced

¼ cup fresh chervil, chopped

Salt and freshly ground black pepper

Preheat the oven to 400°F.

Scrub the potatoes well to clean them, then rub with olive oil and bake them for about an hour, until soft to the touch. Remove from the oven, and set aside to cool.

Once cool enough to handle, skin the potatoes, place in a large stockpot, and mash with a potato masher.

Place the stockpot over medium-low heat. Add the Garlicky White Beans, garlic paste, garlic powder, and MimicCreme. Stir well to combine.

Use either an immersion blender, hand mixer, or a strong arm to whip the potatoes until all the ingredients are fully blended and the mashed potatoes are fluffy. Add the black garlic and chervil.

Taste for salt and pepper, then serve.

FENNEL, VIDALIA ONION, AND ROASTED GARLIC POTATO LATKES WITH MOM'S APPLESAUCE

⇒ Serves 6 ⇐

MOM'S APPLESAUCE
4 medium-size cooking apples (Mom uses McIntosh), peeled, pared, quartered, and cored

1 cup water

½ cup vegan brown sugar, packed tightly

¼ teaspoon ground cinnamon

⅛ teaspoon freshly grated nutmeg

LATKES
2 bulbs garlic

2 large russet potatoes

1 bulb fennel

1 large Vidalia onion

1 leek, trimmed, halved lengthwise, cleaned well, and sliced

¼ cup fresh parsley, minced

1 cup MimicCreme or alternative (page 3)

4 teaspoons Ener-G Egg Replacer powder (do not add water)

Salt and freshly ground black pepper

½ cup potato starch

A shit-ton of canola oil, for frying

Vegan sour cream, to serve

Oh, to be a Jew on Christmas. Personally, I don't think enough people realize the annual struggle I endure every December 25 to find the open Chinese restaurant and decent B movie(s) that will help the day be more tolerable.

This past year, I made a pledge. I would not sulk over my toaster-reheated latkes while watching A Christmas Story *for the ninth time. I would not eat Chinese food with my family while longing for a taste of comforting mashed potatoes and vegan gravy. I would participate.*

My mother and I made vegan waffles together. My family set aside Hanukkah presents for Christmas morning just so we'd know what the joy was all about. We spent all day in the kitchen together preparing a feast that left us so full, watching A Christmas Story *for the ninth time seemed like an appealing idea.*

And I still ate these Fennel, Vidalia Onion, and Roasted Garlic Potato Latkes reheated in my toaster for lunch the next day, but I didn't mind one bit. They were so good, even my mom passed up her own recipe to down about five of mine.

(continues)

Fennel, Vidalia Onion, and Roasted Garlic Potato Latkes . . . (continued)

Make the applesauce: In a medium-size saucepan, heat the apples and water over medium heat until boiling. Lower the heat to a simmer and cook, stirring occasionally, for 5 to 10 minutes, until tender. Stir in the brown sugar, cinnamon, and nutmeg, and heat to boiling.

Serve piping hot, room temperature or cool . . . whatever floats your boat.

Make the latkes: Preheat the oven to 400°F. Peel away the outer layers of the garlic bulbs' skin, making sure to leave the skins of the individual cloves intact. Cut off the top quarter of each garlic bulb so that the individual cloves of garlic are exposed. Place on individual sheets of aluminum foil, drizzle and rub well with olive oil, then wrap each garlic head in foil. Place on a baking sheet and bake for 30 to 35 minutes, or until the cloves feel soft when pressed. Set aside to cool.

Lower the oven temperature to 200°F.

Cut the potatoes, fennel, and onion into pieces small enough to fit through the shute of your food processor. Using the grater attachment, shred the potatoes, fennel, and onion, then place the grated goodness in a large bowl. If you really want to get in touch with your inner bubbe, use the big holes on a cheese grater to grate the potatoes by hand.

Combine the leek slices with the grated vegetables and parsley in a large mixing bowl. Add the salt, Ener-G powder, MimicCreme, and black pepper to taste. Squeeze the roasted garlic bulbs out of their skins and into the bowl, and combine well. Sprinkle the potato starch over the vegetables, then stir to combine thoroughly. Taste for salt.

Cover the bottom of a heavy skillet with ⅓ to ½ inch of canola oil, and heat over high heat until just below the smoking point. Scoop a spoonful of batter onto a slotted spatula and use a second spatula to smash the latke into a thin pancake. It should be ⅓ to ½ inch thick. Carefully push the latke into the oil. If it falls apart a little, just press it together with the spatula. Also press down on the latke to flatten it out. The first batch is always the hardest, so go easy on yourself. Add a few more latkes but don't crowd the pan. Fry until golden brown on the bottom and outside corners, then flip and brown the other side. Or, if you're my sister, fry until black and burned.

Transfer the latkes to a plate lined with paper towels to absorb the oil. If you're not serving immediately, place them on a baking sheet and keep warm in the oven. Top with vegan sour cream and serve with Mom's Applesauce!

PUMPKIN TARTARE OVER CHICKPEA–BLACK CUMIN CREPE CRISPS WITH VEGAN SAGE AND WHITE ALE BROWNED BUTTER SAUCE

 Serves 6

CREPE CRISPS
1¼ cups chickpea flour
¾ cup unbleached all-purpose flour
1 teaspoon salt
1 teaspoon ground black cumin
½ cup almond milk
1 cup water
3 tablespoons vegan margarine, melted, plus extra for cooking
1 tablespoon olive oil, plus extra for cooking
Cracked black pepper

The term leftovers is not one that pops up in my daily vocabulary. Now, "left-on-the-table-after-meal-but-devoured-before-refrigeration" or "in-box-after-dinner-and-eaten-on-drive-home-despite-others-staring-and-laughing"—those are phrases that resonate. To be perfectly honest, leftovers kind of haunt me. In a one-woman household, it's easy to have a lot of wasted food. I do my best to see that I throw away as little as possible.

Last Thanksgiving, I gave myself a challenge: Get creative.

This dish was created almost entirely from my Thanksgiving leftovers, satisfying both my self-imposed dare and budding neurosis.

(continues)

Pumpkin Tartare over Chickpea-Black Cumin Crepe Crisps . . . (continued)

TARTARE

2 cups butternut squash, peeled, seeded, and cut into ¼-inch cubes

½ teaspoon grated fresh ginger, plus a pinch extra for steaming

1½ cups cooked fresh pumpkin, or 1½ cups canned pumpkin puree

3 tablespoons coconut milk

2½ tablespoons freshly squeezed lemon juice

1 tablespoon freshly squeezed orange juice

1 teaspoon rice wine vinegar

⅓ cup toasted almond slivers, chopped

½ teaspoon minced garlic

1 small apple, cored, seeded, and diced into ¼-inch cubes

1 tablespoon stone-ground mustard

1 tablespoon olive oil

Salt and freshly ground black pepper

SAUCE

8 tablespoons (1 stick) vegan margarine

½ tablespoon white ale

10 to 12 fresh sage leaves

⅛ cup freshly squeezed lemon juice

⅛ cup freshly squeezed orange juice

1 tablespoon Dijon mustard

1 tablespoon coconut milk

1 teaspoon sugar

Salt and freshly ground black pepper

Prepare the crepes: In a bowl, combine the flours, salt, and black cumin. In another bowl, combine the almond milk, water, 3 tablespoons of melted margarine, and olive oil. Mix the wet ingredients into the dry, whisking constantly. Let stand at room temperature for an hour.

In a skillet, combine a drizzle of olive oil and about ½ teaspoon of the margarine and heat over medium heat. Swirl the pan around as the margarine melts, to coat the pan and blend the oil and margarine well. Give the batter a good stir. Working as quickly as you can, pour 2 to 3⅛ cups of batter into the pan (depending on pan size and how quick you really are) to create a thin pancake. Loosen the crepe with a spatula and flip as soon as the batter starts to set and brown around the edges.

When both sides are golden brown, transfer to a paper towel–lined plate. Repeat the process until you have enough crepe crisps, or run out of batter, occasionally adding more olive oil and margarine to the pan. The crepes can be stacked until ready to use. (These are also great plain with agave nectar. So yum.)

Prepare the tartare: Steam the squash cubes in a steamer basket for 8 to 10 minutes over water that has been mixed with the fresh ginger. When the squash has softened, remove from the steamer and aside to cool. Once the squash has cooled, mix it with the remaining tartare ingredients in a large bowl. Season with salt and pepper to taste.

Make the ale sauce: Heat the margarine in a small skillet over low heat until it browns, 15 to 20 minutes.

Add the ale and sage leaves and lower heat to medium low. Simmer until reduced, about 3 minutes.

In a blender, combine the fresh lemon and orange juice, mustard, coconut milk, and sugar, and blend until pureed. While the machine is running, slowly add the ale mixture to create an emulsion.

Season with salt and pepper and set aside.

To assemble the dish, place a crepe crisp on a plate, top with a scoop of the tartare, then ladle with a few tablespoons of the sauce. Serve immediately.

5

GRILLIN' & CHILLIN': SIT BACK, RELAX, AND LIGHT UP A . . . GRILL

I love the versatility of grilled food. You can use a charcoal, gas, indoor stove-top grill pan, or get really creative and place a grill rack over an open fire. And who's to say it's just for omnivores? Not this kid, that's for sure.

One fact I know is that barbecues happen. We vegans will be invited, then faced with the awkward moment of asking the host if they're buying a pack of vegan frozen burgers. Then of course you have to make sure all the buns and condiments are vegan, that they're using a separate grill surface, and then we have to trust that all will run smoothly. Sound like a hassle? You bet your sweet fanny it is.

I find that when it comes to family picnics, company barbecues, or any other event that's not already suited to fit our needs, it is best to BYOF (bring your own food).

Grillin' & Chillin' provides you with more ways than ten to bring an enjoyable meal for not only yourself, but everyone else who shares your picnic table. With "meaty" recipes for such main dishes as Mini Vegan Veal, Black Peppercorn, and Basil Sliders with Artichoke and Avocado Tapenade, and for great salads such as Vegan Tuna and Garlic Cannellini Bean Salad, you can sit back, relax, and enjoy the party.

Why should omnivores have all the fun at the company picnic? A good friend made my Orecchiette and Wild Arugula Salad in Vegan Basil-Mint Aioli and Vegan Prosciutto-Wrapped Greens, and was promptly promoted from file clerk to office manager (her chief responsibility being to organize and cater all future office parties).

MINI VEGAN VEAL, BLACK PEPPERCORN, AND BASIL SLIDERS WITH ARTICHOKE AND AVOCADO TAPENADE

≥ Makes 8 sliders ≤

BURGER PATTIES
1 batch Veal Chop–Style Seitan (page 10)
1 flaxseed egg (1 tablespoon ground flaxseed mixed with 1 tablespoon water; see page 29 for how to prepare)
1/3 cup seasoned vegan bread crumbs
1/8 cup MimicCreme or alternative (page 3)
1/4 cup fresh basil, chopped
1/8 cup shallots, diced finely
2 cloves garlic, pressed or minced
1 1/2 tablespoons Dijon mustard
1 tablespoon freshly cracked black pepper
1 teaspoon truffle oil or olive oil
1 1/4 teaspoons kosher salt

With summertime picnics in our midst, I thought I'd try out a recipe that could seduce the hunky carnivore pool boy your aunt Gloria invites to the next family soiree. Enjoy!

SHAGGY KITCHEN TIP You can use an additional 1/2 tablespoon of lemon juice if you don't have limes lying around.

Prepare the patty mixture: Allow the veal chops to drain well, then cut into about 1/2-inch dice. Place the veal cubes in a food processor, and run the machine until the meat is almost pureed, about 2 minutes. Transfer the ground veal to a large bowl and carefully drain off about half of the

160

TAPENADE

1 (16-ounce) can artichoke hearts, drained well

1 small Haas avocado, pitted

1/4 cup extra-virgin olive oil

4 cloves garlic

1/2 tablespoon freshly squeezed lemon juice

1/2 tablespoon freshly squeezed lime juice (see tip)

Salt and freshly ground black pepper

ADDITIONAL BURGER INCIDENTALS

2 teaspoons olive oil

8 shiitake mushrooms, stemmed and sliced

Salt and freshly ground black pepper

8 miniature vegan buns, bagels, or dinner rolls

8 slices vegan cheese (optional)

8 slices vine-ripened tomatoes

8 small pieces red leaf lettuce

excess liquid by pressing firmly on the meat while tilting the bowl over a sink.

Add the flaxseed egg, bread crumbs, and Mimic-Creme to the ground veal, and use your hands to mix it well. Place in the refrigerator for 10 minutes to set.

Remove the veal mixture from the refrigerator, then add the remaining burger patty ingredients. Use your hands to mix well, then taste for salt.

Form the mixture into 2-inch-diameter, 1-inch-thick patties, and set aside.

Prepare the tapenade: Puree all the tapenade ingredients in a food processor. Taste for salt and pepper. Squeeze a little lime or lemon juice over the top, cover tightly with a lid, then place in the refrigerator until ready to use.

Preheat and grease your grill well. Place a small skillet over the flame (or over medium-high heat if using the stove top), and warm the 2 teaspoons of the olive oil until hot. Quickly sauté the shiitake mushrooms until cooked, then season with salt and pepper. Set them aside.

Cook each burger patty for 4 to 5 minutes per side, or until cooked through to your liking. At this point, I like to grill the buns over the flame while melting a small slice of vegan cheese on top. Serve patties on grilled buns with the rest of the burger incidentals and the Artichoke and Avocado Tapenade.

VEGAN ORANGE-SESAME GRILLED CHICKEN TENDERS

⋙ Serves 6 to 8 ⋘

2 batches Chicken-Style Seitan (page 5)

3 tablespoons Dijon mustard

3 tablespoons frozen organic orange juice concentrate, thawed

3 tablespoons light agave nectar

2 teaspoons light sesame oil

1 teaspoon freshly ground white peppercorns

Salt

1 package wooden or bamboo skewers, presoaked for 20 minutes

Sesame seeds for garnish

My little sister has always been the harshest food critic in the family. That's my really eloquent way of saying she was one hell of a picky eater. If it's mushy, sauce covered, or smells funny, she scrunches up her nose in disgust. Did I mention she's twenty-one?

If I can impress her, I know I've cooked up something really special.

As a little girl, her go-to meal was chicken fingers and French fries—but not just any French fries. They had to be fried crispy on the outside, the potato still creamy on the inside. And she wouldn't eat potatoes any other way. Have I overkilled yet about my sister's pickiness? Okay, I should apologize to both you and her.

With age, she's slowly becoming more adventurous. She loved my Seitan Meatballs, which really made my day. So I created these Vegan Chicken Tenders with her in mind, knowing she'd be my harshest critic, especially since she'd probably compare them to the "real" chicken fingers of her childhood . . . how do you trump nostalgia? Well, guess what, folks? She cleaned her plate and asked for more—and I think you'll really enjoy them as well.

Cut each seitan chicken breast crosswise into strips about 3/4 inch wide. In a large bowl, whisk together the Dijon, orange juice concentrate, agave, sesame oil, pepper, and salt to taste. Add the chicken strips and toss well. Cover and marinate in the refrigerator for 15 minutes.

If you've got a gas or charcoal grill, fantastic! Get it heating. Of course, you can also preheat a grill pan, skillet, or broiler. Lightly oil the grill rack. Then remove the chicken strips from the marinade, and insert the skewers through their centers for easy grilling.

I reserved the marinade to use as a dipping sauce, and found it to be quite delicious. Grill or broil the chicken until golden brown, 2 to 3 minutes on each side. Sprinkle with sesame seeds, and enjoy!

FAUX CHICKEN COCONUT-BASIL BURGERS WITH CILANTRO-MINT CHUTNEY

> Makes 6 large or 8 small burger patties <

CHUTNEY
1 (1-inch) piece fresh ginger, peeled
3 green onions, white and green parts, chopped into large pieces
1 cup fresh mint
1 cup fresh cilantro
1/4 cup plain soy yogurt
1 jalapeño, stemmed (optional)
1 tablespoon freshly squeezed lime juice
1/2 teaspoon kosher salt

First, prepare the chutney: Take your handy-dandy food processor (or blender if you don't have one), start the machine running, and drop in the ginger. Once the ginger is coarsely chopped, turn off the machine and scrape down the sides. Add the rest of the chutney ingredients and blend well, scraping down the sides once more for good measure.

Next, make the burgers: Take your chicken-style seitan, drain it as well as possible, then grind well in a food processor. Set aside.

(continues)

163

Faux Chicken Coconut-Basil Burgers . . . (continued)

BURGERS

1½ batches Chicken-Style Seitan (page 5)

1 (14-ounce) can unsweetened coconut milk

Zest of 1 lime (see page 37 for how to zest a lime)

1 tablespoon freshly squeezed lime juice

½ tablespoon cornstarch mixed with ½ tablespoon cold water

1 teaspoon Thai red curry paste

½ cup chopped fresh basil (sweet basil works really well!)

2 flaxseed eggs (2 tablespoons ground flaxseed mixed with 2 tablespoons water; see page 29 for how to prepare)

½ cup toasted wheat germ

½ cup vegan panko-style bread crumbs

1 to 2 teaspoons sea salt (let your taste buds do the talking)

6 to 8 Rudi's Organic Bakery White Hamburger Buns

Combine the coconut milk, lime zest, lime juice, and the cornstarch mixture in a 10-inch skillet. Bring to a simmer. Continue cooking with some occasional stirring until the mixture is reduced to ⅔ cup. This takes 15 to 20 minutes. Add the red curry paste to the reduced liquid and stir until well blended. Transfer the contents of the skillet to a small bowl, and set aside to cool completely.

If you're using a grill, start heating it up now.

Once the coconut milk mixture has cooled to room temperature, combine it in a large bowl with the chicken, basil, flaxseed eggs, wheat germ, panko, and salt. (You may need to add a little more wheat germ or flaxseed egg to help the patties form. It doesn't affect the flavor much, so use your own discretion.) Form into thin patties, place one sheet of foil on each side of each patty, and place on the grill top. Cook for 4 to 5 minutes per side until golden brown and warmed through.

You can also cook these under the broiler, flipping once during cooking, or give a skillet a little grease down and get those babies golden brown.

Put these bad boys on a bun with some of that delicious chutney and whatever else tickles your toenails.

BASIC BURGERS: To make just a plain ole American hamburger, follow the instructions for Vegan Meatballs on page 11, but instead form the mixture into patties. Cook as instructed above for the Faux Chicken Coconut-Basil Burgers, or follow the oven-baking directions for the Vegan Meatballs.

GRILLED SAGE-RUBBED PORK CHOPS WITH WARM APPLE SLAW

> Serves 6 <

4 teaspoons chopped fresh sage, or
1 ½ teaspoons dried

1 large clove garlic, minced

1 teaspoon salt

Freshly ground black pepper

1 batch Pork Chop–Style Seitan (page
7)

2 teaspoons olive oil

1 large white onion, sliced thinly

1 large Granny Smith apple, cored and
sliced thinly

½ head green cabbage, cored and
sliced thinly

3 large carrots, julienned

2 tablespoons apple cider vinegar

¾ cup prepared Better Than Bouillon
No Chicken Base (see page xvi for
how to prepare)

Grilling's the way to go here, but if you're flame deprived, you can also easily make these on the stove top. Just brown the chops in a skillet with a couple of teaspoons of oil prior to adding the slaw.

Start heating up your grill. If you don't have a skillet that can be placed on top of a grill, you'll have to make the slaw on your cooking range.

Combine 3 teaspoons of the fresh sage (or 1 teaspoon dried), the garlic, ½ teaspoon of the salt, and a few grinds of fresh pepper. Rub this mixture all over the pork chops, and let the chops sit at room temperature for 10 minutes.

When the grill is hot, place a sheet of greased aluminum foil on the rack, then place the chops on top and brown on both sides, 3 to 4 minutes per side. Remove from the grill and set aside.

Place your grill-safe skillet on top of the grill and heat the oil. Add the onion, apples, and the remaining teaspoon of fresh sage (or ½ teaspoon dried). Cook, stirring occasionally, until the mixture is soft and golden brown, 4 to 5 minutes. Add the

(continues)

Grilled Sage-Rubbed Pork Chops . . . (continued)

cabbage, carrots, vinegar, and the remaining ½ teaspoon salt, and continue cooking until the cabbage and carrots begin to soften, about 5 minutes. Add the No Chicken broth and place the pork chops in the pan, burying them in the vegetable mixture. Cover and cook for 5 minutes longer.

To serve, arrange the warm slaw on individual plates and top each portion with a pork chop and all the good stuff in the pan.

BOURBON BUFFALO MOLE CHICKEN WINGS WITH VEGAN BLEU CHEESE–AVOCADO OIL AIOLI

≥ Serves 6 to 8 ≤

In my small community of Youngstown, Ohio, Tuesday night was wing night. Meat-hungry, hormone-driven teenage boys would pile into their F150s and S10s, then make the trek across the state line to Sharon, Pennsylvania, to a popular NASCAR-themed chicken establishment for "All You Can Eat Wing Night." They would starve themselves for days, take enough bong rips to intensify their already inhuman hunger, then slam down as many chicken wings as their growing bodies could handle, in hopes of being crowned Wing-Eating Champ (Slob?).

In any event, no matter where you live, the summer months are pegged as "Barbecue Season." Company picnic, family reunion, and beach party invitations flood our mailboxes and Facebook event pages, and 90 percent of them require us to BYOFSV (bring your own food, silly vegan). Most of us have grown quite accustomed to whipping up a salad and buying a box of veggie burgers for our own peace of mind. We're also quite accustomed to the weird stares from everyone chowing down on T-bones, wings, and potato salad.

Well, not anymore. Stand over those hot coals and grill with pride . . . and a little mischievous FU glint in your eyes. You'll feel the satisfaction of a job well done when your omni friends bite into a cruelty-free chicken wing and jump in amazement at how delicious (and spicy!) vegan BBQ can really be.

AIOLI
1 (6-ounce) package Sunergia Soyfoods Soy Bleu Cheese Alternative

2 cloves garlic

½ cup MimicCreme or alternative (page 3)

½ cup vegan sour cream

⅓ cup vegan mayo

¼ cup chopped fresh parsley

¼ cup avocado oil

1 tablespoon fresh dill

Salt and freshly ground black pepper

SAUCE
3 tablespoons vegan margarine

½ large shallot, chopped finely

2 cloves garlic, minced

2 ounces bourbon

3 tablespoons organic vegan light brown sugar

½ cup agave nectar

4 ounces chili sauce

4 ounces barbecue sauce (see page xvi for suggestions)

1½ teaspoons chili powder

1½ teaspoons unsweetened cocoa powder

¼ teaspoon ground cinnamon

¼ cup hot sauce

½ teaspoon kosher salt

Freshly ground black pepper

CHICKEN WINGS
1½ batches Chicken-Style Seitan (page 5), cut into chicken wing–shaped pieces (see tip)

Cooking oil, enough to deep-fry the wings

SHAGGY KITCHEN TIP If you're really in the mood to go all-out, find a cake supply store or craft store and buy some sucker sticks to use as the "bones" in the chicken wings. They make them easier to eat, too!

Prepare the aioli: First, place the Soy Bleu and garlic cloves in a food processor or blender, and pulse about ten times to break them up a bit.

Then add the remaining aioli ingredients, except the avocado oil, to the food processor, and turn the machine on high. While the machine is running, slowly pour in the avocado oil until all the ingredients are fully incorporated. Keep chilled until ready to serve.

Keeps covered in the refrigerator for up to one week.

Prepare the sauce: In a large saucepan, melt the margarine. Add the shallot and garlic cloves and sauté, for 2 to 3 minutes. Stir in the bourbon, brown sugar, and agave, and heat through, 1 minute. Next, add the chili sauce, barbecue sauce, chili powder, cocoa powder, cinnamon, and hot sauce. Cook, stirring occasionally, for 2 minutes. Taste for salt and pepper. Keep warm until ready to serve.

(continues)

Bourbon Buffalo Mole Chicken Wings . . . (continued)

As the sauce cooks, prepare the chicken wings: Heat a good amount of oil (1 to 2 inches) in a deep, heavy skillet or deep fryer. Drop the chicken wings in batches (the amount you drop in at one time will depend on the size of your fryer; don't overcrowd) into the deep fryer. Fry until golden brown on both sides. Remove the wings from the oil and drain.

Place the fried wings in a large mixing bowl and toss with the sauce, coating each wing well.

Serve with the aioli as a dipping sauce, and with Frisée, Carrot, and Celery Stick Salad with Toasted Garlic and Cumin Vinaigrette (recipe follows).

FRISÉE, CARROT, AND CELERY STICK SALAD WITH TOASTED GARLIC AND CUMIN VINAIGRETTE

 Serves 6

2 heads frisée, torn into pieces
Salt and freshly ground black pepper
2 medium-size carrots, cut into matchstick-size pieces
4 ribs celery, cut into matchstick-size pieces
1 small red onion, cut into matchstick-size pieces
½ cup corn kernels
2½ tablespoons olive oil
2 cloves garlic, minced or pressed
1 teaspoon ground cumin
3 tablespoons brown rice vinegar
3 tablespoons freshly squeezed lemon juice
2 tablespoons chopped fresh cilantro leaves

Toss the frisée with a touch of salt and pepper, then combine with the other veggies.

Heat the olive oil in a large skillet over medium heat. Add the garlic and cumin and cook for about 1 minute. Remove from the heat, then whisk in the vinegar and lemon juice. Add to the veggie mixture, along with the cilantro, and toss to coat. Season to taste with salt and black pepper.

Serve immediately, or store covered with a wet paper towel in the refrigerator until ready to serve.

COLUMBIAN ALE-SAUTÉED VEGAN STEAK WITH SWEET ONIONS AND GARLIC-GINGER-AJÍ-AVOCADO SAUCE

≥ Serves 6 ≤

SAUTÉED VEGAN STEAKS
1 batch Beef-Style Seitan (page 6), cut into steak-shaped pieces
1 teaspoon ground cumin
1 teaspoon dried oregano
Pinch of ground coriander
Pinch of garlic powder
Pinch of chili powder
Pinch of salt and pepper
2 tablespoons extra-virgin olive oil
2 cloves garlic, minced
1 large sweet Maui onion, halved and sliced thinly
6 ounces dark ale
$\frac{1}{8}$ cup vegan Worcestershire sauce

SAUCE
1 jalapeño, seeded and chopped
3 cloves garlic, quartered
$\frac{1}{4}$ teaspoon crystallized ginger, chopped
$\frac{1}{3}$ cup sweet onion, chopped roughly
$\frac{1}{2}$ cup green onions, chopped roughly
$\frac{1}{2}$ cup fresh cilantro leaves
1 tablespoon red wine vinegar
$1\frac{1}{2}$ tablespoons freshly squeezed lime juice
1 large Haas avocado
Sea salt and fresh cracked black pepper

Prepare the steaks: After making the seitan steaks, drain well and set on a flat surface.

In a shallow bowl, stir the cumin, oregano, coriander, garlic powder, chili powder, salt, and pepper until fully mixed. Sprinkle each side of the steaks with the spice blend, then rub in the spices well.

Heat the olive oil in a large skillet over medium-high heat, then add the garlic and onions. Sauté until the garlic is fragrant, about 30 seconds, then add the steaks to the pan.

Cook the steaks on one side until golden brown, then flip over. Add the dark ale and Worcestershire sauce to the pan and continue to sauté until both sides are golden brown and the steaks are cooked through.

Remove the pan from the heat and prepare the ají sauce: Place the jalapeño, garlic, ginger, sweet onion, green onion, and cilantro in a blender or food processor. Blend until the mixture begins to form a paste, scraping the sides down two or three times during the blending process. Add the red

(continues)

169

Columbian Ale–Sautéed Vegan Steak . . . (continued)

wine vinegar, lime juice, and avocado, and blend until fully incorporated. Add salt and pepper to taste, pulse a few times more, then taste for salt and pepper. Serve atop the steaks and onions.

CURRIED PORK, ENOKI MUSHROOM, AND PURPLE BASIL POT STICKERS WITH A PORCINI, SHOYU, AND SAKE REDUCTION

⋝ Serves 12 as an appetizer, 6 as a meal ⋜

REDUCTION
Handful of dried porcini mushrooms
1 cup hot water
½ cup shoyu or soy sauce
½ cup sake
¼ cup brown rice vinegar
½ cup mirin

These little gems definitely don't fall under the Grillin' section of this chapter. They are purely for Chillin's sake. Make a batch of these as appetizers for your next house party, and you'll be lucky if your guests leave room for dinner.

SHAGGY KITCHEN TIP You are going to need to grind the pork seitan shortly after it's finished cooking, so don't make it a day in advance, if possible. Alternatively, you can buy packaged vegan chicken or beef instead of making seitan. Grind up as directed for the vegan pork.

Once the vegan pork has cooked, remove it from the pot with a slotted spoon instead of draining off all the broth. Immediately place the pieces of pork seitan in a food processor, then pour 1 tablespoon of the broth into the food processor. Grind to the texture of ground beef, then place in a bowl and cover with plastic wrap until ready to use.

POT STICKERS

- I batch Pork Chop–Style Seitan, cut into 2- to 3-inch pieces (page 7; see tip)
- 2 cups green cabbage, shredded
- ½ tablespoon salt
- 2 tablespoons vegetable oil
- 1.5 ounces enoki mushrooms, cut into 1-inch pieces
- I leek, trimmed removed, halved lengthwise, cleaned well, and sliced thinly
- ¼ cup green onions, sliced thinly
- I tablespoon curry powder
- I tablespoon tamari
- I tablespoon mirin
- 2 cloves garlic, grated finely
- I teaspoon fresh ginger, grated finely
- I cup tightly packed purple basil leaves, chopped finely
- 2 tablespoons chives, minced
- I teaspoon dark sesame oil
- Freshly ground black pepper (optional)
- I (48-count) package vegan pot sticker wrappers
- Vegetable oil, enough to deep-fry the pot stickers
- ½ cup hot prepared Better Than Bouillon No Chicken or Vegetable Base (see page xvi for how to prepare), or water

Prepare the sauce reduction: Place the dried porcinis in a deep bowl, then pour the hot water over top of them. Use a heavy object to ensure that the porcinis are submerged in the hot water. Let the porcinis soak in the hot water for 30 minutes.

Place a bowl in your sink to catch the soaking liquid. Pour the porcinis over a mesh strainer so that the soaking liquid is captured in the bowl. You can save the porcinis for another recipe, or discard them.

Place the porcini soaking liquid, shoyu, sake, brown rice vinegar, and mirin in a large saucepan over high heat. Bring the mixture to a boil, and boil until the mixture reduces by two-thirds. Set aside.

While the porcinis soak and cook, prepare the pot stickers: Grind your pork, as described in the tip. Take the chopped cabbage, and place it in a large bowl. Sprinkle the salt over the top, then let it stand for 30 minutes while you prep the rest of your ingredients. At the end of the 30 minutes, use a cheesecloth, a dish towel, or paper towels to drain as much liquid from the cabbage as possible. Set the drained cabbage aside to dry further.

Heat the vegetable oil in a large skillet over medium-high heat.

Add the ground pork, enoki mushrooms, leek, and green onions to the skillet, and sauté for 3 to

(continues)

Curried Pork, Enoki Mushroom, and Purple Basil Pot Stickers . . . (continued)

4 minutes until the leeks are soft and translucent. Lower the heat to medium low, then add the cabbage and stir. Add the curry powder, tamari, mirin, garlic, and ginger to the pan, stir well, then sauté for another 2 to 3 minutes. Remove from the heat, transfer the mixture to a large bowl, and allow it to cool to room temperature.

Once cooled, add the purple basil, chives, and sesame oil, then use your hands to mix completely. Taste for salt and pepper.

To assemble the pot stickers, prepare a small bowl of water for moistening the wrappers. Take a wrapper and lay it out on a flat surface. Place a small spoonful of the filling in the center of the wrapper. Dip your finger in the bowl of water, then run your finger around the outside edge of half of the wrapper. Making sure that the wet and dry side don't meet yet, carefully fold the wrapper in half like a taco.

Start at one end, and carefully pinch the sides together. Work your way around to the other end, making sure the pot sticker is completely sealed so that the filling remains inside. Repeat with each pot sticker, then set aside with the fold side up so that the bottom becomes flat. Let sit until you're ready to cook them.

You can cook the pot stickers one of several ways. I used the steam/pan-fry method, but you can also feel free to use other methods:

To steam/pan-fry: Using a large skillet with a lid, pour in enough vegetable oil to cover the bottom of the pan. Heat the oil over high heat until it's shining, then place enough pot stickers in the pan so that it is filled but not overcrowded.

Add ¼ cup of the No Chicken broth to the pan, lower the heat to medium, then cover with a lid. Allow the pot stickers to cook for 4 minutes, then remove the lid and add an additional ¼ cup of broth. Let the pot stickers cook until the water fully evaporates. Once the water is evaporate, let cool for an additional minute, then remove from the pan and serve.

Repeat the process until all of the pot stickers are cooked.

To deep-fry: Heat several inches of oil in a large stockpot or deep fryer until it registers 350°F. Carefully drop the pot stickers into the heated oil, then fry until golden brown (5 to 7 minutes). Carefully remove them with a mesh strainer or slotted spoon, then place on a towel to drain and cool. Serve.

To steam: Place 2 to 3 cups of water (depending on the width of the pot) in the bottom of a rice cooker that has a steamer basket. Place the steamer basket in the cooker, then place enough pot stickers in the basket so that it is full but the pot stickers do not overlap. Turn the rice cooker to the COOK setting, and let the pot stickers steam for 10 to 12 minutes, until cooked through. Check that the water doesn't fully evaporate.

Once the pot stickers are done steaming, carefully remove the steamer basket, then pour the remaining liquid in the cooking pot over the top of them to help unstick.

Serve immediately, with the sauce reduction (use as a dip or drizzle over the pot stickers).

WHITE PEPPER VEGAN TURKEY SHAWARMA WITH CHIPOTLE-TOMATO RELISH AND ROASTED GARLIC, SAGE, AND ARTICHOKE TAHINI PASTE

⇒ Serves 8 ⇐

Why should omnis get to have all the fun with Thanksgiving leftovers? After I severely over-estimated my need for vegan turkey at this year's festivities, I was glad to see the opportunity for recipe creation. And don't think you can lazy out and not bake the pitas. When they're warm and chewy, it makes all the difference.

(continues)

White Pepper Vegan Turkey Shawarma . . . (continued)

SHAWARMA

1 batch Turkey-Style Seitan (page 8),
    cooked in one large piece
1 tablespoon turmeric
2 teaspoons kosher salt
2 teaspoons ground coriander
1 teaspoon ground cumin
2 teaspoons white pepper
1 teaspoon cayenne
2 yellow onions, sliced $\frac{1}{4}$ inch thick
$\frac{1}{2}$ cup extra-virgin olive oil

RELISH

1$\frac{1}{4}$ pounds vine-ripened tomatoes,
    chopped finely
$\frac{3}{4}$ cup red onion, chopped finely
2 dried chipotle peppers, seeded and
    chopped finely
$\frac{1}{4}$ cup olive oil
$\frac{1}{8}$ cup plus 1 tablespoon freshly
    squeezed lemon juice
Handful of Flat-Leaf Italian Parsley,
    chopped
Salt and freshly ground pepper

TAHINI PASTE

1 bulb garlic
1 (14-ounce) can artichoke hearts,
    drained
1$\frac{1}{2}$ cups tahini
Olive oil
2 teaspoons fresh sage, chopped finely
$\frac{1}{2}$ cup freshly squeezed lemon juice
1 cup hot water
Salt and freshly ground pepper

Slice the giant piece of turkey seitan into eight cutlets. Take a large, shallow baking dish that's big enough for all the cutlets and place the cutlets in the baking dish.

Combine all the spices in a small bowl.

Place the sliced onions in a 9 by 13-inch baking dish. Sprinkle with a heaping tablespoon of the spice blend and drizzle 2 tablespoons of the olive oil over the top of them, turning them over to make sure both sides are coated well.

Sprinkle the remainder of the spice blend over both sides of the Vegan Turkey cutlets, using your hands to rub in the spice blend well. Drizzle 4 tablespoons of olive oil over the top of the cutlets, again turning to make sure both sides are coated.

Cover both the turkey and the onions, then place in the refrigerator for 4 to 8 hours.

Prepare the relish: Combine all of the relish ingredients in a medium-size bowl, then taste for salt and pepper. Keep covered and refrigerated until ready to use.

Prepare the tahini paste: Preheat the oven to 400°F.

Peel away the outer layers of skin on the garlic bulb, then slice off the top $\frac{1}{4}$ to $\frac{1}{2}$ inch of the bulb so that the cloves are exposed. Place the piece of garlic on a sheet of aluminum foil, then drizzle the bulb with olive oil so that it's coated well.

> **TO ASSEMBLE**
> 8 whole pitas
> 1 cup pickled eggplant or cucumber, sliced thinly

Wrap the garlic in foil and bake for 30 minutes. Set aside to cool.

Pulse the artichoke hearts several times in a food processor or blender to break them up a bit.

Once the garlic is cool, squeeze out the cloves into a food processor or blender, then add the remaining ingredients. Blend until the mixture becomes a smooth paste.

Taste for salt and pepper.

Store in the refrigerator until ready to use.

Grill and assemble the pita sandwiches: Preheat the oven to between 150° and 200°F, or the "Keep Warm" setting.

After the 4 to 8 hours of chilling time, rub a grill pan or your grill rack with olive oil and preheat it. Brush each pita bread with enough olive oil to coat well. Grill the onion slices until they begin to soften, about 4 minutes per side. Then grill the turkey cutlets until browned and warmed through, about 3 minutes per side. Finally, grill the pita bread until you get some nice grill marks, about 2 minutes per side. Place on a baking rack in the oven to keep warm until ready to assemble the shawarma.

Place the grilled cutlets and onions on a cutting surface. Make a kind of sandwich, placing a cutlet on the top and bottom, with onion slices in the middle. Thinly slice the cutlet sandwich crosswise, repeating the process until all the turkey and onions have been thinly sliced. Carefully transfer the sandwiched strips to a large bowl.

Place equal amounts of the sandwiched strips on each pita bread, and top with Chipotle Tomato Relish, Pickled Eggplant, and Roasted Garlic, Sage, and Artichoke Tahini Sauce.

SUMMERTIME HEIRLOOM TOMATO AND HERB SALAD

⇒ Serves 6 ⇐

4 large heirloom tomatoes (I use black and pineapple tomatoes), cored and cut into wedges

2 large English cucumbers, peeled, halved lengthwise, and cut in ¼-inch-thick cubes

1 cup kalamata olives, pitted and sliced

1 small red onion, sliced thinly and chopped

2 tablespoons chiffonaded fresh basil (see instructions on page 43)

1 tablespoon fresh mint leaves, finely chopped

½ teaspoon minced fresh oregano

3 tablespoons Italian red wine vinegar

1 tablespoon freshly squeezed lemon juice

1 teaspoon freshly squeezed lime juice

1½ teaspoons lemon zest (see page 37 for how to zest a lemon)

1¼ teaspoons salt

½ teaspoon sugar

¼ teaspoon freshly ground black pepper

¾ cup olive oil

1 (6-ounce) package Sunergia Soyfoods Soy Feta Alternative (Optional)

If I could have sex with a fruit, it would be with an a heirloom tomato. It's firm on the outside, soft, sweet, and pretty on the inside. If you end up going through a bad breakup, you can make it boil, then peel away its tough exterior and mash it to bits. The perfect companion.

This is one of my all-time favorite salads. The tomatoes, herbs, oil, and vinegar are such a winning combination. Bring this to your next gathering, and it'll be gone before you have time to give the stud-muffin bartender your number.

In a large salad bowl place the tomatoes, cucumber slices, olives, red onion, basil, mint, and oregano.

Place the vinegar, lemon juice, lime juice, lemon zest, salt, sugar, and pepper in a small bowl, and whisk until the salt and sugar have dissolved. Add the oil slowly, whisking while pouring, until completely incorporated. Pour the dressing over the vegetables and toss.

Allow the salad to sit for about 10 minutes before serving. If you're making this in advance, don't dress the salad until just before serving, instead covering and storing the dressing and vegetables separately in the fridge.

....

HEIRLOOM TOMATO, BLACK GARLIC, AND MARSALA-ROASTED CHICKPEA PANZANELLA

≥ Serves 6 ≤

MARSALA-ROASTED CHICKPEAS

1 (15-ounce) can chickpeas, drained well

2½ teaspoons olive oil

2 teaspoons Marsala wine

1 teaspoon tamari

1½ teaspoons freshly squeezed lemon juice

1 teaspoon herbes de Provence

¼ teaspoon garlic powder

¼ teaspoon kosher salt

Pinch of vegan cane sugar

PANZANELLA

1 pound of day-old Tuscan bread

3 mixed heirloom tomatoes, cut into large dice

1 large cucumber, peeled and diced

1 red onion, halved and sliced thinly

1 batch Marsala-Roasted Chickpeas

3 cloves black garlic, minced

2 cloves garlic, mincedAbout ⅓ cup olive oil

2 tablespoons sherry vinegar

2 tablespoons balsamic vinegar

Handful of fresh basil leaves, chiffonaded (see how on page 43)

Salt and freshly ground black pepper

First, make the roasted chickpeas: Preheat the oven to 400°F. Place the drained chickpeas in a 9-inch square casserole dish.

In a small bowl, whisk together the remaining ingredients and pour over the chickpeas. Toss well to coat the chickpeas.

Roast the chickpeas for 25 to 30 minutes, stirring twice during the roasting process. Set aside to cool.

Make the panzanella: Take the bread and lightly moisten it with running water from your faucet. It should be slightly moistened the whole way through. If it's too wet, squeeze out the excess liquid.

Use your hands to tear the moistened bread into small pieces, then set in a large bowl while the chickpeas cool.

Once the chickpeas are cool, add them and all the vegetables and garlic to the large bowl with the torn bread and toss.

Whisk together the olive oil and vinegar, then pour over the top of the salad and toss well. Taste for salt and pepper and add the basil.

Serve immediately, or place in the refrigerator for 30 minutes before serving.

CUMIN AND AVOCADO OIL–RUBBED PORTOBELLO TORTAS WITH DRAGON FRUIT PICO DE GALLO AND PURPLE BASIL–WHITE PEPPERCORN MAYO

≥ Makes 4 large or 8 small tortas ≤

TORTAS

3 tablespoons avocado oil, plus more for the grill pan

1 teaspoon ground cumin

1/2 teaspoon chili powder

2 cloves garlic, minced

1/4 to 1/2 teaspoon salt

Freshly cracked black pepper

4 portobello mushroom caps, halved

2 tablespoons dry white wine

Shredded vegan mozzarella (preferably Daiya brand)

OTHER SANDWICH INCIDENTALS

4 torta rolls (or kaiser rolls), sliced like a hamburger bun

Romaine lettuce

Purple Basil–White Peppercorn Mayo (recipe follows)

Dragon Fruit Pico de Gallo (recipe follows)

I'm not just white, I'm saltine cracker soaked in soy milk white. I like Scrabble. And musicals. And scarves—plaid scarves. Whenever I attempt to make an ethnic dish, I feel as if I'm doing something dirty. How dare I tread on another culture's territory because my skin reflects more light than quartz does during a solar eclipse.

For as far back as I can remember, there was always an endless amount of amazing Italian food in my home town. Up until I was thirteen, though, the only options for Mexican were Taco Bell and Ch-Chi's.

Then, all of a sudden, Cancún appeared on the scene in the late '90s. It was delicious. It was authentic. You could eat a full meal for less than you make in an hour working minimum wage in Ohio. Their chips were free and always fresh. The margaritas are amazing.

Okay . . . there was a slight catch. They may have been shut down once (or twice) for health code violations. I don't eat animals, so I figure I escaped danger. But on the plus side, they always reopen with a vengeance! You've gotta respect their determination.

Enjoy making the tortas! They rock socks.

MAYO

1 cup tightly packed purple (opal) basil leaves

½ teaspoon freshly squeezed lemon juice

1 cup Vegenaise

½ teaspoon sherry vinegar

½ teaspoon ground white peppercorns

PICO DE GALLO

1 small or ½ large dragon fruit, peeled and chopped roughly

4 Roma tomatoes, diced

½ red onion, chopped finely

1 jalapeño, seeded and chopped finely (optional)

3 radishes, chopped

½ cup chopped cilantro leaves

1 clove garlic, minced

Juice of ½ lime, or more if desired

A touch of salt and freshly ground black pepper

Whisk together the 3 tablespoons of avocado oil, cumin, chili powder, garlic, salt, and pepper to taste. Using your hands, rub each piece of portobello with the oil mixture to coat on both sides.

Drizzle enough avocado oil to coat the bottom of the grill pan (1 to 2 teaspoons), and heat over medium-high heat.

Grill the portobellos on each side until browned and softened, 4 to 5 minutes per side, adding the white wine about halfway through the cooking process to deglaze the pan. Top with however much you want of vegan mozzarella during the last few minutes so that it has time to melt.

To prepare the mayo: Combine all the mayo ingredients, in order, in a food processor. Blend until the basil leaves are finely minced and the mixture is fully combined. Add salt if desired.

To prepare the pico de gallo: Combine all of the pico de gallo ingredients in a large bowl, then toss well. Taste for salt, pepper, and lime juice.

Keeps covered in the refrigerator for up to one week.

1. Bottom half of roll
2. Romaine
3. Portobello with cheese
4. Dragon Fruit Salsa
5. Purple Basil Mayo, smeared on top half of roll
6. Top half of roll

ORECCHIETTE AND WILD ARUGULA SALAD IN VEGAN BASIL-MINT AIOLI

⇒ Serves 6 ⇐

1 pound orecchiette

1 cup tightly packed fresh basil leaves

8 to 10 fresh whole mint leaves, plus 5 to 6 leaves, chopped finely

3 cloves garlic

¾ cup extra-virgin olive oil (the fruitier, the better)

¾ cup vegan mayo

Juice of 1 small lemon

3 ounces fresh wild arugula

2 large or 3 small heirloom tomatoes (Black Brandywines rock!), seeded and chopped

½ cup chiffonaded fresh basil (see page 43 for instructions)

¼ cup pine nuts, toasted

Salt and freshly ground black pepper to taste

I'm going to allow this to serve as a disclaimer to all those romantically interested in me: I smell. Yes, you heard me correctly. Unless you catch me fresh out of the shower, expect our make-out sessions to taste like a tour of little Italy. Our first passionate kiss will have strong undertones of fresh garlic. After the second, deeper kiss, you'll probably have to pick some chunks of basil out of your teeth.

Still interested?

Good! We're off to a great start, you and I.

Maybe it's the hidden Italian in me, but I know of no such thing as "too much garlic." I love it. During a visit to my parents' place in San Francisco, I stole a cookbook from their library that's aptly titled The Garlic Lover's Cookbook. I don't think there's a single recipe in the whole damn book that calls for less than twelve cloves. It's so stink-tastic, and they've yet to call and ask me why it mysteriously disappeared. Needless to say, it inspired me, so here you go. You might need some after-dinner mints when you're finished. You've been warned.

Cook the orecchiette according to package directions, until just al dente. Drain well in a colander over your sink, then rinse with cold water. Drain well again. Toss the noodles with a bit of olive oil to prevent sticking. Set aside.

Combine the basil, 8 to 10 whole mint leaves, garlic, olive oil, mayo, and lemon juice in a blender or food processor. Now whip it—whip it good (ha-ha . . . you know that song's totally stuck in your head now).

Place the orecchiette in a large serving bowl, and toss with the arugula, tomatoes, basil, and mint. Pour the sauce over the pasta, and toss well. Taste for salt and pepper.

Garnish with pine nuts, and serve.

VEGAN GALBI (KOREAN SHORT RIBS) AND BULGOGI (GRILLED STEAK)

⋛ Serves 8 ⋚

Seitan is awesome here, but you can also make this recipe using extra-firm tofu or prepackaged vegan beef products. This marinade is also excellent for veggies or making a stir-fry.

(continues)

Vegan Galbi and Bulgogi (continued)

> 2 batches Beef-Style Seitan (page 6)
> 2 cups tamari or soy sauce
> 1 cup mirin (sherry will work as well)
> 1⅓ cups sugar
> 2 heads garlic, minced
> 2 tablespoons dark sesame oil
> 1 teaspoon freshly squeezed kiwi juice, or 1 teaspoon freshly squeezed lime juice mixed with ¼ teaspoon sugar
> 4 to 6 cups steamed white rice

Make sure the beef seitan is drained well. Cut half of the seitan into 1-inch-thick strips for the galbi, and cut the other half into the thinnest slices possible for the bulgogi.

Make the seitan marinade by mixing all the ingredients, except the seitan in a large bowl. Place the seitan and marinade in either an airtight container or plastic bag, making sure the seitan is fully submerged. Let it sit in the refrigerator as long as possible. Overnight is ideal, 3 to 4 hours should be the minimum.

Then fire up the grill (or grill pan) and go to town! Reserve the marinade to use as a dipping sauce. If you're feeling extra fancy, you can boil the extra marinade in a small saucepan until it reduces and thickens up a bit. For the galbi, place either Popsicle sticks, two presoaked kabob skewers, or two toothpicks in the end of each "rib" prior to grilling, to make them seem extra authentic, and easier to cook and eat.

Grease your grill rack or pan well.

Grill each rib on each side, 3 to 4 minutes, until browned and heated through. Grill each slice of bulgogi for about 1 minute on each side, until browned.

Serve with the rice and Black Sesame–Spinach Banchan (recipe follows).

··

BLACK SESAME–SPINACH BANCHAN (SIDE DISH) SALAD

> Serves 8

---

4 bunches spinach leaves
2 tablespoons sesame oil
4 cloves garlic, minced
2 tablespoons black sesame seeds
2 teaspoons salt

Banchan are traditional Korean small plates of food served with cooked rice. Below is a recipe for one of my favorites.

Prepare an ice bath (large bowl of ice water), and set aside.

Bring a large pot of water to a boil, and blanch the spinach for 30 to 40 seconds. Immediately drain and then plunge the spinach into the ice bath to stop the greens from cooking. Drain well again and place in a medium-size bowl. Add the rest of the ingredients, mix well, and serve.

PAN-ASIAN BLACK SESAME–CABBAGE SLAW TOSSED WITH ROSE WATER, CILANTRO, AND MINT PESTO

> Serves 6 to 8 as a side salad

SHAGGY KITCHEN TIP The rosewater, cilantro, and mint pesto is great by itself on pasta or crackers. I like to make a double batch and save some for a day when I'm feeling lazy.

(continues)

Pan-Asian Black Sesame-Cabbage Slaw . . . (continued)

SLAW

½ napa cabbage, cored, sliced thinly and chopped

½ red onion, sliced thinly

1 (15-ounce) can chickpeas, rinsed and drained

1 (8-ounce) can bamboo shoots, drained and chopped coarsely

1 to 2 teaspoons French white wine vinegar

1 to 2 teaspoons freshly squeezed lemon juice

Salt and freshly ground black pepper

1 to 2 tablespoons black sesame seeds

1 green onion, sliced thinly (for garnish)

PESTO

1½ cups tightly packed fresh cilantro leaves,

½ cup fresh mint leaves

2 cloves of garlic, chopped roughly

1 (³⁄₈-inch) piece fresh ginger, peeled and chopped roughly

2 garlic chives, cut into thirds

2 teaspoons rose water

1 teaspoon Dijon mustard

3 teaspoons toasted sesame oil

1 teaspoon freshly squeezed lemon juice

½ teaspoon freshly squeezed lime juice

A pinch of salt and freshly ground black pepper

First, toss the cabbage, red onion, chickpeas, and bamboo shoots together in a large bowl.

Next, make the pesto by combining all of the pesto ingredients in a food processor, and blending until fully combined and a paste is formed.

Top the cabbage mixture with the pesto, then drizzle with the wine vinegar and lemon juice. Add some salt and pepper, then toss well.

Taste for additional salt and pepper, then toss with the black sesame seeds.

Allow the slaw to sit for about half an hour prior to serving garnished with the green onions.

Keeps covered in the refrigerator for four to five days.

VEGAN BLACK CUMIN CRAB TOSTADAS OVER CABBAGE SALAD WITH LIME, MINT, AND WASABI DRESSING

≥ Serves 8 ≤

CRAB
½ teaspoon ground black cumin
½ teaspoon ground coriander
½ teaspoon ground cumin
¼ teaspoon shallot or onion powder
¼ teaspoon garlic powder
2 (16-ounce) cans young green jack-
    fruit, packed in brine (see page 19)
2 tablespoons canola oil, plus more for
    pan-frying
Salt and freshly ground black pepper
1 cup pico de gallo salsa (I love the
    Trader Joe's variety)

CABBAGE SALAD AND DRESSING
½ head green or purple cabbage, sliced
    thinly
⅓ cup freshly squeezed lime juice
¼ cup fresh mint, chopped finely
2 tablespoons fresh cilantro leaves,
    chopped
½ teaspoon ground cumin
¼ teaspoon wasabi paste
⅛ teaspoon salt
Pinch of sugar

TOSTADAS
8 (6-inch) corn tortillas
¼ cup canola oil
½ teaspoon salt
¼ teaspoon ground cumin

Prepare the crab: First, make your black cumin blend, by combining the black cumin, coriander seeds, cumin, shallot powder, and garlic powder in a small bowl. Set aside.

Drain the cans of jackfruit well by squeezing over a colander. Break up the jackfruit into smaller pieces as you squeeze out the liquid. Once well drained and broken down, place into a bowl and drizzle with the canola oil. Mix well. Slowly stir in the spice blend until it coats all the jackfruit, then taste for salt and pepper.

Heat a little more canola oil in a large skillet over medium-high heat. Pan-fry the jackfruit until it's browned and some of the pieces are crispy, then set aside to cool.

Once it reaches room temperature, return the jack-fruit to a bowl, and stir in the pico de gallo.

Prepare the cabbage: Place the cabbage in a bowl. Combine all the remaining salad ingredients, then pour over the cabbage and toss well.

Prepare the tostadas: Preheat the oven to 350°F.

(continues)

Vegan Black Cumin Crab Tostadas . . . (continued)

In a small bowl, combine the canola oil, salt, and cumin. Using a basting brush, paintbrush, or your fingers, rub each tortilla on both sides with the oil blend, then place on a large baking sheet.

Bake for 15 to 20 minutes, flipping over once during the baking process, until the tortillas are crisp and browning around the edges.

Serve the crab over the cabbage salad on top of the tortillas.

HARVEST TIME SALSA

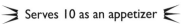 Serves 10 as an appetizer

½ tart red apple, seeded
10 baby tomatillos
1 (¼-inch-thick) slice red onion, chopped
2 cloves garlic, quartered
3 Roma tomatoes, quartered
4 to 5 fresh basil leaves
4 to 5 fresh mint leaves
Handful of cilantro sprigs
Juice of 1 lime
Salt and freshly ground black pepper

First, pulse the apples a few times in a food processor.

Add the rest of the ingredients, and blend the shi . . . I mean . . . blend well.

Pour the finished salsa into a bowl, then serve with tortilla chips or fresh cut veggies.

Keeps covered in the refrigerator for up to one week.

VEGAN DILL AND CHIVE CASHEW CHEESE

≥ Serves 6 to 8 as an appetizer ≤

This cheese works really well as a dip for fresh veggies, crackers, or chips, or as a spread on bread and toast. It's an easy recipe to throw together that really stands out on the appetizer table at the party. Oh, and try the leftovers in place of vegan mayo on a sandwich. You'll thank me later.

1½ cups raw cashew pieces

2 teaspoons freshly squeezed lemon juice

2 teaspoons fresh dill, or 1 teaspoon dried

2 to 3 chives, chopped

3 cloves garlic

½ teaspoon salt

Freshly ground black pepper

⅓ cup water

Place the cashews in a bowl or deep container, and submerge under water. They should be covered by at least 2 to 3 inches. Allow the cashews to sit for about 3 hours. Drain well in a colander over your sink, then place in a food processor.

Add the lemon juice, dill, about three-quarters of the chives, and the garlic, salt, and pepper to taste, and let it run at high speed for 1 minute. (This gets loud—don't make this at night if you have thin walls.) Scrape down the sides of the food processor with a spatula, add the water, and let it run at high speed for another 4 to 5 minutes, pausing every minute or two to scrape down the sides again.

Transfer to a bowl, and garnish with the remaining chives. Let it stand out at room temperature, covered, for 1 to 2 days before serving, if possible. That's when the cheese is at its finest. After two days, you can throw it into the fridge for up to about a week.

Serve with warm, chewy fresh bread (La Brea Bakery French baguettes are my favorite!), top on pizza, eat with crackers, and so on.

VEGAN TUNA AND GARLIC CANNELLINI BEAN SALAD

⋟ Serves 6 ⋞

TUNA
1 batch Vegan Canned Tuna Packed in Oil (page 19)
1 batch Garlicky White Beans (page 142)
1 medium-size red onion, sliced thinly
1 cup kalamata olives, sliced
1/3 scant cup red wine vinegar
The leaves from 3 sprigs of fresh oregano, chopped
Salt and freshly ground black pepper

Combine the prepared tuna and beans with the onion, kalamatas, red wine vinegar, oregano, and salt and pepper to taste.

Taste to ensure salt and pepper amounts are correct, then serve immediately or keep chilled in the refrigerator until ready to serve.

Keeps covered in the refrigerator for up to one week.

CHIPOTLE ADOBO BARBECUED CHICKEN

⋟ Serves 4 to 5 ⋞

Bobby Flay is kind of like the Billy Mays of the grilling world. He not only promotes it, he "brings it." Throw in the term chipotle infused and you've got yourself a Flay signature dish. Well, Mr. Flay, I'm here to let you know that I, too, can toss an adobo-infused masterpiece on the grill and have it kick some serious tushie.

Drain about half of the adobo sauce from the can of chipotle peppers, remove the chipotles from the remaining sauce (reserve the sauce), and dice finely on a cutting surface.

Melt the margarine in a medium-size saucepan over medium-high heat, then add the chipotle peppers and sauté for about 3 minutes. Add all the remaining ingredients,

1 (7-ounce) can chipotle peppers in adobo sauce

1 tablespoon vegan margarine

1 1/4 cups vegan ketchup

1/4 cup chili sauce

1 tablespoon Colgin Liquid Smoke, Natural Hickory Flavor

3 1/2 tablespoons vegan brown sugar

3 1/2 tablespoons molasses

1 tablespoon vegan Worcestershire sauce

2 tablespoons stone-ground mustard

1 teaspoon chili powder

1 tablespoon freshly squeezed lime juice

1/2 teaspoon garlic powder

1/2 teaspoon salt

A few grinds of cracked black pepper

A pinch of cumin

A pinch of cayenne

1 batch Chicken-Style Seitan (page 5)

except the seitan, including the reserved remaining adobo sauce.

Lower the heat to a simmer, and allow the sauce to cook for about 15 minutes. Taste for seasonings.

Cut up the chicken seitan however you like, then either coat or allow it to marinate in the sauce for a few hours.

Grill, or cook on a grill pan or under the broiler for 3 to 4 minutes on each side until the desired char and temperature is achieved.

VEGAN ROASTED GARLIC CAESAR DRESSING WITH HOMEMADE BUTTERY CROUTONS

 Serves 6

Preheat the oven to 400°F. Peel away the outer layers of skin on the garlic bulb, then slice off the top 1/4 to 1/2 inch of the bulb so that the cloves are exposed. Place the piece of garlic on a sheet of aluminum foil, then drizzle the bulb with olive oil so that it's coated well.

Wrap the garlic in foil and bake for 30 minutes. Set aside to cool.

(continues)

Vegan Roasted Garlic Caesar Dressing . . . (continued)

DRESSING

1 head fresh garlic

¼ cup extra-virgin olive oil, plus extra for roasting the garlic

¼ cup slivered raw almonds

⅛ cup raw cashew pieces

1 (15-ounce) can chickpeas (canning liquid reserved)

½ cup freshly squeezed lemon juice

2 tablespoons capers (brine reserved)

1 tablespoon caper brine

½ cup chickpea liquid

1 teaspoon sugar

½ teaspoon yellow mustard powder

¼ teaspoon garlic powder

Salt and freshly ground black pepper

CROUTONS

1 medium-size French baguette, cut into ½-inch cubes

2 cloves fresh garlic, pressed or minced

2 tablespoons vegan margarine, melted

SALAD

1 head romaine lettuce, chopped roughly

Vegan Parmesan (optional) (I like Dr-Cow Aged Tree Nut Cheese grated finely using my Microplane grater, but you can also use the recipe on page 22.)

Take a food processor and blend the almonds and cashews until they're almost a powder. Squeeze in the cloves of roasted garlic, then add the chickpeas and olive oil. Blend until combined, scraping the sides down once during the process.

Add the rest of the ingredients to the food processor, and blend until completely combined. Taste for salt and pepper, and feel free to add more lemon juice or water if the consistency doesn't suit your fancy.

You won't need all of this dressing. I like to save some for rainy (read: lazy) days.

Make the croutons: Preheat the oven to 375°F. Place the cubed bread to an airtight container or plastic bag, and press the whole garlic cloves over the bread cubes. I like to use this method because you allow the fresh juice from the pressed garlic to also be added to the mixture, but mincing will work just fine if you don't have a garlic press.

Pour the melted margarine over the bread cubes, and toss well. I usually just slap the lid on and give it a few good shakes.

Place on a baking sheet, and bake for 5 to 10 minutes, flipping the croutons once during the process. Keep a close eye on them, though. Everyone's oven is different. Some toast faster than others.

Toss an adequate amount of dressing with the romaine, add the croutons, and garnish with Parmesan, if desired.

VEGAN RANCH DRESSING: MY WAY

⫸ Makes 2 to 3 cups of dressing ⫷

¾ cup Vegenaise

¼ cup vegan cream cheese

⅓ cup vegan sour cream

½ cup soy milk (or more, depending on how thick you like it)

2 to 3 tablespoons fresh dill, or 1 tablespoon dried

2 tablespoons fresh flat-leaf parsley leaves

1 tablespoon fresh chives, chopped

2 cloves fresh garlic

1 teaspoon onion salt

1 tablespoon vanilla soy creamer

Salt and freshly ground black pepper

Plenty of vegan ranch dressing recipes are available today. Some aren't bad, others taste like salty glue. I find that it's key to put the time and a little extra cash into making one hell of a vegan ranch. Truthfully, this recipe makes more dressing than two bottles of the store-bought variety. If you do the math, it actually costs you less and tastes a hell of a lot better.

SHAGGY KITCHEN TIP To make this dressing more like a dip for chips and veggies, reduce the amount of soy milk by half.

Combine all the ingredients in a blender or food processor, and puree until completely blended. Adjust the soy milk amounts to achieve your desired thickness. Taste for salt and pepper.

Keeps covered in the refrigerator for up to two weeks.

VEGAN GREEN PAPAYA SALAD (SOM TUM)

⟩ Serves 6 ⟨

2 small tomatoes, seeded and cut into
  wedges
1 cup fresh, long green beans, sliced
  into 2-inch segments
¾ cup cucumber, seeded and julienned
1 carrot, julienned
4 cups green papaya, julienned
6 cloves garlic, mashed
Juice of 2 to 3 limes
¼ cup tamarind juice concentrate
2 to 3 tablespoons Au Lac Vegetarian
  Fish Sauce or light soy sauce
3 tablespoons palm sugar
1 tablespoon water
¼ cup unsalted peanuts, chopped finely
4 to 6 Thai chiles, chopped finely
  (optional)

SHAGGY KITCHEN TIP The authentic version calls for actual fish sauce, but if you can't find Au Lac Vegetarian Fish Sauce, you can use light soy sauce instead.

While I was perusing my neighborhood farmers' market one week, I spotted a sign that read GREEN PAPAYAS FOR SALE. I rubbed my eyes really hard, trying to make sure the previous evening's libations weren't still affecting my vision. Nope! The sign was still there, clear as day. I was in a state of shock. I walked over, picked up one of the emerald gems, and smiled wider than a kid let loose in a chocolate swimming pool.

You see, I have this obsession with green papaya salad—known in its native country of Thailand as som tum. Its flavor graces every one of the taste buds with its deliciousness. It's savory, sweet, spicy, and served chilled. It is the perfect dish on a hot summer evening. Green papaya salad is simply fantastic. Bless your poor little soul should you dine at a Thai restaurant with me and try to take a bite. Having a chopstick impale your hand is not a pleasant experience.

I decided to spare my friends the pain, and spare myself from having to share and just made my own. All right, maybe I shared a little with them.

Reserve a few of the tomatoes, green beans, cucumber slices, and carrots for garnish. Place the rest and the papaya in a large bowl.

To make the dressing, mix together the garlic, lime juice, tamarind juice concentrate, and fish sauce in a small bowl.

In a small saucepan, melt the palm sugar with the water until it forms a syrup. Combine with the rest of the dressing and mix well.

Pour the dressing over the salad and toss well. Garnish with the reserved vegetables, peanuts, and chiles, if using. Serve immediately, or keep chilled until ready to serve.

WARM SPINACH AND RED ONION SALAD WITH GREEN APPLE, MEYER LEMON, AND FRESH MINT VINAIGRETTE

 Serves 4

VINAIGRETTE
Zest of 2 medium-size Meyer lemons (see page 37 for how to zest a lemon)
4 sprigs fresh mint
2 teaspoons sugar
2 tablespoons freshly squeezed Meyer lemon juice
¼ cup green apple or apple cider vinegar
Salt and freshly ground black pepper

SALAD
2 pounds baby spinach leaves, washed well
I small red onion, halved and sliced thinly
I to 2 cloves garlic, minced
2 heirloom or vine-ripened tomatoes, cut into wedges
I tablespoon fresh mint, chopped finely
5 tablespoons olive oil

The combo of vinegar and green apple gives this salad a sweet-and-sour kick. If you can't find green apple vinegar, just substitute apple cider vinegar.

First, make the vinaigrette: Combine the lemon zest and mint in a food processor or blender. Once they are both chopped finely, add the rest of the dressing ingredients and blend completely. Taste for salt and pepper.

Prepare the salad: In a large bowl, mix the spinach, onion, garlic, tomatoes, and mint. Heat the oil in a large skillet over medium-high heat, then add the spinach mixture. Toss in the olive oil for 1 minute. As the spinach leaves are just beginning to wilt, immediately transfer the salad to a serving dish. Toss with the vinaigrette and serve immediately.

GRILLED STEAK AND CREMINIS WITH GARLIC, SHERRY, AND ROSEMARY SAUCE

⇒ Serves 4 to 5 ⇐

SAUCE

6 cloves garlic

1/3 cup water (or more, if needed)

2 tablespoons fresh rosemary

1/2 teaspoon kosher salt

I small crusty French baguette (about 8 inches long), sliced

1/3 cup slivered almonds

2 tablespoons sherry vinegar

1/2 cup olive oil

Freshly cracked black pepper

GRILLED STEAK AND MUSHROOMS

3 teaspoons ground black sea salt or kosher salt

1 1/2 teaspoons garlic powder

I teaspoon onion powder

Freshly cracked black pepper

I batch Beef-Style Seitan (page 6)

I pound cremini mushrooms, cleaned and sliced

I tablespoon vegan margarine

Even though I don't date men, I find it incredibly sexy when they are manly enough to step away from meat. Many male vegans and vegetarians I have met voiced their fear of being embarrassed by their homeboys when they had to order a baked potato and side salad at a steak restaurant.

This is a great recipe to put your homeboys on shut mouth. It's meaty, full of flavor, and beats a baked potato and side salad any day of the week.

First things first, make the sauce. Place the garlic in a food processor and process until finely minced. Add the rest of the sauce ingredients and puree until smooth. Scrape down the sides, and taste for salt, pepper, and desired thickness. Add more water if it's too thick for your liking. Warm in a saucepan on the grill, stove top, or microwave just prior to serving.

Get your grill heated to about medium-high heat.

In a small bowl, combine the black salt, garlic powder, onion powder and black pepper.

Rub each steak with a little of the seasonings, then set aside.

194

Take two 20-inch-long sheets of heavy-duty aluminum foil, and place half of the sliced creminis in the center of each sheet. Sprinkle the creminis liberally with some of the seasonings, then place ½ tablespoon of margarine on top of each mushroom pile.

Wrap the foil around the creminis just as you would wrap a present. Keep the corners sealed and tight, but leave a bit of space between the creminis and the top of the foil, for heat circulation. Place the creminis on the grill rack and grill for 20 to 25 minutes, until soft and delicate.

Place the steaks directly on the grill rack, and cook for 4 to 5 minutes on each side, until well browned and warmed thoroughly.

Top with the grilled creminis and the sauce.

VEGAN PROSCIUTTO-WRAPPED GREENS

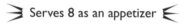 Serves 8 as an appetizer

I selflessly admit to having a schoolgirl crush on Giada De Laurentiis. In the past, I've rambled about my Italian-loving side. Sure, it was fostered in an environment where the overwhelming mob population spawned the popularity of the cuisine. I like to think that's why the Italian food I ate as a kid was so damn authentic. Mafia influence aside, Youngstown's Italian food was (and still is) some of the best I've ever eaten.

Now, back to Giada. Although many of the recipes in her cookbooks border on the cliché side of Italy's foodscape, that doesn't mean I can't use them as a blank canvas to spruce up and veganize. Special thanks to Giada for giving me some inspiration and being someone who looks prettier than Mario Batalli when shimmying about a kitchen.

This is a great (and fancy!) appetizer for the holidays. The dark, peppery flavor of the wild arugula really complements the season and your glass of straight brandy.

(continues)

Vegan Procuitto-Wrapped Greens (continued)

3 tablespoons olive oil

1 clove garlic, pressed or minced

2 teaspoons sherry vinegar

2 teaspoons freshly squeezed lemon juice

½ teaspoon stone-ground Dijon mustard

5 ounces wild arugula or mesclun greens (or mixed)

Kosher salt and freshly ground black pepper

2 tablespoons finely grated Dr-Cow Aged Tree Nut Cheese, any flavor, or Vegan Parmesan Blend (page 22)

1 batch Crispy Vegan Prosciutto (page 14), but with the tofu sliced lengthwise into large rectangles instead of small

Mix the olive oil, garlic, sherry vinegar, lemon juice, and mustard together in a small bowl.

In a separate large bowl, gently toss the greens with salt and pepper. Toss in the grated cheese and enough dressing to gently coat the greens. Taste for salt and pepper.

Roll up in the prosciutto and fasten with a toothpick or decorative fastener of choice. (Believe me . . . if I found those little plastic swords, I'd use them!)

6

GET BAKED

No, silly stoner. I'm talking about baked goods. My wise father once told me that "baking is like chemistry, except in chemistry class you can't lick the spoon." Baking wasn't always my favorite way to get down in the kitchen. It requires one to be more exact in one's measurements, and I like the freedom to be creative.

Yet, the more I baked, the more I began to love the art. I found ways to be creative within the boundaries, and you can, too! My basic cake recipe used for the Vegan Twinkies is adaptable in more ways than you can imagine. There are even some savory baked goods if you lack a sweet tooth, like me (I know . . . weird for a Jewish girl).

Just like in science class, there's plenty of room to experiment. Baking is about having fun and satisfying yourself. So go ahead now—get baked!

> The economy is in shambles. Don't spend thirty dollars on a vegan pie when you can make your own Fire-Roasted Pumpkin, Hazelnut, and Black Cumin Pie with Vanilla Bean Crème Fraîche! This chapter even includes a DIY guide to homemade vegan marshmallows.

VEGAN TWINKIES

Makes 14 cakes

CAKE
Organic canola oil spray, for greasing the pan

2⅛ cups unbleached all-purpose flour

1⅛ cups organic sugar

2 teaspoons baking powder

½ teaspoon baking soda

1 teaspoon Nature's Flavors Butter Flavor Powder

½ teaspoon sea salt

1½ cups MimicCreme or vegan buttermilk (page 4)

½ cup canola oil

1½ teaspoons vanilla extract

FILLING
½ cup vegan vegetable shortening

8 tablespoons (1 stick) vegan margarine

2 cups organic confectioners' sugar

2 teaspoons vanilla extract

2 tablespoons barley malt powder or ¼ cup Ricemellow Crème Fluff

I could seriously devote an entire book to my cake recipes. For those living in the Los Angeles area, you probably know me as "the Vegan Twinkie Baker." I can say with pride that I spent at least two months perfecting my Twinkie recipe. I would toil away in my kitchen, then use my best friend Leigh as a guinea pig. Without her, I don't believe I would have known when to "just stop" because the recipe had been "perfected."

I started with the readily available Vegan Lunch Box recipe. I made it once, then tasted the results, but I wanted them to taste a little more dense and sticky like the packaged variety. I tried once, twice, thirty times. Finally, I had a winner. Jennifer McCann, I owe you a serious debt of gratitude for helping me on my way. The frosting recipe is entirely yours. By the way, barley malt powder can usually be found at beer brewing supply stores or online, but sub Ricemellow Crème Fluff if you can't locate some.

This is the original vanilla-flavored version. As you can imagine, or have had the opportunity to taste, there are countless other variations. Get creative and have some fun!

SHAGGY KITCHEN TIP If you're in need of a specialty pan to make these, Norpro manufactures the best cream canoe pan on the market (www.norpro.com).

Preheat the oven to 365°F. Yes, 365. It's the perfect Twinkie temperature.

Apply three or four streams of canola oil spray to a paper towel or dish towel, then grease half of the 9 by 12-inch cream canoe baking pan very well. Reapply another three or four sprays of the canola oil spray to the towel, then grease the second half of the pan. Your pan should be looking shiny and ready for action!

Prepare the cakes: In the bowl of a stand mixer or a large mixing bowl, combine the flour, sugar, baking powder, baking soda, butter flavor powder, and salt. Stir gently until all of the dry ingredients are fully mixed.

In a separate mixing bowl, whisk together the MimicCreme, canola oil, and vanilla until they're fully combined. Pour the wet ingredients into the dry, and stir together until there are no lumps and you have a smooth cake batter.

Pour ¼ cup of the batter into each Twinkie spot on the pan. Bake for 16 to 18 minutes. Insert a toothpick into the center of one of the Twinkles, then pull it out. If there's no batter stuck to the toothpick, these bad boys are finished.

Place the pan on a cooling rack, then allow the Twinkies to cool for 15 minutes. Using an icing spatula or an oyster shucker, gently work the Twinkies out of the pan, then place them on a cooling rack.

Prepare your filling: Beat together the shortening and margarine until they're fluffy and fully combined. Add the confectioners' sugar in ½-cup batches, stirring in well before adding the next. Finally, add the vanilla and barley malt powder, and beat until all the ingredients are whipped together completely.

Using an icing injector (the cream canoe pans usually include one), inject a little bit of filling into three different spots along the underside of each Twinkie. Enjoy!

VEGAN BUTTERNUT SQUASH, APPLE, AND ONION GALETTE WITH BLUE CHEESE

⇒ Makes 2 galettes; serves 8 to 10 ⇐

DOUGH

1¼ cups unbleached all-purpose flour

1½ teaspoons Ener-G Egg Replacer powder (do not add water), or 1 flaxseed egg (1 tablespoon ground flaxseed mixed with 1 tablespoon water; see page 29 for how to prepare)

Pinch of salt

8 tablespoons (1 stick) cold vegan margarine, diced

¼ cup MimicCreme or alternative (page 3), plus more if needed

FILLING

1 large baking apple (I used Jonagold), halved and cored

1 small or ½ medium-size butternut squash (about ¾ pound), halved, seeded, but unpeeled

1 small yellow onion, peeled

3 tablespoons vegan margarine, melted

2 teaspoons chopped fresh rosemary

2 teaspoons chopped fresh thyme

Kosher salt and freshly cracked black pepper

2 tablespoons stone-ground mustard

⅓ cup Sunergia Soyfoods Soy Bleu Cheese Alternative, crumbled (optional)

Ah, Paris. The City of Lights. Last winter, I went through a serious quarter-life crisis. I booked a flight to England, bought some train tickets, located some overseas couches to crash on, filled a backpack, and away I went! It was easily one of the best months of my life. I met some amazing people, saw some awesome sights, and ate fantastic food. I don't even really have much of a sweet tooth and I'm still craving those delectable French pastries.

Being a vegan in Paris was definitely a challenge. I did quite a bit of homework before my travels, after being warned that Parisian restaurants are less willing than others to help veganize your meal. I can now personally verify the aforementioned statement as truth.

I couldn't find a place to crash my last two nights in Paris, so I found a cheap hostel in the Marais District. It was just my luck that the hotel was run by one of the followers of the Supreme Master Ching Hai, teacher of the Quan Yin Method, known to many as "the Vegan Cult." He hooked me up with directions to a hole-in-the-wall where I could buy all-vegan pastries! Baguettes, éclairs, croissants, and of course . . . galettes! To say the least, it was an inspirational trip.

Prepare the dough: Pulse the flour, egg replacer, and salt together in a food processor. Add the margarine and pulse about ten times, until the mixture resembles a coarse cornmeal with a few larger bits of margarine. Add the MimicCreme and pulse one or two times more; don't let the dough form a mass around the blade. If the dough seems very dry, add 1 teaspoon more MimicCreme at a time, pulsing briefly between additions. Remove the blade and bring the dough together by hand. Shape the dough into a disk, wrap it in plastic wrap, and refrigerate at least 1 hour.

Prepare the filling: Preheat the oven to 400°F.

Cut each apple half into eight wedges and put them in a large bowl. Slice the squash and onion into wedges as thick as the apple wedges and add them to the bowl. Add the melted margarine, rosemary, and thyme, and toss gently. Season with salt and pepper, and toss again.

Roll the dough on a well-floured surface into a 12-inch round. Transfer the dough to a baking sheet and brush lightly with the mustard. Starting 2 inches from the edge, alternate pieces of apple, squash, and onion in overlapping circles. Fold and pleat the dough over the edge of the filling so it looks pretty, fancy, and French.

Bake until the crust is browned and the filling is tender and caramelized, about 50 minutes. Scatter the optional cheese over the filling and bake until melted, about 5 minutes more. Cool the galette briefly on a wire rack. Cut into wedges and serve.

RAINIER CHERRY, LEMON, AND SWEET RICOTTA GRATIN

> Serves 6 ⬱

SWEET RICOTTA (SEE TIP)
12 ounces extra-firm silken tofu

I tablespoon fresh lemon zest (see page 37 for how to zest a lemon)

½ teaspoon sea salt

¼ teaspoon organic sugar

I teaspoon freshly squeezed lemon juice

GRATIN
I tablespoon freshly squeezed lemon juice

I tablespoon black currant–or raspberry-flavored liqueur

¼ teaspoon freshly cracked black pepper

6 tablespoons organic sugar

1½ pounds Rainier cherries, pitted and halved

½ cup plus 2 tablespoons MimicCreme or alternative (page 3)

⅛ teaspoon sea salt

2 teaspoons agar powder

3 tablespoons slivered almonds, toasted

SHAGGY KITCHEN TIP The vegan ricotta is different in this recipe than the one in the seitan chapter because it's used for a sweet, not savory, dish. I also highly recommend serving this with some vegan vanilla ice cream or soy whipped cream.

Preheat the broiler.

In a large bowl, use a fork to mash together all of the vegan ricotta ingredients until the mixture has the texture of cottage cheese. Set aside.

In a separate small bowl, combine the lemon juice, liqueur, and pepper. Set aside.

Place 3 tablespoons of the sugar in a large skillet and heat over medium-high heat until the sugar begins to melt (translucent spots will start to appear), about 2 minutes. Add the cherries to the pan and let them cook for 2 minutes without stirring. Pour the lemon juice mixture over the cherries, stir once, then cook for an additional 2 minutes, until thickened. Remove from the heat.

In the bottom part of a double boiler, bring 2 cups of water to a boil. Do not place the top part of the

202

double boiler over the water yet. In the top half of the double boiler, place the remaining 3 tablespoons of sugar, MimicCreme, and salt. Sprinkle the agar powder over the top of the MimicCreme mixture, and allow to sit for 5 minutes.

Lower the heat of the boiling water to a fast simmer, stir the agar powder into the MimicCreme mixture, then place the top half of the double boiler over the bottom half with the simmering water. Cook the MimicCreme mixture, whisking constantly, until it has thickened considerably to a pastelike texture, 2 to 3 minutes.

Remove from the heat, and beat at high speed with a hand mixer or vigorously with a whisk until the MimicCreme mixture is fluffy and forms peaks.

Pour the contents of the cherry skillet into a gratin or casserole dish, then fold the MimicCreme mixture into the ricotta until combined. Spoon the ricotta evenly over the top of the cherries, then toast under the preheated broiler until the topping is browned.

Sprinkle the toasted almond slivers over the top, then allow to cool briefly before serving.

Keeps covered in the refrigerator for four to five days.

VEGAN BELGIAN WAFFLES

≥ Makes about 4 waffles ≤

While I was growing up, mornings in my house were less than sensational. My little sister and I each had a fair amount of quirky tenacity that always spiced life up a bit. I'm not going to say we argued, but two preteen girls sharing a bathroom can cause a tad of friction, to say the least.

We definitely had our share of joyous early risings—particularly if Mom was making breakfast. For years, her specialty was French toast. She knew just the right combination of batter, bread, and frying time. Then, for one of my parents' anniversaries, my dad bought

(continues)

Vegan Belgian Waffles (continued)

1½ cups all-purpose flour

2 teaspoons baking powder

1 teaspoon tapioca or potato starch

½ teaspoon baking soda

¾ teaspoon salt

1⅓ cups MimicCreme or alternative (page 3)

2 tablespoons agave nectar

2 tablespoons vegan margarine, melted

½ cup water

Nonstick canola spray or 2 tablespoons canola oil, for greasing the waffle iron

her a full-on professional waffle maker. Unfortunately for me, I'd already moved three thousand miles away from Youngstown to Los Angeles. I finally got my chance to have my way with that waffle maker, and we made hot, sweet love one Christmas morning. I walked out of the kitchen sweaty, satisfied, and actually cured of the Jew Blues I experience from knowing my friends are probably opening awesome presents. It was a far cry from the elementary school mornings, indeed.

In a medium-size bowl, combine the flour, baking powder, tapioca starch, baking soda, and salt. In a small bowl, combine the MimicCreme and agave. Pour the wet ingredients into the dry and stir lightly until it comes together. Add the margarine and mix well.

Add ¼ cup of the water and incorporate well. If the batter seems too thick to pour, add as much as necessary of the remaining ¼ cup of water and mix together. You can also add whatever fixin's you'd like to the batter now (do I hear bananas, anyone?).

Spray the waffle iron well with either no-stick canola spray, or rub the iron with a light coating of canola oil.

Make sure you consult your waffle iron's manual before using, and cook your waffles according to the instructions.

Depending on the brand/type of waffle maker you're using, the results may vary. The consistency of the batter, temperature, and "browning" setting all factor into the cooking time. Making waffles is an art form that takes practice. Don't beat yourself up if the first one turns out more like a giant, round biscotti.

SWEET BAGUETTE HAZELNUT FRENCH TOAST WITH VEGAN AUNT JEMIMA SYRUP

 Serves 6 ⋹

FRENCH TOAST
½ cup MimicCreme or vegan butter-milk (page 4)

½ cup Silk Hazelnut, Plain, or Vanilla Soy Creamer

1 cup Vegan Egg Mix, minus the garlic powder (page 28)

Pinch of ground cinnamon

Pinch of freshly grated nutmeg

1 to 2 tablespoons vegan margarine

1 large sweet vegan baguette, cut into 1-inch-thick slices

Vegan confectioners' sugar, for garnish (optional)

SYRUP (OPTIONAL)
¾ cup Madhava Amber Organic Agave Nectar

¼ cup pure maple syrup

2 tablespoons vegan margarine, melted

Pinch of kosher salt

SHAGGY KITCHEN TIP If you're making a large amount of French toast or not planning to eat immediately, preheat your oven to 200°F or its "Keep Warm" setting, and place a cooling rack on top of a baking sheet. Place the finished slices of French toast on the cooling rack, then place the baking sheet in the oven to keep the French toast fresh and warm until serving.

In a medium-size bowl, whisk together the Mimic-Creme, soy creamer, egg mix, cinnamon, and nutmeg until fully combined.

Melt the margarine in a large skillet over medium-high heat. Dip each slice of baguette in the MimicCreme mixture, making sure the slices are coated on all sides. Place the coated bread into

(continues)

Sweet Baguette Hazelnut French Toast . . . (continued)

the hot skillet, being careful not to overcrowd the pan. You can make the French toast in batches, if necessary. Add a little bit more margarine to the skillet before cooking the next set.

Allow each slice of French toast to cook on each side for 2 to 3 minutes, or until golden brown and crisped to your liking.

Sprinkle the French toast with confectioners' sugar (optional), and serve with Vegan Aunt Jemima Maple Syrup, if desired.

To make the syrup: Whisk all of the syrup ingredients together until fully combined. Serve with French toast, waffles, or—if you're a Midwestern cracker like me—vegan sausage patties.

GARLIC FRENCH TOAST

 Serves 6

½ cup MimicCreme or vegan butter-milk (page 4)

½ plain soy creamer

1 cup Vegan Egg Mix (page 28)

1 to 2 tablespoons vegan margarine, for cooking

6 slices white bread

Vegan confectioners' sugar, for garnish (optional)

"What on earth?!" you must be asking yourself. Yes. Garlic French toast. I made this by happy accident for my lady one weekend. She was hungry, and wanted French toast ASAP. Damn hormones. Anyway, I went into the kitchen and whipped up a batch of French toast using my typical egg mix with the garlic powder. I was hoping she wouldn't notice the difference, but lo and behold, I was wrong. She takes a bite . . .

Jane: "This tastes like there's garlic in it—"

Me: "Oh shit."

Jane: "—and it's awesome!"

Me: "Uh . . . really? I mean, I meant to do that."

Garlic French toast has become a favorite in our household, and I hope it will in yours as well.

In a large bowl, whisk the MimicCreme, soy creamer, and egg mix together until fully combined.

Melt the margarine in a large skillet over medium-high heat. Dip each slice of bread in the MimicCreme mixture, making sure the slices are coated on each side.

Place the bread in the hot skillet, being careful not to overcrowd the pan. You can make the French toast in batches, if necessary. Add a little bit more margarine to the skillet before cooking the next set.

Allow each slice of French toast to cook on each side for 2 to 3 minutes, or until golden brown and crisped to your liking.

Sprinkle with confectioners' sugar and serve with Vegan Aunt Jemima Maple Syrup (on page 205), if desired.

RUSTIC SUNFLOWER SEED AND LIME PESTO QUICHE TARTLETS WITH ROMA TOMATOES AND BLACK OLIVES

⇒ Makes 4 tartlets ⇐

While I like a homemade crust as much as the next gal, you can also simplify this recipe by purchasing premade vegan piecrusts, letting them thaw, then rolling out and molding to tartlet pans.

Prepare the crust dough: Pulse the flour, egg replacer, salt, garlic, and cayenne together in a food processor. Add the margarine and pulse about ten times, until

(continues)

Rustic Sunflower Seed and Lime Pesto Quiche Tartlets ... (continued)

CRUST DOUGH

1⅓ cups plus 4 tablespoons pastry or all-purpose flour

1½ teaspoons Ener-G Egg Replacer powder (do not add water)

¼ teaspoon salt

2 cloves garlic, pressed or minced

Pinch of cayenne

8 tablespoons (1 stick) cold vegan margarine, diced into cubes

¼ cup cold MimicCreme or coconut milk, plus more if needed

PESTO

¼ cup raw sunflower seeds

¼ cup pine nuts

3 cloves fresh garlic

4 ounces fresh basil leaves

Juice of ½ lime

Salt and freshly ground black pepper

¼ cup extra-virgin olive oil

TO ASSEMBLE

1 batch Crust Dough

2 cups Vegan Scrambled Eggs (page 27)

½ cup sunflower seed and lime pesto

2 to 3 Roma tomatoes, sliced thinly

Black olives, sliced

Salt and freshly ground black pepper

Fresh basil, for garnish (optional)

the mixture resembles coarse cornmeal with a few bean-size chunks of margarine still in it. Add the MimicCreme, and pulse one or two times more; don't let the dough form a mass around the blade. If the dough seems dry, add 1 teaspoon at a time of more MimicCreme, pulsing briefly.

Remove the blade and bring the dough together by hand. Shape the dough into a disk, wrap it in plastic wrap, and refrigerate at least 1 hour.

While the dough chills, prepare the pesto: Clean your food processor or blender, then throw in the sunflower seeds, pine nuts, and garlic. Let the food processor run for about 30 seconds to break everything up into smaller pieces. Add the basil, lime juice, and some salt and pepper.

Turn the food processor back on, and slowly pour all of the olive oil down the shute (or through the center of the blender lid, if you are using a blender) until the mixture is fully combined. Taste to see if more salt or pepper is needed.

To prepare the quiche tartlets: Preheat the oven to 375°F. Grease your tartlet pans well.

Roll out the crust dough, then mold enough dough into each tartlet pan so that it's about ¼ inch thick on the bottom and sides. Prebake in the oven for 12 to 13 minutes, then set aside to cool.

Combine the scrambled eggs and the pesto well. Spread about ⅛ cup of the mixture evenly in the bottom of each cooled, prebaked tart shell. Top with a layer of sliced Romas and black olives. Spread another ⅛ cup of the mixture on top of the veggies, then add a second layer of sliced Romas and olives. Sprinkle the top layer of tomatoes with a touch of salt and pepper.

Bake for about 30 minutes, until fully set and cooked through. Allow to cool to room temperature before removing from the pans and serving.

Garnish with fresh basil, if desired.

MOM'S CARROT PUDDING

Makes 1 (8-inch) square pan; serves 10 to 12

12 tablespoons (1½ sticks) vegan margarine, melted
1 cup vegan brown sugar
¼ cup MimicCreme or alternative (page 3)
1½ cups all-purpose flour
1½ teaspoons baking powder
1½ cups grated carrots
Juice of ½ lemon
1 teaspoon baking soda dissolved in 1 tablespoon hot water

Before you say, "Carrot? Pudding? No," listen to me when I say that this is one of the most delicious, comforting foods you will ever eat. It's not really pudding, per se. It's more like a dense, moist cake. My mother used to make this for special occasions, but I would bother her all year long to make a batch "just for the family" (a.k.a. "just me").

SHAGGY KITCHEN TIP If you don't eat the whole pan in one sitting, toast some of the carrot pudding in the toaster oven until it's crisp around the edges.

Preheat the oven to 350°F. Grease an 8-inch square pan and set aside.

(continues)

209

Mom's Carrot Pudding (continued)

Beat the margarine, brown sugar, and MimicCreme together by hand.

In a separate bowl, combine the flour and baking powder.

Add the flour mixture, grated carrots, and lemon juice to the margarine mixture, but not the baking soda yet. Mix together well, then add baking soda mixture.

Spread evenly in the prepared pan and bake for 30 to 35 minutes. Allow it to cool in the pan for about 10 minutes prior to serving.

VEGAN BRIOCHE

 Makes 1 loaf of brioche

2 cups all-purpose flour, plus more for dusting the pan

2¼ teaspoons dry active yeast

2 tablespoons warm water

1 tablespoon sugar

1 teaspoon salt

½ cup MimicCreme or vegan buttermilk (page 4), at room temperature

2 to 3 tablespoons high-fat (4 to 5 g per serving) soy milk

6 tablespoons (¾ stick) vegan margarine, plus more for greasing the pan

Egg wash (2 tablespoons melted vegan margarine mixed with 1 tablespoon MimicCreme or vegan buttermilk [page 4])

In a large mixing bowl, mix ½ cup of the flour with the yeast and water. Cover the bowl with a kitchen towel and set in a warm place (no hotter than 85°F). Let the dough rise until it has doubled in size.

Knead the remaining ½ cup of flour with the sugar, salt, MimicCreme, and soy milk. This mixture needs to be forcefully kneaded for about 15 minutes for the appropriate amount of gluten to develop in the dough. Once the dough has come together with a smooth consistency, work in the softened 6 tablespoons of margarine. Now work the two dough mixtures together (the one you just kneaded plus the one you set aside to rise) until you have one smooth ball of dough. Place the ball in a floured bowl, cover, and place in the refrigerator for 1 hour.

Preheat the oven to 450°F. Grease a loaf pan with vegan margarine and dust with flour.

Form the chilled dough into a log, then place in the prepared pan. Place the pan in a warm area and allow the dough to rise again until doubled in size.

Brush the top of the brioche loaf with the egg wash, then bake for 25 to 30 minutes until golden dark brown and set. Remove from the oven and set the pan on a cooling rack until cool enough to handle.

Keeps in an airtight container for up to a week.

FIRE-ROASTED PUMPKIN, HAZELNUT, AND BLACK CUMIN PIE WITH VANILLA BEAN CRÈME FRAÎCHE

⋟ Makes 1 pie; serves 6 to 8 ⋞

CRÈME FRAÎCHE
1 batch Vegan Crème Fraîche (page 25), prepared to step prior to refrigeration
½ vanilla bean, split lengthwise
4½ teaspoons sugar

When I see or smell a pie, I kind of morph into Eric Cartman. No other thoughts can really permeate my carnal lust for a plate, fork, slice, and silence. And maybe a scoop of Organic Coconut Bliss Naked Coconut vegan ice cream.

When I cook for or eat with my friends, silence is how I know we're thoroughly satisfied with our food. I fondly remember moments from my teenage years when, following a recreational joint smoking session in my car parked behind a grocery store, we'd drive around laughing and chattering like five-year-olds. Then we'd go through a drive-through window and . . .

UTTER SILENCE.

Well, except for the sound of crunching French fries.

(continues)

Fire-Roasted Pumpkin, Hazelnut, and Black Cumin Pie . . . (continued)

PIECRUST

1¼ cups unbleached all-purpose flour

1½ teaspoons Ener-G Egg Replacer powder (do not add water), or 1 flaxseed egg (1 tablespoon ground flaxseed mixed with 1 tablespoon water; see page 29 for how to prepare)

Pinch of salt

8 tablespoons (1 stick) cold vegan margarine, diced

¼ cup cold MimicCreme or alternative (page 3), plus more if needed

ROASTED PUMPKIN PUREE

2 to 3 tablespoons olive oil

1 (3- to 4-pound) sugar pie pumpkin, quartered, stemmed, and seeded (see tip)

Salt

SHAGGY KITCHEN TIP You can substitute 1½ cups of canned pumpkin, and just skip to the "Prepare the Filling" part of the recipe.

When my best friend and I first took bites of this pie, we were able to revisit the bliss of the famous "Delicious Silence."

Okay . . . so the pumpkin's not really roasted over a fire, per se, but doesn't it sound more riveting? The black cumin seeds add to the slightly smoky undertones, but if you can't find them, the pie will taste just dandy anyway.

Prepare the crème fraîche: Using a sharp knife, scrape the seeds from the vanilla bean. Combine the crème fraîche with the vanilla bean seeds and the sugar. Cover and refrigerate for at least 1 hour. (May be prepared up to three days ahead, covered and refrigerated.)

Prepare the piecrust: Pulse the flour, egg replacer, and salt together in a food processor. Add the margarine and pulse about ten times, until the mixture is coarse with a few bean-size bits of margarine. Add the MimicCreme, and pulse one or two times more; don't let the dough form a mass around the blade.

If the dough seems very dry, add 1 teaspoon at a time of more MimicCreme, pulsing briefly. Remove the blade and bring the dough together by hand. Shape the dough into a disk, wrap it in plastic wrap, and refrigerate at least 1 hour.

PIE FILLING

2 cups toasted hazelnuts

¾ cup vegan brown sugar

1 teaspoon salt

1 tablespoon arrowroot powder or cornstarch

4½ teaspoons Ener-G Egg Replacer powder (do not add water), or 3 flaxseed eggs (3 tablespoons ground flaxseed mixed with 3 tablespoons water; see page 29 for how to prepare)

1 teaspoon ground cinnamon

1 teaspoon ground black cumin seeds

A few pinches of ground ginger

A few pinches of fresh grated nutmeg

2 whole cloves, ground

1½ cups Roasted Pumpkin Puree

1 teaspoon vanilla extract

¾ cup MimicCreme or alternative (page 3)

1 cup coconut milk

Prepare the pumpkin puree: Preheat the oven to 400°F. Brush on and rub in the olive oil all over the pumpkin, sprinkle generously with salt, and then bake on a baking sheet until soft, about 1 hour. Remove the skins, and puree the good stuff in a food processor or with a mixer. Set aside.

Preheat the oven to 350°F. Pies bake best in the center of your oven, so make sure the racks are properly placed.

Prepare the filling: Puree only 1½ cups of the hazelnuts and the ¼ cup of the brown sugar in a food processor until it turns into a paste. Set aside. Chop the remaining ½ cup of hazelnuts with a chopper or knife, and set aside separately for sprinkling on top after baking.

In a large bowl, mix together the remaining ½ cup of brown sugar, the salt, arrowroot, egg replacer, black cumin, nutmeg, cinnamon, cloves, and ginger. Stir in the pumpkin puree and vanilla. Now stir in the MimicCreme and coconut milk until just combined. Set aside.

Roll out the piecrust on a well-floured surface and flip into your pan of choice.

Before filling the crust, crumble the hazelnut paste evenly on top of the pie dough and press down to create a layer across the entire bottom. Use a fork to prick the piecrust a few times to prevent air bubbles. Fill the piecrust evenly with the filling. Bake for about 50 minutes, until the edges are set and the center barely wiggles.

Let it cool, and serve with Vanilla Bean Crème Fraîche.

VEGAN PEANUT BUTTER DREAM PIE

> Serves 6 to 8 >

⅓ cup plus 1½ teaspoons Mimic-Creme or coconut milk

½ tablespoon vegan margarine, melted

1 (9-inch) Arrowhead Mills Graham Cracker Pie Crust

4 ounces vegan cream cheese

½ cup vegan sour cream

1 (10-ounce) container Ricemellow Crème Fluff

1 cup organic confectioners' sugar

1 cup peanut butter

½ teaspoon chocolate extract (optional)

½ cup vegan chocolate chips (optional—see additional step below if using).

Peanut Butter. Dream. Pie. "Why the ethereal name?" you ask. One bite of this divine creation, and you'll be dreaming about another slice (or five) for days. I know I was, but only because my friends devoured the rest before I had a chance to have a second helping.

Preheat the oven to 375°F.

Combine 1½ teaspoons of the MimicCreme with the melted margarine, then lightly brush onto the inside of the graham cracker piecrust. Bake for 5 minutes, then set aside on a cooling rack to cool.

Using either a hand mixer or a whisk, beat together the cream cheese, sour cream, Ricemellow Crème Fluff, confectioners' sugar, peanut butter, chocolate extract (if using), and remaining ⅓ cup of MimicCreme. Make sure the mixture is fully blended with no lumps of confectioners' sugar remaining.

Pour the mixture into the prebaked piecrust, then place in the freezer to set.

Remove the pie from the freezer 30 to 45 minutes prior to serving.

Optional chocolate topping: Once the pie has sat in the freezer for about an hour, melt the chocolate chips and pour into a heavy-duty zippered plastic bag. Snip off a tiny piece of one of the bottom corners of the bag, then drizzle the melted chocolate over the pie in a snazzy pattern.

BUBBE'S PINWHEEL COOKIES

 Makes about 20 servings

---

16 tablespoons (2 sticks) vegan
    margarine
1 cup sugar
¼ cup MimicCreme or alternative,
    (page 3)
2½ teaspoons vanilla extract
1½ teaspoons Ener-G Egg Replacer
    powder (do not add water)
2¾ cups sifted all-purpose flour
1 teaspoon baking powder
⅔ teaspoon salt
2 (1-ounce) squares vegan baking
    chocolate, melted, or 2 (1-ounce)
    packets liquid vegan baking
    chocolate

These cookies are very special to me. My very Yiddische bubbe (great-grandmother on my father's side) started feeding these to me before I had the teeth needed to chew them. When Bubbe . . . well, let's just say when she went to God's Delicatessen, my father inherited the recipe. In what proved to be an excellent father-daughter bonding experience, I helped him veganize the recipe. They tasted exactly, if not better, than I remembered.

Beat the margarine and sugar together in a large bowl. Add the MimicCreme and vanilla, and mix well. Add the egg replacer, flour, baking powder, and salt. Mix well to form a dough. Divide into five equal portions.

Take one portion of the dough and place it in a small bowl. Add the melted chocolate and stir thoroughly to make a chocolate dough.

(continues)

215

Bubbe's Pinwheel Cookies . . . (continued)

Take one-quarter (one portion) of the remaining plain dough, roll it into a ball, and place it between two 15-inch-long sheets of waxed paper. Roll the ball with a rolling pin into a circle between $\frac{1}{8}$ and $\frac{1}{6}$ inch thick.

Take one-quarter of the chocolate dough, place between two sheets of waxed paper, and roll with a rolling pin until it's about the same size as the plain dough. Peel off the top sheet of waxed paper from the chocolate dough, then flip it over on top of the plain dough so that it kind of looks like a pizza. Gently peel the waxed paper from the chocolate dough, patting down with your fingers so that it sticks to the plain dough. Then, using the waxed paper under the plain dough, carefully roll the dough up as you would a jellyroll.

Repeat three times more with the remaining plain and chocolate dough, to create four rolls in all. Freeze the rolls for 3 to 4 hours, until firm, then slice to a thickness of about $\frac{1}{8}$ inch.

Preheat the oven to 375°F.

Place the cookie slices on a cookie sheet (they can be close together . . . they won't spread) and bake for 10 to 15 minutes.

Keep in mind that there really is no correct way to bake these cookies. I like mine extra crispy! The end result should look a little something like the cookies in the photo, but no single roll of pinwheel cookies looks exactly the same.

VEGAN COCONUT ICE-CREAM PIE

⋟ Makes 1 pie; serves 6 to 8 ⋞

1 premade vegan piecrust, or 1 Piecrust (page 212)

1 (14-ounce) can coconut milk

1 (8-ounce) package vegan cream cheese

½ cup sugar

1 teaspoon vanilla extract

1 teaspoon coconut extract (optional)

2 tablespoons water

½ vanilla bean

2 teaspoons agar powder

2 tablespoons coconut oil, melted

¼ cup sweetened, grated coconut

I'm not much of a raw foodie, but I occasionally like to be a lazy foodie. Don't get me wrong. I bust my butt almost daily in the kitchen. Sometimes I just need a recipe that takes the heat out of the kitchen. This pie is so perfect on a hot summer day, or even to cool down your tummy after a hot, savory meal.

Bake the premade vegan piecrust as directed on the package, then set aside to cool. If you're making a homemade crust, prep this first.

In a blender, combine the coconut milk, cream cheese, ¼ cup of the sugar, vanilla and coconut extracts, and water. Make a slit down the center of the vanilla bean, then gently scrape out the seeds and add to the blender. Cover tightly and blend the mixture until smooth.

Pour the contents of the blender into a small saucepan. Sprinkle the agar powder on top and let stand for 5 minutes.

Bring the contents of the pan to a boil, stirring frequently, then immediately remove from the heat and then stir in the melted coconut oil.

Pour the mixture into the prepared crust. Cover and chill in the freezer until firm, 4 to 5 hours.

Before serving, toast the shredded coconut in a nonstick skillet over low heat until golden. Allow the pie to sit at room temperature for 10 to 15 minutes before garnishing with the toasted coconut and serving.

HOMEMADE VEGAN MARSHMALLOWS

⋙ Makes 20 to 30 marshmallows, depending on how large you slice them ⋘

¼ cup cornstarch

⅓ cup confectioners' sugar

⅛ cup tapioca starch

⅓ cup plus 1 heaping tablespoon light corn syrup

Pinch of salt

1 teaspoon vanilla extract

3 teaspoons Ener-G Egg Replacer powder (do not add water)

2 tablespoons barley malt powder

1 teaspoon xanthan gum

2½ tablespoons water

2½ tablespoons plain soy creamer

3 teaspoons agar powder

1 cup granulated sugar

My dad the culinary chemist first shined the light on the ease of homemade confections. Well, it was not always 100 percent easy, but it was always fun. I'll never forget the time we formed a human taffy pull in our kitchen—getting every family member except the dog (he shed too much) in on the action. When I was a little Shaglet, Dad showed us how to make marshmallows the real way, and I took it upon myself to perfect a cruelty-free version so that vegans can share in the experience.

In a small bowl, sift together the cornstarch, confectioners' sugar, and tapioca starch. Lightly grease a 9 by 13-inch baking pan, then sprinkle with 1 tablespoon of the cornstarch mixture and shake the pan around to coat the sides and the bottom well.

In the bowl of your stand mixer, (or use a very large bowl and hand mixer), combine the corn syrup, salt, vanilla, egg replacer, barley malt powder, and xanthan gum. Make sure your stand mixer's wire whisk attachment is sitting out. You'll need it soon. Set aside.

Take the smallest saucepan you have, and pour in the water and soy creamer. Sprinkle the agar powder over the top and allow it to sit for 5 minutes. Add the granulated sugar, then heat over medium-low heat until the sugar dissolves and the mixture is beginning to boil.

Remove from the heat and immediately pour into the bowl of the stand mixer. Whisk at high speed for 2 to 3 minutes until all the ingredients are blended and fluffy.

Pour into the prepared baking pan, then smooth out the top with a spatula. Let set for a few hours, then use a damp knife to cut the marshmallows into whatever size or shape you choose. Roll each marshmallow in the remaining cornstarch mixture, then let them stand on a wire cooling rack overnight to dry.

Keeps in an airtight container for up to two weeks.

SOUTHERN SEA SALT–PECAN PRALINES

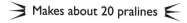 Makes about 20 pralines

2 cups sugar
½ cup MimicCreme (see tip)
½ cup soy milk (see tip)
⅛ teaspoon table salt
2 tablespoons vegan margarine
2½ cups pecan halves
A few teaspoons sea salt

The final recipe in my book is dedicated to Jane. Together, we veganized her grandmother's recipe. I added a little flair, because that's just how I roll.

SHAGGY KITCHEN TIP For the MimicCreme substitution in this recipe, omit the MimicCreme and soy milk, and replace with 1 cup of coconut milk.

Line a large, flat surface with waxed paper.

In a large saucepan, combine the sugar, MimicCreme, soy milk, and table salt, making sure that everything is well incorporated and not sticking to the bottom of the pan.

If you have a candy thermometer, great. Place it in the pan now, making sure it's not directly touching the bottom. If you don't have a thermometer, that's okay, too.

(continues)

Southern Sea Salt–Pecan Pralines . . . (continued)

Have ready a glass of cold water, and keep it near your oven. Cook the mixture over low to medium heat, stirring constantly, making sure to scrape the bottom and sides of the pan.

When the mixture hits 210°F (or after about 20 minutes), add the margarine and pecans, and continue to cook and stir until the temperature reaches 234°F (soft ball stage). If you don't have a candy thermometer, or even if you do, drop a little bit of the mixture into the water. If it solidifies, remove the pan from the heat and spoon out the mixture onto the waxed paper.

You can make the pralines as big or small as you'd like. Sprinkle each praline with a tiny pinch of sea salt, and allow to cool and set.

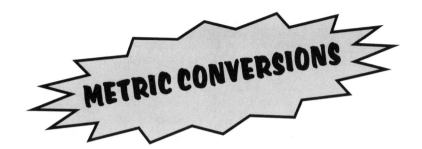

METRIC CONVERSIONS

THE RECIPES IN THIS BOOK have not been tested with metric measurements, so some variations might occur.

Remember that the weight of dry ingredients varies according to the volume or density factor: 1 cup of flour weighs far less than 1 cup of sugar, and 1 tablespoon doesn't necessarily hold 3 teaspoons.

GENERAL FORMULA FOR METRIC CONVERSION

Ounces to grams	Multiply ounces by 28.35
Grams to ounces	Multiply grams by 0.035
Pounds to grams	Multiply pounds by 453.5
Pounds to kilograms	Multiply pounds by 0.45
Cups to liters	Multiply cups by 0.24
Fahrenheit to Celsius	Subtract 32 from Fahrenheit temperature, multiply by 5, divide by 9
Celsius to Fahrenheit	Multiply Celsius temperature by 9, divide by 5, add 32

VOLUME (LIQUID) MEASUREMENTS

1 teaspoon = $\frac{1}{6}$ fluid ounce = 5 milliliters
1 tablespoon = $\frac{1}{2}$ fluid ounce = 15 milliliters
2 tablespoons = 1 fluid ounce = 30 milliliters
$\frac{1}{4}$ cup = 2 fluid ounces = 60 milliliters
$\frac{1}{3}$ cup = $2\frac{2}{3}$ fluid ounces = 79 milliliters
$\frac{1}{2}$ cup = 4 fluid ounces = 118 milliliters
1 cup or $\frac{1}{2}$ pint = 8 fluid ounces = 250 milliliters
2 cups or 1 pint = 16 fluid ounces = 500 milliliters
4 cups or 1 quart = 32 fluid ounces = 1,000 milliliters
1 gallon = 4 liters

METRIC CONVERSIONS

VOLUME (DRY) MEASUREMENTS

¼ teaspoon = 1 milliliter

½ teaspoon = 2 milliliters

¾ teaspoon = 4 milliliters

1 teaspoon = 5 milliliters

1 tablespoon = 15 milliliters

¼ cup = 59 milliliters

⅓ cup = 79 milliliters

½ cup = 118 milliliters

⅔ cup = 158 milliliters

¾ cup = 177 milliliters

1 cup = 225 milliliters

4 cups or 1 quart = 1 liter

½ gallon = 2 liters

1 gallon = 4 liters

WEIGHT (MASS) MEASUREMENTS

1 ounce = 30 grams

2 ounces = 55 grams

3 ounces = 85 grams

4 ounces = ¼ pound = 125 grams

8 ounces = ½ pound = 240 grams

12 ounces = ¾ pound = 375 grams

16 ounces = 1 pound = 454 grams

LINEAR MEASUREMENTS

½ inch = 1⅓ cm

1 inch = 2½ cm

6 inches = 15 cm

8 inches = 20 cm

10 inches = 25 cm

12 inches = 30 cm

20 inches = 50 cm

OVEN TEMPERATURE EQUIVALENTS, FAHRENHEIT (F) AND CELSIUS (C)

100°F = 38°C

200°F = 95°C

250°F = 120°C

300°F = 150°C

350°F = 180°C

400°F = 205°C

450°F = 230° C

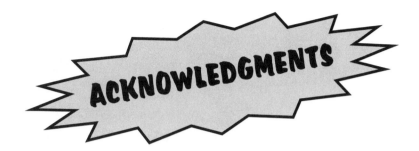

ACKNOWLEDGMENTS

FIRST AND FOREMOST, I thank my Mom and Dad. They've always supported my decisions and endeavors, emotionally and financially.

Mom, without your concern for my well-being* and amazing ability to whip up culinary mastery after a hard 9 hour work day, I firmly believe I wouldn't have the love for food that I do today.

Dad, you are a true home chef in every sense of the word. You taught me how to make taffy, pasta from scratch, paella . . . I could go on for hours. On your days off, you were always in the kitchen challenging yourself to make the most complicated recipes. I definitely absorbed this quality from you. And hot damn can you make a cheesecake.

My little sister, Alli. I'm in awe of your strength and intelligence. You are so much wiser than I am, which was a very hard fact for me to admit on paper. You will make a huge impact on this world with both your powerful mind and pure heart.

Jane, you are my rock. Together, we are a creative force. While our dietary interests couldn't lie on more opposite ends of the spectrum, you never bat a lash when

* *(aka Shoving food down my throat like a good Jewish mother.)*

ACKNOWLEDGMENTS

I explain that I "just need to cook." You have a genuinely beautiful heart and soul. I love you.

Amy, my best friend and the first vegetarian I knew. You are an amazing human being. Your soul is deeper than anyone else I know. No one knows me better than you. We've shared moments of laughter that no one else can even come close to understanding.

Tina, my best friend and professional ass-kicker. You always give me the advice I need to hear. You truly deserve the nickname "Tenacious D." You fight the good fight, and I love you for it.

Leigh, my first guinea pig. You tasted so many of my culinary creations and helped me improve my skills. I'm sorry you had to eat so many Vegan Twinkies prior to their perfection. Thank you for being an amazing friend . . . even when the tequila got the best of me.

Ashley and Nick, my first publicists. You've promoted my culinary endeavors from the beginning. I can't thank you enough. Thank you for testing my recipes at the drop of a hat, and for inviting me into your home to use your bitchin' oven.

Sita, my first and best friend in the state of California. I can count on no one more than you. Your unique sense of style, personality, and determination never cease to amaze me.

Meg at LJK Literary: You have been my rock-star since day one. You were the first to believe that my book could go somewhere, and you worked with me day and night to assure it would fall into the right hands. You're an amazing human being. Thank you for all you've done. I know we'll only continue to accomplish great things together. Renée at Da Capo Press: I cannot thank you enough for standing behind my writing. You've been so incredibly passionate about my material, and it's been an absolute joy working together. You always know the right words to help me truck through my edits. Thank you for believing in me and my cooking.

Collin, my Project Editor: Thank you so much for making this process a smooth one. You were always understanding when my chaotic life interfered with deadlines, and I can't thank you enough for helping me balance my life. Pauline Brown, my Interior Designer: You, m'dear, are amazing. I couldn't have imagined the book looking any more amazing and "like me." You did such an incredible job bringing *Veganize This!* to life. Thank you so much. Steve Cooley, my Cover Designer: Steve, you made *Veganize This!* look like the most bad-ass vegan cookbook on the shelf. Than you for truly understanding my vision. I'm so excited about how enticingly you designed the cover.

And last, but most certainly not least, Mike K., for being quite possibly the most supportive, wise human being on earth. I don't think there are even words to describe what a fantastic influence you've been in my life. Thank you, thank you, thank you.

INDEX

Aioli:
  Bourbon Buffalo Mole Sauce Chicken
    Wings with Vegan Bleu Cheese–Avocado
    Aioli, 166–168
  Orecchiette and Wild Arugula Salad in
    Vegan Basil-Mint Aioli, 180–181
Ale:
  Belgian Ale and Roasted Garlic–Infused
    White Chicken Chili Gumbo, 116–117
  Colombian Ale-Sautéed Vegan Steak and
    Sweet Onions with Garlic-Ginger-Ají-
    Avocado Sauce, 169–170
  Juniper Berry and White Peppercorn–
    Rubbed Field Roast with Sage-Infused
    Vegetables and Balsamic Ale-Cranberry
    Reduction, 144–145
  Pumpkin Tartare over Chickpea–Black
    Cumin Crepe Crisps with Vegan Sage
    and White Ale Browned Butter Sauce,
    155–157
  Roasted Garlic Caesar Dressing with
    Homemade Buttery Croutons, 189–190
  Sausage and Beer Gravy over Cheddar,
    Green Onion, and Cilantro Buttermilk
    Biscuits with Fried Dill and Dandelion
    Greens, 96–98

  Turkey-Style Seitan, 8
  Veal Chop–Style Seitan, 10
Almonds:
  Grilled Steak and Creminis with Garlic,
    Sherry, and Rosemary Sauce, 194–195
  Pumpkin Tartare over Chickpea–Black
    Cumin Crepe Crisps with Vegan Sage
    and White Ale Browned Butter Sauce,
    155–157
Apples:
  Butternut Squash, Apple, and Onion Galette
    with Blue Cheese, 200–201
  Chicken-Apple Sausage, 12–13
  Fennel, Vidalia Onion, and Roasted Garlic
    Potato Latkes with Mom's Applesauce,
    153–155
  Grilled Sage-Rubbed Pork Chops with
    Warm Apple Slaw, 165–166
  Pumpkin Tartare over Chickpea–Black
    Cumin Crepe Crisps with Vegan Sage
    and White Ale Browned Butter Sauce,
    155–157
Artichoke hearts:
  Lemon-Artichoke Cavatelli in an Heirloom
    Tomato–Cream Vinaigrette with English
    Peas and Vegan Prosciutto, 78–80

Mini Vegan Veal, Black Peppercorn, and Basil Sliders with Artichoke and Avocado Tapenade, 160–161

White Pepper Vegan Turkey Shawarma with Chipotle-Tomato Relish and Roasted Garlic, Sage, and Artichoke Tahini Paste, 173–175

Arugula:
Orecchiette and Wild Arugula Salad in Vegan Basil-Mint Aioli, 180–181
Prosciutto-Wrapped Greens, 195–196
White Lasagne with Basil Ricotta, Spinach, Young Rocket, and Diced Vegan Pancetta, 70–71

Asparagus: Orzo with Vegan Chicken-Apple Sausage, Asparagus, Baby Tomatoes, and Ricotta Salata in a White Tomato Sauce, 40–41

Aunt Jemima Syrup, Sweet Baguette Hazelnut French Toast with, 205–206

Avocado oil:
Bourbon Buffalo Mole Sauce Chicken Wings with Vegan Bleu Cheese–Avocado Aioli, 166–168
Cumin and Avocado Oil–Rubbed Portobello Tortas with Dragon Fruit Pico de Gallo and Purple Basil–White Peppercorn Mayo, 178–179

Avocados:
Carnitas and Caramelized Shallot and Mushroom Enchiladas with Tomatillo, Green Apple, and Avocado Sauce and Lime Crème Fraîche, 82–83
Colombian Ale-Sautéed Vegan Steak and Sweet Onions with Garlic-Ginger-Ají-Avocado Sauce, 169–170
Heirloom Bean, Red Russian Kale, and Wheat Berry Chili, 117–118
Mini Vegan Veal, Black Peppercorn, and Basil Sliders with Artichoke and Avocado Tapenade, 160–161

Bacon:
Morel Mushroom and Bacon White Macaroni and Cheese, 92–94
Saffron, Oregano, and Garlic Chive–Infused Vegan Sea Bass, Clams, Bacon, and Beech Mushrooms in White Wine, 61–62
Vegan Bacon, 15

Banchan (Side Dish) Salad, Black Sesame-Spinach, 183

Basil:
Coconut Vinegar–Cured Tofu Scallops with Lemongrass-Basil Cream Sauce and Cilantro-Garlic Coconut Rice, 42–43
Cumin and Avocado Oil–Rubbed Portobello Tortas with Dragon Fruit Pico de Gallo and Purple Basil–White Peppercorn Mayo, 178–179
Curried Pork, Enoki Mushroom, and Purple Basil Pot Stickers with a Porcini, Shoyu, and Sake Reduction, 170–173
Faux Chicken Coconut-Basil Burgers with Cilantro-Mint Chutney, 163–164
Orecchiette and Wild Arugula Salad in Vegan Basil-Mint Aioli, 180–181
Oregano and Basil-Rubbed Marsala Flank Steak Stuffed with Saffron Wild Mushrooms, 143–144
Pan-Seared White Pepper Tofu Scallops with Basil Cream Sauce Served over Linguine, 74–75
Thai Tofu, Vegetable, and Coconut Soup, 113–114
White Lasagne with Basil Ricotta, Spinach, Young Rocket, and Diced Vegan Pancetta, 70–71

Bean sprouts:
Pineapple Five-Spice Bun with Pineapple-Orange Sherry-Glazed Tofu, 35–37
Taiwanese Minced Pork and Garlic Chive Chow Mein, 129–131

Beans:

Belgian Ale and Roasted Garlic–Infused White Chicken Chili Gumbo, 116–117

Garlicky White Beans, 142

Green Papaya Salad (Som Tum), 192–193

Heirloom Bean, Red Russian Kale, and Wheat Berry Chili, 117–118

Heirloom Cannellini Beans with Sage, Crispy Vegan Prosciutto, and Fava Bean Pesto Ragout, 33–35

Heirloom Tomato, Black Garlic, and Marsala-Roasted Chickpea Panzanella, 177

Pan-Asian Black Sesame–Cabbage Slaw Tossed with Rose Water, Cilantro, and Mint Pesto, 183–184

Pan-Roasted Tempeh with White Bean Broth, Cilantro Pesto, and Roasted Shallots with Sautéed Kale, 48–50

Quattro Garlic Mashed Potatoes and White Beans, 152

Roasted Garlic Caesar Dressing with Homemade Buttery Croutons, 189–190

Sautéed Shallot, Cremini, and Fennel Green Bean Casserole, 138–140

Tuna and Garlic Cannellini Bean Salad, 188

Beef:

Beef-Style Seitan, 6

Braciole, 99–100

Chicken-Fried Tofu Steaks with Rosemary-Thyme Chicken Gravy, Two Ways: Gluten Free and Regular, 108–111

Coffee-Rubbed Vegan Steak Tacos with Grilled Lobster Mushroom, Heirloom Cherry Tomato, and Corn Salsa, 105–107

Colombian Ale-Sautéed Vegan Steak and Sweet Onions with Garlic-Ginger-Ají-Avocado Sauce, 169–170

Dijonaise-Crusted Beef Tenderloin Medallions with Vegan Béarnaise Sauce over Roasted Eggplant and Garlic Smashed Potatoes, 86–88

Galbi (Korean Short Ribs) and Bulgogi (Grilled Steak), 181–182

Grilled Steak and Creminis with Garlic, Sherry, and Rosemary Sauce, 194–195

Lemon-Thyme-Agave–Braised Vegan Short Ribs and Seared Tofu Scallops with Mineola Tangelo–Saffron Sauce, 80–81

Oregano and Basil-Rubbed Marsala Flank Steak Stuffed with Saffron Wild Mushrooms, 143–144

Red Wine and Peppercorn-Braised Brisket, 146–147

Spanish Purple Pepper Vegan Beef Stew, 94–96

Beets: Pork Chops and Cranberries in Oregon Pinot Noir Reduction with Wild Mushroom, Kale, Beet, and Hazelnut Hash, 127–129

Belgian Ale and Roasted Garlic–Infused White Chicken Chili Gumbo, 116–117

Belgian Waffles, 203–205

Bell peppers:

Red Chard, Roasted Garlic, and Ricotta–Stuffed Peppers with Sun-Dried Tomato and Toasted Pine Nut Marinara, 76–78

Spanish Purple Pepper Vegan Beef Stew, 94–96

Thai Tofu, Vegetable, and Coconut Soup, 113–114

Biscuits: Sausage and Beer Gravy over Cheddar, Green Onion, and Cilantro Buttermilk Biscuits with Fried Dill and Dandelion Greens, 96–98

Black Cumin Crab Tostadas over Cabbage Salad with Lime, Mint, and Wasabi Dressing, 185–186

Black Sesame–Spinach Banchan (Side Dish) Salad, 183

Blue cheese:

Bourbon Buffalo Mole Sauce Chicken Wings with Vegan Bleu Cheese–Avocado Aioli, 166–168

INDEX

Blue cheese (*continued*)
    Butternut Squash, Apple, and Onion Galette
        with Blue Cheese, 200–201
Bourbon Buffalo Mole Sauce Chicken Wings
    with Vegan Bleu Cheese–Avocado Oil
    Aioli, 166–168
Braciole, 99–100
Breads:
    Belgian Waffles, 203–205
    Brioche, 210–211
    Cilantro Buttermilk Biscuits, 97
    Garlic Pizza Dough, 101
    No-Yeast Pizza Crust, 104–105
Breakfast foods:
    Belgian Waffles, 203–205
    Eggs Benedict Florentine Omelets with
        Sage Hollandaise Sauce, 53–54
    Garlic French Toast, 206–207
    Matzo Brei, 148–149
    Scrambled Eggs, 27
    Sweet Baguette Hazelnut French Toast with
        Vegan Aunt Jemima Syrup, 205–206
Brioche, 210–211
Brisket, Red Wine and Peppercorn-Braised,
    146–147
Broccoli, Cheddar, and Rice Casseroles in a
    Chanterelle and Rosemary Cream Sauce,
    Individual, 149–150
Broccoli Rabe and Chanterelles, Kugel with,
    137–138
Bubbe's Pinwheel Cookies, 215–216
Buffalo Mole Sauce Chicken Wings, Bourbon,
    with Vegan Bleu Cheese–Avocado Aioli,
    166–168
Bulgogi (Grilled Steak), Galbi (Korean Short
    Ribs) and, 181–182
Bun, Pineapple Five-Spice, with Pineapple-
    Orange Sherry-Glazed Tofu, 35–37
Burgers:
    Faux Chicken Coconut-Basil Burgers with
        Cilantro-Mint Chutney, 163–164
    Mini Vegan Veal, Black Peppercorn, and
        Basil Sliders with Artichoke and Avocado
        Tapenade, 160–161
Butternut squash:
    Butternut Squash, Apple, and Onion Galette
        with Blue Cheese, 200–201
    Butternut Squash and Vanilla Bean Risotto,
        150–151
    Pumpkin Tartare over Chickpea–Black
        Cumin Crepe Crisps with Vegan Sage
        and White Ale Browned Butter Sauce,
        155–157
    Quinoalenta and Rosemary Squash Chips
        with Wild Mushrooms and Vegan
        Mascarpone, 83–85

Cabbage:
    Black Cumin Crab Tostadas over Cabbage
        Salad with Lime, Mint, and Wasabi
        Dressing, 185–186
    Curried Pork, Enoki Mushroom, and Purple
        Basil Pot Stickers with a Porcini, Shoyu,
        and Sake Reduction, 170–173
    Grilled Sage-Rubbed Pork Chops with
        Warm Apple Slaw, 165–166
    Pan-Asian Black Sesame–Cabbage Slaw
        Tossed with Rose Water, Cilantro, and
        Mint Pesto, 183–184
Café de Paris Butter, Escargots à la
    Bourguignonne en Croûte Vegan Brioche
    with, 73
Cakes:
    Mom's Carrot Pudding, 209–210
    Twinkies, 198–199
Cannellini beans (white beans):
    Belgian Ale and Roasted Garlic–Infused
        White Chicken Chili Gumbo, 116–117
    Garlicky White Beans, 142
    Heirloom Cannellini Beans with Sage,
        Crispy Vegan Prosciutto, and Fava Bean
        Pesto Ragout, 33–35

Pan-Roasted Tempeh with White Bean Broth, Cilantro Pesto, and Roasted Shallots with Sautéed Kale, 48–50

Quattro Garlic Mashed Potatoes and White Beans, 152

Tuna and Garlic Cannellini Bean Salad, 188

Caponata, Veal Chops with Sunchoke, 66–67

Carnitas and Caramelized Shallot and Mushroom Enchiladas with Tomatillo, Green Apple, and Avocado Sauce and Lime Crème Fraîche, 82–83

Carrots:

Frisée, Carrot, and Celery Stick Salad with Toasted Garlic and Cumin Vinaigrette, 168

Mom's Carrot Pudding, 209–210

Cashews:

Dill and Chive Cashew Cheese, 187

Egg Mix, 28

Parmesan Blend, 22

Cavatelli, Lemon-Artichoke, in an Heirloom Tomato–Cream Vinaigrette with English Peas and Vegan Prosciutto, 78–80

Celery Stick, Frisée, and Carrot Salad with Toasted Garlic and Cumin Vinaigrette, 168

Champagne-Lemon Cream Sauce and Sun-Dried Tomato and Roasted Red Pepper Salsa, Free-Form Wild Mushroom Lasagne with, 68–69

Chard, Roasted Garlic, and Ricotta–Stuffed Peppers with Sun-Dried Tomato and Toasted Pine Nut Marinara, 76–78

Cheddar:

Doritos, 123–124

Individual Broccoli, Cheddar, and Rice Casseroles in a Chanterelle and Rosemary Cream Sauce, 149–150

Morel Mushroom and Bacon White Macaroni and Cheese, 92–94

Quattro Formaggio White Truffle Macaroni and Cheese, 91–92

Sausage and Beer Gravy over Cheddar, Green Onion, and Cilantro Buttermilk Biscuits with Fried Dill and Dandelion Greens, 96–98

Cheese alternatives:

Dill and Chive Cashew Cheese, 187

DIY Vegan Mozzarella That Melts!, 21–22

Fontina, 24

Goat Cheese, 23–24

Mascarpone, 23

Parmesan Blend, 22

Ricotta, 22

vegan products, xvii

Cheese dishes:

Bourbon Buffalo Mole Sauce Chicken Wings with Vegan Bleu Cheese–Avocado Oil Aioli, 166–168

Braciole, 99–100

Butternut Squash, Apple, and Onion Galette with Blue Cheese, 200–201

Cheesy Sweet Onion and Heirloom Tomato Pie, 120–121

Crab and Oyster Mushroom Mezzelune in a Roasted Hatch Chile and Walnut Cream Sauce, 58–60

Dill and Chive Cashew Cheese, 187

Doritos, 123–124

Goat Cheese, Spinach, and Sun-Dried Tomato–Stuffed Pork Chops with Roasted Garlic Fingerling Potatoes and Pearl Onions, 38–39

Herbes de Provence and Roasted Garlic Pizza with Melting Vegan Cheese Blend, 100–102

Individual Broccoli, Cheddar, and Rice Casseroles in a Chanterelle and Rosemary Cream Sauce, 149–150

Lemon-Artichoke Cavatelli in an Heirloom Tomato–Cream Vinaigrette with English Peas and Vegan Prosciutto, 78–80

Cheese dishes *(continued)*

Morel Mushroom and Bacon White Macaroni and Cheese, 92–94

Orzo with Vegan Chicken-Apple Sausage, Asparagus, Baby Tomatoes, and Ricotta Salata in a White Tomato Sauce, 40–41

Quattro Formaggio White Truffle Macaroni and Cheese, 91–92

Quinoalenta and Rosemary Squash Chips with Wild Mushrooms and Vegan Mascarpone, 83–85

Rainier Cherry, Lemon, and Sweet Ricotta Gratin, 202–203

Red Chard, Roasted Garlic, and Ricotta–Stuffed Peppers with Sun-Dried Tomato and Toasted Pine Nut Marinara, 76–78

Sausage and Beer Gravy over Cheddar, Green Onion, and Cilantro Buttermilk Biscuits with Fried Dill and Dandelion Greens, 96–98

White Lasagne with Basil Ricotta, Spinach, Young Rocket, and Diced Vegan Pancetta, 70–71

Cherry, Lemon, and Sweet Ricotta Gratin, 202–203

Chestnut, Marble Rye, and Pancetta Stuffing with Sherry, Leeks, and Blue Foot and Shiitake Mushrooms, 140

Chicken:

Belgian Ale and Roasted Garlic–Infused White Chicken Chili Gumbo, 116–117

Bourbon Buffalo Mole Sauce Chicken Wings with Vegan Bleu Cheese–Avocado Oil Aioli, 166–168

Chicken Marsala Masala with Fresh Morels, 72

Chicken Paprikash, 122–123

Chicken-Apple Sausage, 12–13

Chicken-Style Seitan, 5

Chipotle Adobo Barbecued Chicken, 188–189

Faux Chicken Coconut-Basil Burgers with Cilantro-Mint Chutney, 163–164

Green Garlic Gumbo, 114–115

Hatch Chile Chicken Cacciatore with Black Garlic–Tomato Sauce, 56–57

Lemongrass, Ginger, and Coriander-Infused Matzo Ball Soup, 134–136

Orange-Sesame Grilled Chicken Tenders, 162–163

Orzo with Vegan Chicken-Apple Sausage, Asparagus, Baby Tomatoes, and Ricotta Salata in a White Tomato Sauce, 40–41

Chicken-Fried Tofu Steaks with Rosemary-Thyme Chicken Gravy, Two Ways: Gluten Free and Regular, 108–111

Chickpeas:

Heirloom Tomato, Black Garlic, and Marsala-Roasted Chickpea Panzanella, 177

Pan-Asian Black Sesame–Cabbage Slaw Tossed with Rose Water, Cilantro, and Mint Pesto, 183–184

Roasted Garlic Caesar Dressing with Homemade Buttery Croutons, 189–190

Chili, Heirloom Bean, Red Russian Kale, and Wheat Berry, 117–118

Chili Gumbo, Belgian Ale and Roasted Garlic-Infused White Chicken, 116–117

Chipotle Adobo Barbecued Chicken, 188–189

Chipotle-Tomato Relish and Roasted Garlic, Sage, and Artichoke Tahini Paste, White Pepper Vegan Turkey Shawarma with, 173–175

Chocolate:

Bubbe's Pinwheel Cookies, 215–216

Eggplant Parmesan Ravioli with Heirloom Tomato, Strawberry, and Chocolate Marinara, 46–48

Peanut Butter Dream Pie, 214–215

Chow Mein, Taiwanese Minced Pork and Garlic Chive, 129–131

Cilantro:

Belgian Ale and Roasted Garlic–Infused White Chicken Chili Gumbo, 116–117

Carnitas and Caramelized Shallot and
Mushroom Enchiladas with Tomatillo,
Green Apple, and Avocado Sauce and
Lime Crème Fraîche, 82–83

Coconut Vinegar–Cured Tofu Scallops with
Lemongrass-Basil Cream Sauce and
Cilantro-Garlic Coconut Rice, 42–43

Colombian Ale-Sautéed Vegan Steak and
Sweet Onions with Garlic-Ginger-Ají-
Avocado Sauce, 169–170

Cumin and Avocado Oil–Rubbed Portobello
Tortas with Dragon Fruit Pico de Gallo
and Purple Basil–White Peppercorn
Mayo, 178–179

Faux Chicken Coconut-Basil Burgers with
Cilantro-Mint Chutney, 163–164

Heirloom Bean, Red Russian Kale, and
Wheat Berry Chili, 117–118

Pan-Asian Black Sesame–Cabbage Slaw
Tossed with Rose Water, Cilantro, and
Mint Pesto, 183–184

Pan-Roasted Tempeh with White Bean
Broth, Cilantro Pesto, and Roasted
Shallots with Sautéed Kale, 48–50

Sausage and Beer Gravy over Cheddar,
Green Onion, and Cilantro Buttermilk
Biscuits with Fried Dill and Dandelion
Greens, 96–98

Clams:
Clams and Clamshells, 18–19
Saffron, Oregano, and Garlic Chive–
Infused Vegan Sea Bass, Clams, Bacon,
and Beech Mushrooms in White Wine,
61–62

Coconut:
Coconut Ice-Cream Pie, 217
Coconut Vinegar–Cured Tofu Scallops
with Lemongrass-Basil Cream Sauce
and Cilantro-Garlic Coconut Rice,
42–43
Faux Chicken Coconut-Basil Burgers with
Cilantro-Mint Chutney, 163–164

Fire-Roasted Pumpkin, Hazelnut, and Black
Cumin Pie with Vanilla Bean Crème
Fraîche, 211–213

Thai Tofu, Vegetable, and Coconut Soup,
113–114

Coffee-Rubbed Vegan Steak Tacos with Grilled
Lobster Mushroom, Heirloom Cherry
Tomato, and Corn Salsa, 105–107

Collard greens: Belgian Ale and Roasted
Garlic–Infused White Chicken Chili
Gumbo, 116–117

Colombian Ale-Sautéed Vegan Steak and
Sweet Onions with Garlic-Ginger-Ají-
Avocado Sauce, 169–170

Comfort foods:
Belgian Ale and Roasted Garlic–Infused
White Chicken Chili Gumbo, 116–117
Braciole, 99–100
Cheesy Sweet Onion and Heirloom Tomato
Pie, 120–121
Chicken Paprikash, 122–123
Chicken-Fried Tofu Steaks with Rosemary-
Thyme Chicken Gravy, Two Ways: Gluten
Free and Regular, 108–111
Coffee-Rubbed Vegan Steak Tacos with
Grilled Lobster Mushroom, Heirloom
Cherry Tomato, and Corn Salsa, 105–107
Creamy Roasted Pumpkin, Sherry, and
Tarragon Soup, 119–120
Doritos, 123–124
Eggplant Lasagna–Style Vegan Deep-Dish
Pizza, 103–104
Green Garlic Gumbo, 114–115
Heirloom Bean, Red Russian Kale, and
Wheat Berry Chili, 117–118
Herbes de Provence and Roasted Garlic
Pizza with Melting Vegan Cheese Blend,
100–102
Louisiana-Style Yellow Rice, 111
Mom's Carrot Pudding, 209–210
Morel Mushroom and Bacon White
Macaroni and Cheese, 92–94

INDEX

Comfort foods (*continued*)

No-Yeast Pizza Crust, 104–105

Pork Chops and Cranberries in Oregon Pinot Noir Reduction with Wild Mushroom, Kale, Beet, and Hazelnut Hash, 127–129

Quattro Formaggio White Truffle Macaroni and Cheese, 91–92

Sausage and Beer Gravy over Cheddar, Green Onion, and Cilantro Buttermilk Biscuits with Fried Dill and Dandelion Greens, 96–98

Spaghetti and Meatballs with San Marzano and Port Wine Marinara Sauce, 112

Spanish Purple Pepper Vegan Beef Stew, 94–96

Spicy No-Tuna Sushi Roll, 125–127

Taiwanese Minced Pork and Garlic Chive Chow Mein, 129–131

Thai Tofu, Vegetable, and Coconut Soup, 113–114

Cookies, Bubbe's Pinwheel, 215–216

Cool Whip, 25

Corn Salsa, Coffee-Rubbed Vegan Steak Tacos with Grilled Lobster Mushroom, Heirloom Cherry Tomato, and, 105–107

Crab:

Black Cumin Crab Tostadas over Cabbage Salad with Lime, Mint, and Wasabi Dressing, 185–186

Crab and Oyster Mushroom Mezzelune in a Roasted Hatch Chile and Walnut Cream Sauce, 58–60

Jumbo Lump Jackfruit Crab Cakes with Spanish Garlic Mayonnaise and Warm Saffron Nage, 50–52

Cranberries, dried: Pork Chops and Cranberries in Oregon Pinot Noir Reduction with Wild Mushroom, Kale, Beet, and Hazelnut Hash, 127–129

Cranberries, fresh: Juniper Berry and White Peppercorn–Rubbed Field Roast with Sage-Infused Vegetables and Balsamic Ale-Cranberry Reduction, 144–145

Crème fraîche:

Carnitas and Caramelized Shallot and Mushroom Enchiladas with Tomatillo, Green Apple, and Avocado Sauce and Lime Crème Fraîche, 82–83

Chicken Paprikash, 122–123

Fire-Roasted Pumpkin, Hazelnut, and Black Cumin Pie with Vanilla Bean Crème Fraîche, 211–213

Kugel with Broccoli Rabe and Chanterelles, 137–138

Vegan Crème Fraîche, 25

Crepe crisps: Pumpkin Tartare over Chickpea–Black Cumin Crepe Crisps with Vegan Sage and White Ale Browned Butter Sauce, 155–157

Croutons, Homemade Buttery, Roasted Garlic Caesar Dressing with, 189–190

Cumin and Avocado Oil–Rubbed Portobello Tortas with Dragon Fruit Pico de Gallo and Purple Basil–White Peppercorn Mayo, 178–179

Curried Pork, Enoki Mushroom, and Purple Basil Pot Stickers with a Porcini, Shoyu, and Sake Reduction, 170–173

Dairy alternatives:

Cool Whip, 25

Crème Fraîche, 25

Dill and Chive Cashew Cheese, 187

DIY Vegan Mozzarella That Melts!, 21–22

Fontina, 24

Goat Cheese, 23–24

Mascarpone, 23

MimicCreme, xix–xx

MimicCreme alternatives, 3–4

Parmesan Blend, 22

Ricotta, 22

vegan products, xvii, xix–xx, xxi–xxii

Dandelion greens: Sausage and Beer Gravy over Cheddar, Green Onion, and Cilantro Buttermilk Biscuits with Fried Dill and Dandelion Greens, 96–98

Desserts:
Bubbe's Pinwheel Cookies, 215–216
Coconut Ice-Cream Pie, 217
Cool Whip, 25
Fire-Roasted Pumpkin, Hazelnut, and Black Cumin Pie with Vanilla Bean Crème Fraîche, 211–213
Homemade Vegan Marshmallows, 218–219
Mom's Carrot Pudding, 209–210
Peanut Butter Dream Pie, 214–215
Rainier Cherry, Lemon, and Sweet Ricotta Gratin, 202–203
Southern Sea Salt–Pecan Pralines, 219–220
Twinkies, 198–199

Dijonaise-Crusted Beef Tenderloin Medallions with Vegan Béarnaise Sauce over Roasted Eggplant and Garlic Smashed Potatoes, 86–88

Dill and Chive Cashew Cheese, 187

Dips:
Dill and Chive Cashew Cheese, 187
Harvest Time Salsa, 186

DIY Vegan Mozzarella That Melts!, 21–22

Doritos, 123–124

Dragon fruit: Cumin and Avocado Oil–Rubbed Portobello Tortas with Dragon Fruit Pico de Gallo and Purple Basil–White Peppercorn Mayo, 178–179

Egg alternatives:
Egg Mix, 28
Egg Yolk Mix, 28
Ener-G, xviii
Flaxseed Egg, 29
Scrambled Eggs, 27

Egg dishes:
Eggs Benedict Florentine Omelets with Sage Hollandaise Sauce, 53–54

Kugel with Broccoli Rabe and Chanterelles, 137–138
Matzo Brei, 148–149
Rustic Sunflower Seed and Lime Pesto Quiche Tartlets with Roma Tomatoes and Black Olives, 207–209

Eggplant:
Dijonaise-Crusted Beef Tenderloin Medallions with Vegan Béarnaise Sauce over Roasted Eggplant and Garlic Smashed Potatoes, 86–88
Eggplant Lasagna–Style Vegan Deep-Dish Pizza, 103–104
Eggplant Parmesan Ravioli with Heirloom Tomato, Strawberry, and Chocolate Marinara, 46–48
Red Chard, Roasted Garlic, and Ricotta–Stuffed Peppers with Sun-Dried Tomato and Toasted Pine Nut Marinara, 76–78
Roasted White Eggplant Fettuccine Alfredo with Fresh Fennel and Spinach, 62–64
Veal Chops with Sunchoke Caponata, 66–67

Enchiladas: Carnitas and Caramelized Shallot and Mushroom Enchiladas with Tomatillo, Green Apple, and Avocado Sauce and Lime Crème Fraîche, 82–83

Escargots à la Bourguignonne en Croûte Vegan Brioche with Café de Paris Butter, 73

Faux Chicken Coconut-Basil Burgers with Cilantro-Mint Chutney, 163–164

Fava Bean Pesto Ragout, Heirloom Cannellini Beans with Sage, Crispy Vegan Prosciutto, and, 33–35

Fennel:
Fennel, Vidalia Onion, and Roasted Garlic Potato Latkes with Mom's Applesauce, 153–155
Roasted White Eggplant Fettuccine Alfredo with Fresh Fennel and Spinach, 62–64

Fire-Roasted Pumpkin, Hazelnut, and Black Cumin Pie with Vanilla Bean Crème Fraîche, 211–213

Fish. *See* Seafood dishes

Flaxseed Egg, 29

Fontina cheese:
Cheesy Sweet Onion and Heirloom Tomato Pie, 120–121
Vegan Fontina, 24

Free-Form Wild Mushroom Lasagne with Champagne-Lemon Cream Sauce and Sun-Dried Tomato and Roasted Red Pepper Salsa, 68–69

French toast:
Garlic French Toast, 206–207
Sweet Baguette Hazelnut French Toast with Vegan Aunt Jemima Syrup, 205–206

Frisée, Carrot, and Celery Stick Salad with Toasted Garlic and Cumin Vinaigrette, 168

Galbi (Korean Short Ribs) and Bulgogi (Grilled Steak), 181–182

Galette with Blue Cheese, Butternut Squash, Apple, and Onion, 200–201

Garlic:
Fennel, Vidalia Onion, and Roasted Garlic Potato Latkes with Mom's Applesauce, 153–155
Frisée, Carrot, and Celery Stick Salad with Toasted Garlic and Cumin Vinaigrette, 168
Garlic French Toast, 206–207
Garlicky White Beans, 142
Green Garlic Gumbo, 114–115
Hatch Chile Chicken Cacciatore with Black Garlic–Tomato Sauce, 56–57
Heirloom Tomato, Black Garlic, and Marsala-Roasted Chickpea Panzanella, 177
Quattro Garlic Mashed Potatoes and White Beans, 152
Roasted Garlic Caesar Dressing with Homemade Buttery Croutons, 189–190

Gluten Free Chicken-Fried Tofu Steaks with Rosemary-Thyme Chicken Gravy, 108–109

Goat cheese:
Goat Cheese, Spinach, and Sun-Dried Tomato–Stuffed Pork Chops with Roasted Garlic Fingerling Potatoes and Pearl Onions, 38–39
Vegan Goat Cheese, 23–24

Green beans:
Green Papaya Salad (Som Tum), 192–193
Sautéed Shallot, Cremini, and Fennel Green Bean Casserole, 138–140

Green Garlic Gumbo, 114–115

Green Papaya Salad (Som Tum), 192–193

Greens, Prosciutto-Wrapped, 195–196

Gumbo:
Belgian Ale and Roasted Garlic–Infused White Chicken Chili Gumbo, 116–117
Green Garlic Gumbo, 114–115

Ham-Style Seitan, 9

Harvest Time Salsa, 186

Hatch chile peppers, 54–55

Hazelnut French Toast, Sweet Baguette, with Vegan Aunt Jemima Syrup, 205–206

Hazelnuts:
Fire-Roasted Pumpkin, Hazelnut, and Black Cumin Pie with Vanilla Bean Crème Fraîche, 211–213
Pork Chops and Cranberries in Oregon Pinot Noir Reduction with Wild Mushroom, Kale, Beet, and Hazelnut Hash, 127–129

Heirloom Bean, Red Russian Kale, and Wheat Berry Chili, 117–118

Heirloom Cannellini Beans with Sage, Crispy Vegan Prosciutto, and Fava Bean Pesto Ragout, 33–35

Heirloom Tomato, Black Garlic, and Marsala-Roasted Chickpea Panzanella, 177

Herbes de Provence and Roasted Garlic Pizza
with Melting Vegan Cheese Blend,
100–102
Holiday dishes:
Butternut Squash and Vanilla Bean Risotto,
150–151
Fennel, Vidalia Onion, and Roasted Garlic
Potato Latkes with Mom's Applesauce,
153–155
Garlicky White Beans, 142
Individual Broccoli, Cheddar, and Rice
Casseroles in a Chanterelle and Rosemary
Cream Sauce, 149–150
Juniper Berry and White Peppercorn–
Rubbed Field Roast with Sage-Infused
Vegetables and Balsamic Ale-Cranberry
Reduction, 144–145
Kugel with Broccoli Rabe and Chanterelles,
137–138
Lemongrass, Ginger, and Coriander-Infused
Matzo Ball Soup, 134–136
Matzo Brei, 148–149
Oregano and Basil-Rubbed Marsala Flank
Steak Stuffed with Saffron Wild
Mushrooms, 143–144
Pumpkin Tartare over Chickpea–Black
Cumin Crepe Crisps with Vegan Sage
and White Ale Browned Butter Sauce,
155–157
Quattro Garlic Mashed Potatoes and White
Beans, 152
Red Wine and Peppercorn-Braised Brisket,
146–147
Roasted Chestnut, Marble Rye, and Pancetta
Stuffing with Sherry, Leeks, and Blue
Foot and Shiitake Mushrooms, 140
Sautéed Shallot, Cremini, and Fennel Green
Bean Casserole, 138–140
Hollandaise sauce: Eggs Benedict Florentine
Omelets with Sage Hollandaise Sauce,
53–54
Homemade Vegan Marshmallows, 218–219

Ice-Cream Pie, Coconut, 217
Individual Broccoli, Cheddar, and Rice
Casseroles in a Chanterelle and Rosemary
Cream Sauce, 149–150

Jackfruit:
Black Cumin Crab Tostadas over Cabbage
Salad with Lime, Mint, and Wasabi
Dressing, 185–186
Canned Tuna Packed in Oil, 19–20
Crab and Oyster Mushroom Mezzelune in a
Roasted Hatch Chile and Walnut Cream
Sauce, 58–60
Jumbo Lump Jackfruit Crab Cakes with
Spanish Garlic Mayonnaise and Warm
Saffron Nage, 50–52
Spicy No-Tuna Sushi Roll, 125–127
Jumbo Lump Jackfruit Crab Cakes with
Spanish Garlic Mayonnaise and Warm
Saffron Nage, 50–52
Juniper Berry and White Peppercorn–Rubbed
Field Roast with Sage-Infused Vegetables
and Balsamic Ale-Cranberry Reduction,
144–145

Kale:
Heirloom Bean, Red Russian Kale, and
Wheat Berry Chili, 117–118
Pan-Roasted Tempeh with White Bean
Broth, Cilantro Pesto, and Roasted
Shallots with Sautéed Kale, 48–50
Pineapple Five-Spice Bun with
Pineapple-Orange Sherry-Glazed Tofu,
35–37
Pork Chops and Cranberries in Oregon
Pinot Noir Reduction with Wild
Mushroom, Kale, Beet, and Hazelnut
Hash, 127–129
Korean Short Ribs (Galbi) and Grilled Steak
(Bulgogi), 181–182
Kugel with Broccoli Rabe and Chanterelles,
137–138

INDEX

Lasagne:
  Free-Form Wild Mushroom Lasagne with Champagne-Lemon Cream Sauce and Sun-Dried Tomato and Roasted Red Pepper Salsa, 68–69
  White Lasagne with Basil Ricotta, Spinach, Young Rocket, and Diced Vegan Pancetta, 70–71
Latkes: Fennel, Vidalia Onion, and Roasted Garlic Potato Latkes with Mom's Applesauce, 153–155
Lemon-Artichoke Cavatelli in an Heirloom Tomato–Cream Vinaigrette with English Peas and Vegan Prosciutto, 78–80
Lemongrass, Ginger, and Coriander-Infused Matzo Ball Soup, 134–136
Lemon-Thyme-Agave–Braised Vegan Short Ribs and Seared Tofu Scallops with Mineola Tangelo–Saffron Sauce, 80–81
Linguine, Pan-Seared White Pepper Tofu Scallops with Basil Cream Sauce Served over, 74–75
Louisiana-Style Yellow Rice, 111

Macaroni and cheese:
  Morel Mushroom and Bacon White Macaroni and Cheese, 92–94
  Quattro Formaggio White Truffle Macaroni and Cheese, 91–92
Marinade, Basic Seafood, 16
Marinara:
  Eggplant Parmesan Ravioli with Heirloom Tomato, Strawberry, and Chocolate Marinara, 46–48
  Red Chard, Roasted Garlic, and Ricotta–Stuffed Peppers with Sun-Dried Tomato and Toasted Pine Nut Marinara, 76–78
  Spaghetti and Meatballs with San Marzano and Port Wine Marinara Sauce, 112
Marshmallows, Homemade Vegan, 218–219

Mascarpone cheese:
  Quinoalenta and Rosemary Squash Chips with Wild Mushrooms and Vegan Mascarpone, 83–85
  Vegan Mascarpone, 23
Matzo Ball Soup, Lemongrass, Ginger, and Coriander-Infused, 134–136
Matzo Brei, 148–149
Meat alternatives. *See also specific types of meat*
  Bacon, 15
  Beef-Style Seitan, 6
  Chicken-Apple Sausage, 12–13
  Chicken-Style Seitan, 5
  Crispy Vegan Prosciutto, 14
  Ham-Style Seitan, 9
  Meatballs, 11–12
  Pancetta, 14
  Pork Chop–Style Seitan, 7
  Turkey-Style Seitan, 8
  Veal Chop–Style Seitan, 10
  vegan products, xvi, xix
Meatballs:
  Spaghetti and Meatballs with San Marzano and Port Wine Marinara Sauce, 112
  Turkish Pomegranate Meatball Soup, 64–65
  Vegan Meatballs, 11–12
MimicCreme, xix–xx, 3–4
Mineola Tangelo–Saffron Sauce, Lemon-Thyme-Agave–Braised Vegan Short Ribs and Seared Tofu Scallops with, 80–81
Mini Vegan Veal, Black Peppercorn, and Basil Sliders with Artichoke and Avocado Tapenade, 160–161
Mint:
  Black Cumin Crab Tostadas over Cabbage Salad with Lime, Mint, and Wasabi Dressing, 185–186
  Coconut Vinegar–Cured Tofu Scallops with Lemongrass-Basil Cream Sauce and Cilantro-Garlic Coconut Rice, 42–43
  Faux Chicken Coconut-Basil Burgers with Cilantro-Mint Chutney, 163–164

Pan-Asian Black Sesame–Cabbage Slaw Tossed with Rose Water, Cilantro, and Mint Pesto, 183–184

Pineapple Five-Spice Bun with Pineapple-Orange Sherry-Glazed Tofu, 35–37

Warm Spinach and Red Onion Salad with Green Apple, Meyer Lemon, and Fresh Mint Vinaigrette, 193

Mom's Carrot Pudding, 209–210

Morel Mushroom and Bacon White Macaroni and Cheese, 92–94

Mozzarella cheese:
    Cheesy Sweet Onion and Heirloom Tomato Pie, 120–121

    DIY Vegan Mozzarella That Melts!, 21–22

    Herbes de Provence and Roasted Garlic Pizza with Melting Vegan Cheese Blend, 100–102

    Morel Mushroom and Bacon White Macaroni and Cheese, 92–94

    Quattro Formaggio White Truffle Macaroni and Cheese, 91–92

    White Lasagne with Basil Ricotta, Spinach, Young Rocket, and Diced Vegan Pancetta, 70–71

Munchies. *See* Comfort foods

Mushrooms:
    Belgian Ale and Roasted Garlic–Infused White Chicken Chili Gumbo, 116–117

    Carnitas and Caramelized Shallot and Mushroom Enchiladas with Tomatillo, Green Apple, and Avocado Sauce and Lime Crème Fraîche, 82–83

    Chicken Marsala Masala with Fresh Morels, 72

    Coffee-Rubbed Vegan Steak Tacos with Grilled Lobster Mushroom, Heirloom Cherry Tomato, and Corn Salsa, 105–107

    Crab and Oyster Mushroom Mezzelune in a Roasted Hatch Chile and Walnut Cream Sauce, 58–60

    Cumin and Avocado Oil–Rubbed Portobello Tortas with Dragon Fruit Pico de Gallo and Purple Basil–White Peppercorn Mayo, 178–179

    Curried Pork, Enoki Mushroom, and Purple Basil Pot Stickers with a Porcini, Shoyu, and Sake Reduction, 170–173

    Escargots à la Bourguignonne en Croûte Vegan Brioche with Café de Paris Butter, 73

    Free-Form Wild Mushroom Lasagne with Champagne-Lemon Cream Sauce and Sun-Dried Tomato and Roasted Red Pepper Salsa, 68–69

    Grilled Steak and Creminis with Garlic, Sherry, and Rosemary Sauce, 194–195

    Hatch Chile Chicken Cacciatore with Black Garlic–Tomato Sauce, 56–57

    Kugel with Broccoli Rabe and Chanterelles, 137–138

    Morel Mushroom and Bacon White Macaroni and Cheese, 92–94

    Oregano and Basil-Rubbed Marsala Flank Steak Stuffed with Saffron Wild Mushrooms, 143–144

    Pork Chops and Cranberries in Oregon Pinot Noir Reduction with Wild Mushroom, Kale, Beet, and Hazelnut Hash, 127–129

    Quinoalenta and Rosemary Squash Chips with Wild Mushrooms and Vegan Mascarpone, 83–85

    Roasted Chestnut, Marble Rye, and Pancetta Stuffing with Sherry, Leeks, and Blue Foot and Shiitake Mushrooms, 140

    Saffron, Oregano, and Garlic Chive–Infused Vegan Sea Bass, Clams, Bacon, and Beech Mushrooms in White Wine, 61–62

    Sautéed Shallot, Cremini, and Fennel Green Bean Casserole, 138–140

No-Tuna Sushi Roll, Spicy, 125–127

No-Yeast Pizza Crust, 104–105

INDEX

Nuts:

Crab and Oyster Mushroom Mezzelune in a Roasted Hatch Chile and Walnut Cream Sauce, 58–60

Dill and Chive Cashew Cheese, 187

Egg Mix, 28

Fire-Roasted Pumpkin, Hazelnut, and Black Cumin Pie with Vanilla Bean Crème Fraîche, 211–213

Free-Form Wild Mushroom Lasagne with Champagne-Lemon Cream Sauce and Sun-Dried Tomato and Roasted Red Pepper Salsa, 68–69

Grilled Steak and Creminis with Garlic, Sherry, and Rosemary Sauce, 194–195

Orecchiette and Wild Arugula Salad in Vegan Basil-Mint Aioli, 180–181

Parmesan Blend, 22

Pork Chops and Cranberries in Oregon Pinot Noir Reduction with Wild Mushroom, Kale, Beet, and Hazelnut Hash, 127–129

Pumpkin Tartare over Chickpea–Black Cumin Crepe Crisps with Vegan Sage and White Ale Browned Butter Sauce, 155–157

Red Chard, Roasted Garlic, and Ricotta–Stuffed Peppers with Sun-Dried Tomato and Toasted Pine Nut Marinara, 76–78

Roasted Chestnut, Marble Rye, and Pancetta Stuffing with Sherry, Leeks, and Blue Foot and Shiitake Mushrooms, 140

Roasted Garlic Caesar Dressing with Homemade Buttery Croutons, 189–190

Rustic Sunflower Seed and Lime Pesto Quiche Tartlets with Roma Tomatoes and Black Olives, 207–209

Southern Sea Salt–Pecan Pralines, 219–220

Okra: Green Garlic Gumbo, 114–115

Olives:

Rustic Sunflower Seed and Lime Pesto Quiche Tartlets with Roma Tomatoes and Black Olives, 207–209

Summertime Heirloom Tomato and Herb Salad, 176

Tuna and Garlic Cannellini Bean Salad, 188

Omelets, Eggs Benedict Florentine, with Sage Hollandaise Sauce, 53–54

Onions:

Butternut Squash, Apple, and Onion Galette with Blue Cheese, 200–201

Cheesy Sweet Onion and Heirloom Tomato Pie, 120–121

Colombian Ale-Sautéed Vegan Steak and Sweet Onions with Garlic-Ginger-Ají-Avocado Sauce, 169–170

Fennel, Vidalia Onion, and Roasted Garlic Potato Latkes with Mom's Applesauce, 153–155

Goat Cheese, Spinach, and Sun-Dried Tomato–Stuffed Pork Chops with Roasted Garlic Fingerling Potatoes and Pearl Onions, 38–39

Sautéed Shallot, Cremini, and Fennel Green Bean Casserole, 138–140

Warm Spinach and Red Onion Salad with Green Apple, Meyer Lemon, and Fresh Mint Vinaigrette, 193

Orange-Sesame Grilled Chicken Tenders, 162–163

Orecchiette and Wild Arugula Salad in Vegan Basil-Mint Aioli, 180–181

Oregano and Basil-Rubbed Marsala Flank Steak Stuffed with Saffron Wild Mushrooms, 143–144

Orzo with Vegan Chicken-Apple Sausage, Asparagus, Baby Tomatoes, and Ricotta Salata in a White Tomato Sauce, 40–41

Pan-Asian Black Sesame–Cabbage Slaw Tossed with Rose Water, Cilantro, and Mint Pesto, 183–184

Pancetta:

Hatch Chile Chicken Cacciatore with Black Garlic–Tomato Sauce, 56–57

Roasted Chestnut, Marble Rye, and Pancetta Stuffing with Sherry, Leeks, and Blue Foot and Shiitake Mushrooms, 140

Vegan Pancetta, 14

White Lasagne with Basil Ricotta, Spinach, Young Rocket, and Diced Vegan Pancetta, 70–71

Pan-Roasted Tempeh with White Bean Broth, Cilantro Pesto, and Roasted Shallots with Sautéed Kale, 48–50

Pan-Seared White Pepper Tofu Scallops with Basil Cream Sauce Served over Linguine, 74–75

Pantry list, xv–xxii

Panzanella: Heirloom Tomato, Black Garlic, and Marsala-Roasted Chickpea Panzanella, 177

Parmesan cheese:
    Crab and Oyster Mushroom Mezzelune in a Roasted Hatch Chile and Walnut Cream Sauce, 58–60

    Morel Mushroom and Bacon White Macaroni and Cheese, 92–94

    Parmesan Blend, 22

    White Lasagne with Basil Ricotta, Spinach, Young Rocket, and Diced Vegan Pancetta, 70–71

Pasta and noodles:
    Basic Pasta Dough, 45–46

    Chicken Paprikash, 122–123

    Crab and Oyster Mushroom Mezzelune in a Roasted Hatch Chile and Walnut Cream Sauce, 58–60

    Eggplant Parmesan Ravioli with Heirloom Tomato, Strawberry, and Chocolate Marinara, 46–48

    Free-Form Wild Mushroom Lasagne with Champagne-Lemon Cream Sauce and Sun-Dried Tomato and Roasted Red Pepper Salsa, 68–69

    Heirloom Cannellini Beans with Sage, Crispy Vegan Prosciutto, and Fava Bean Pesto Ragout, 33–35

Lemon-Artichoke Cavatelli in an Heirloom Tomato–Cream Vinaigrette with English Peas and Vegan Prosciutto, 78–80

Orecchiette and Wild Arugula Salad in Vegan Basil-Mint Aioli, 180–181

organic products, xviii

Orzo with Vegan Chicken-Apple Sausage, Asparagus, Baby Tomatoes, and Ricotta Salata in a White Tomato Sauce, 40–41

Pan-Seared White Pepper Tofu Scallops with Basil Cream Sauce Served over Linguine, 74–75

Pineapple Five-Spice Bun with Pineapple-Orange Sherry-Glazed Tofu, 35–37

Quattro Formaggio White Truffle Macaroni and Cheese, 91–92

Roasted White Eggplant Fettuccine Alfredo with Fresh Fennel and Spinach, 62–64

Spaghetti and Meatballs with San Marzano and Port Wine Marinara Sauce, 112

Taiwanese Minced Pork and Garlic Chive Chow Mein, 129–131

White Lasagne with Basil Ricotta, Spinach, Young Rocket, and Diced Vegan Pancetta, 70–71

Peanut Butter Dream Pie, 214–215

Peas: Lemon-Artichoke Cavatelli in an Heirloom Tomato–Cream Vinaigrette with English Peas and Vegan Prosciutto, 78–80

Pecans, Southern Sea Salt–Pecan, 219–220

Peppers, bell. See Bell peppers

Pesto:
    Heirloom Cannellini Beans with Sage, Crispy Vegan Prosciutto, and Fava Bean Pesto Ragout, 33–35

    Pan-Asian Black Sesame–Cabbage Slaw Tossed with Rose Water, Cilantro, and Mint Pesto, 183–184

    Pan-Roasted Tempeh with White Bean Broth, Cilantro Pesto, and Roasted Shallots with Sautéed Kale, 48–50

Pesto (*continued*)
  Rustic Sunflower Seed and Lime Pesto
    Quiche Tartlets with Roma Tomatoes and
    Black Olives, 207–209
Pies, dessert:
  Coconut Ice-Cream Pie, 217
  Fire-Roasted Pumpkin, Hazelnut, and Black
    Cumin Pie with Vanilla Bean Crème
    Fraîche, 211–213
  Peanut Butter Dream Pie, 214–215
Pies, savory:
  Butternut Squash, Apple, and Onion Galette
    with Blue Cheese, 200–201
  Cheesy Sweet Onion and Heirloom Tomato
    Pie, 120–121
  Rustic Sunflower Seed and Lime Pesto
    Quiche Tartlets with Roma Tomatoes and
    Black Olives, 207–209
Pine nuts:
  Free-Form Wild Mushroom Lasagne with
    Champagne-Lemon Cream Sauce and
    Sun-Dried Tomato and Roasted Red
    Pepper Salsa, 68–69
  Orecchiette and Wild Arugula Salad in
    Vegan Basil-Mint Aioli, 180–181
  Red Chard, Roasted Garlic, and Ricotta–
    Stuffed Peppers with Sun-Dried Tomato
    and Toasted Pine Nut Marinara, 76–78
  Rustic Sunflower Seed and Lime Pesto
    Quiche Tartlets with Roma Tomatoes and
    Black Olives, 207–209
Pineapple Five-Spice Bun with Pineapple-
    Orange Sherry-Glazed Tofu, 35–37
Pinot noir: Pork Chops and Cranberries in
    Oregon Pinot Noir Reduction with Wild
    Mushroom, Kale, Beet, and Hazelnut
    Hash, 127–129
Pinwheel Cookies, Bubbe's, 215–216
Pizza:
  Eggplant Lasagna–Style Vegan Deep-Dish
    Pizza, 103–104
  Herbes de Provence and Roasted Garlic
    Pizza with Melting Vegan Cheese Blend,
    100–102
Pizza crust:
  Garlic Pizza Dough, 101
  No-Yeast Pizza Crust, 104–105
Pomegranate Meatball Soup, Turkish, 64–65
Pork. *See also* Bacon; Pancetta; Prosciutto
  Carnitas and Caramelized Shallot and
    Mushroom Enchiladas with Tomatillo,
    Green Apple, and Avocado Sauce and
    Lime Crème Fraîche, 82–83
  Curried Pork, Enoki Mushroom, and Purple
    Basil Pot Stickers with a Porcini, Shoyu,
    and Sake Reduction, 170–173
  Goat Cheese, Spinach, and Sun-Dried
    Tomato–Stuffed Pork Chops with
    Roasted Garlic Fingerling Potatoes and
    Pearl Onions, 38–39
  Grilled Sage-Rubbed Pork Chops with
    Warm Apple Slaw, 165–166
  Ham-Style Seitan, 9
  Pork Chops and Cranberries in Oregon
    Pinot Noir Reduction with Wild
    Mushroom, Kale, Beet, and Hazelnut
    Hash, 127–129
  Pork Chop–Style Seitan, 7
  Taiwanese Minced Pork and Garlic Chive
    Chow Mein, 129–131
Pot stickers: Curried Pork, Enoki Mushroom,
    and Purple Basil Pot Stickers with a
    Porcini, Shoyu, and Sake Reduction,
    170–173
Potatoes:
  Dijonaise-Crusted Beef Tenderloin
    Medallions with Vegan Béarnaise Sauce
    over Roasted Eggplant and Garlic
    Smashed Potatoes, 86–88
  Fennel, Vidalia Onion, and Roasted Garlic
    Potato Latkes with Mom's Applesauce,
    153–155

Goat Cheese, Spinach, and Sun-Dried Tomato–Stuffed Pork Chops with Roasted Garlic Fingerling Potatoes and Pearl Onions, 38–39

Quattro Garlic Mashed Potatoes and White Beans, 152

Pralines, Southern Sea Salt–Pecan, 219–220

Prosciutto:

Crispy Vegan Prosciutto, 14

Heirloom Cannellini Beans with Sage, Crispy Vegan Prosciutto, and Fava Bean Pesto Ragout, 33–35

Lemon-Artichoke Cavatelli in an Heirloom Tomato–Cream Vinaigrette with English Peas and Vegan Prosciutto, 78–80

Prosciutto-Wrapped Greens, 195–196

Puddings:

Kugel with Broccoli Rabe and Chanterelles, 137–138

Mom's Carrot Pudding, 209–210

Pumpkin:

Creamy Roasted Pumpkin, Sherry, and Tarragon Soup, 119–120

Fire-Roasted Pumpkin, Hazelnut, and Black Cumin Pie with Vanilla Bean Crème Fraîche, 211–213

Pumpkin Tartare over Chickpea–Black Cumin Crepe Crisps with Vegan Sage and White Ale Browned Butter Sauce, 155–157

Quattro Formaggio White Truffle Macaroni and Cheese, 91–92

Quattro Garlic Mashed Potatoes and White Beans, 152

Quiche Tartlets, Rustic Sunflower Seed and Lime Pesto, with Roma Tomatoes and Black Olives, 207–209

Quinoalenta and Rosemary Squash Chips with Wild Mushrooms and Vegan Mascarpone, 83–85

Rainier Cherry, Lemon, and Sweet Ricotta Gratin, 202–203

Ranch Dressing: My Way, 191

Ravioli, Eggplant Parmesan, with Heirloom Tomato, Strawberry, and Chocolate Marinara, 46–48

Red Wine and Peppercorn-Braised Brisket, 146–147

Rice:

Belgian Ale and Roasted Garlic–Infused White Chicken Chili Gumbo, 116–117

Butternut Squash and Vanilla Bean Risotto, 150–151

Coconut Vinegar–Cured Tofu Scallops with Lemongrass-Basil Cream Sauce and Cilantro-Garlic Coconut Rice, 42–43

Galbi (Korean Short Ribs) and Bulgogi (Grilled Steak), 181–182

Green Garlic Gumbo, 114–115

Individual Broccoli, Cheddar, and Rice Casseroles in a Chanterelle and Rosemary Cream Sauce, 149–150

Louisiana-Style Yellow Rice, 111

Spicy No-Tuna Sushi Roll, 125–127

Turkish Pomegranate Meatball Soup, 64–65

Ricotta cheese:

Braciole, 99–100

Crab and Oyster Mushroom Mezzelune in a Roasted Hatch Chile and Walnut Cream Sauce, 58–60

Lemon-Artichoke Cavatelli in an Heirloom Tomato–Cream Vinaigrette with English Peas and Vegan Prosciutto, 78–80

Orzo with Vegan Chicken-Apple Sausage, Asparagus, Baby Tomatoes, and Ricotta Salata in a White Tomato Sauce, 40–41

Rainier Cherry, Lemon, and Sweet Ricotta Gratin, 202–203

Red Chard, Roasted Garlic, and Ricotta–Stuffed Peppers with Sun-Dried Tomato and Toasted Pine Nut Marinara, 76–78

Ricotta cheese (*continued*)
  Vegan Ricotta, 22
  White Lasagne with Basil Ricotta, Spinach,
    Young Rocket, and Diced Vegan Pancetta,
    70–71
Risotto, Butternut Squash and Vanilla Bean,
  150–151
Roasted Chestnut, Marble Rye, and Pancetta
  Stuffing with Sherry, Leeks, and Blue
  Foot and Shiitake Mushrooms, 140
Roasted Garlic Caesar Dressing with
  Homemade Buttery Croutons, 189–190
Roasted red peppers: Free-Form Wild Mushroom
  Lasagne with Champagne-Lemon Cream
  Sauce and Sun-Dried Tomato and Roasted
  Red Pepper Salsa, 68–69
Roasted White Eggplant Fettuccine Alfredo
  with Fresh Fennel and Spinach, 62–64
Rustic Sunflower Seed and Lime Pesto Quiche
  Tartlets with Roma Tomatoes and Black
  Olives, 207–209

Saffron:
  Chicken Marsala Masala with Fresh Morels,
    72
  Jumbo Lump Jackfruit Crab Cakes with
    Spanish Garlic Mayonnaise and Warm
    Saffron Nage, 50–52
  Lemon-Thyme-Agave–Braised Vegan Short
    Ribs and Seared Tofu Scallops with
    Mineola Tangelo–Saffron Sauce, 80–81
  Louisiana-Style Yellow Rice, 111
  Oregano and Basil-Rubbed Marsala Flank
    Steak Stuffed with Saffron Wild
    Mushrooms, 143–144
  Saffron, Oregano, and Garlic Chive–Infused
    Vegan Sea Bass, Clams, Bacon, and Beech
    Mushrooms in White Wine, 61–62
Sake: Curried Pork, Enoki Mushroom, and
  Purple Basil Pot Stickers with a Porcini,
  Shoyu, and Sake Reduction, 170–173

Salads and dressings:
  Black Cumin Crab Tostadas over Cabbage
    Salad with Lime, Mint, and Wasabi
    Dressing, 185–186
  Black Sesame–Spinach Banchan (Side
    Dish) Salad, 183
  Frisée, Carrot, and Celery Stick Salad with
    Toasted Garlic and Cumin Vinaigrette, 168
  Green Papaya Salad (Som Tum), 192–193
  Grilled Sage-Rubbed Pork Chops with
    Warm Apple Slaw, 165–166
  Heirloom Tomato, Black Garlic, and
    Marsala-Roasted Chickpea Panzanella,
    177
  Orecchiette and Wild Arugula Salad in
    Vegan Basil-Mint Aioli, 180–181
  Pan-Asian Black Sesame–Cabbage Slaw
    Tossed with Rose Water, Cilantro, and
    Mint Pesto, 183–184
  Ranch Dressing: My Way, 191
  Roasted Garlic Caesar Dressing with
    Homemade Buttery Croutons, 189–190
  Summertime Heirloom Tomato and Herb
    Salad, 176
  Tuna and Garlic Cannellini Bean Salad, 188
  Warm Spinach and Red Onion Salad with
    Green Apple, Meyer Lemon, and Fresh
    Mint Vinaigrette, 193
Salsa:
  Coffee-Rubbed Vegan Steak Tacos with
    Grilled Lobster Mushroom, Heirloom
    Cherry Tomato, and Corn Salsa, 105–107
  Cumin and Avocado Oil–Rubbed Portobello
    Tortas with Dragon Fruit Pico de Gallo
    and Purple Basil–White Peppercorn
    Mayo, 178–179
  Free-Form Wild Mushroom Lasagne with
    Champagne-Lemon Cream Sauce and
    Sun-Dried Tomato and Roasted Red
    Pepper Salsa, 68–69
  Harvest Time Salsa, 186

Sausage:
  Chicken-Apple Sausage, 12–13
  Green Garlic Gumbo, 114–115
  Orzo with Vegan Chicken-Apple Sausage,
    Asparagus, Baby Tomatoes, and Ricotta
    Salata in a White Tomato Sauce, 40–41
  Sausage and Beer Gravy over Cheddar,
    Green Onion, and Cilantro Buttermilk
    Biscuits with Fried Dill and Dandelion
    Greens, 96–98
Scallops:
  Coconut Vinegar–Cured Tofu Scallops with
    Lemongrass-Basil Cream Sauce and
    Cilantro-Garlic Coconut Rice, 42–43
  Lemon-Thyme-Agave–Braised Vegan Short
    Ribs and Seared Tofu Scallops with
    Mineola Tangelo–Saffron Sauce, 80–81
  Pan-Seared White Pepper Tofu Scallops
    with Basil Cream Sauce Served over
    Linguine, 74–75
  Tofu Scallops, 17
Scrambled Eggs, 27
Sea bass:
  Saffron, Oregano, and Garlic Chive–
    Infused Vegan Sea Bass, Clams, Bacon,
    and Beech Mushrooms in White Wine,
    61–62
  Vegan Sea Bass, 20
Seafood alternatives:
  Canned Tuna Packed in Oil, 19–20
  Clams and Clamshells, 18–19
  Sea Bass, 20
  Tofu Scallops, 17
Seafood dishes:
  Black Cumin Crab Tostadas over Cabbage
    Salad with Lime, Mint, and Wasabi
    Dressing, 185–186
  Coconut Vinegar–Cured Tofu Scallops
    with Lemongrass-Basil Cream Sauce
    and Cilantro-Garlic Coconut Rice,
    42–43

Crab and Oyster Mushroom Mezzelune in a
    Roasted Hatch Chile and Walnut Cream
    Sauce, 58–60
  Jumbo Lump Jackfruit Crab Cakes with
    Spanish Garlic Mayonnaise and Warm
    Saffron Nage, 50–52
  Lemon-Thyme-Agave–Braised Vegan Short
    Ribs and Seared Tofu Scallops with
    Mineola Tangelo–Saffron Sauce, 80–81
  Pan-Seared White Pepper Tofu Scallops with
    Basil Cream Sauce Served over Linguine,
    74–75
  Saffron, Oregano, and Garlic Chive–Infused
    Vegan Sea Bass, Clams, Bacon, and Beech
    Mushrooms in White Wine, 61–62
  Spicy No-Tuna Sushi Roll, 125–127
  Tuna and Garlic Cannellini Bean Salad, 188
Seafood Marinade, Basic, 16
Seaweed:
  Basic Seafood Marinade, 16
  Canned Tuna Packed in Oil, 19–20
  Crab and Oyster Mushroom Mezzelune in a
    Roasted Hatch Chile and Walnut Cream
    Sauce, 58–60
  Spicy No-Tuna Sushi Roll, 125–127
Seitan. *See* Meat alternatives
Shawarma, White Pepper Vegan Turkey, with
    Chipotle-Tomato Relish and Roasted Garlic,
    Sage, and Artichoke Tahini Paste, 173–175
Short ribs:
  Galbi (Korean Short Ribs) and Bulgogi
    (Grilled Steak), 181–182
  Lemon-Thyme-Agave–Braised Vegan Short
    Ribs and Seared Tofu Scallops with
    Mineola Tangelo–Saffron Sauce, 80–81
Slaw:
  Grilled Sage-Rubbed Pork Chops with
    Warm Apple Slaw, 165–166
  Pan-Asian Black Sesame–Cabbage Slaw
    Tossed with Rose Water, Cilantro, and
    Mint Pesto, 183–184

INDEX

Sliders, Mini Vegan Veal, Black Peppercorn, and Basil, with Artichoke and Avocado Tapenade, 160–161

Som Tum (Green Papaya Salad), 192–193

Soups:

    Creamy Roasted Pumpkin, Sherry, and Tarragon Soup, 119–120

    Lemongrass, Ginger, and Coriander-Infused Matzo Ball Soup, 134–136

    Thai Tofu, Vegetable, and Coconut Soup, 113–114

    Turkish Pomegranate Meatball Soup, 64–65

Southern Sea Salt–Pecan Pralines, 219–220

Soy products, xxi

Spaghetti and Meatballs with San Marzano and Port Wine Marinara Sauce, 112

Spanish Garlic Mayonnaise and Warm Saffron Nage, Jumbo Lump Jackfruit Crab Cakes with, 50–52

Spanish Purple Pepper Vegan Beef Stew, 94–96

Spicy No-Tuna Sushi Roll, 125–127

Spinach:

    Black Sesame–Spinach Banchan (Side Dish) Salad, 183

    Goat Cheese, Spinach, and Sun-Dried Tomato–Stuffed Pork Chops with Roasted Garlic Fingerling Potatoes and Pearl Onions, 38–39

    Roasted White Eggplant Fettuccine Alfredo with Fresh Fennel and Spinach, 62–64

    Turkish Pomegranate Meatball Soup, 64–65

    Warm Spinach and Red Onion Salad with Green Apple, Meyer Lemon, and Fresh Mint Vinaigrette, 193

    White Lasagne with Basil Ricotta, Spinach, Young Rocket, and Diced Vegan Pancetta, 70–71

Squash:

    Butternut Squash, Apple, and Onion Galette with Blue Cheese, 200–201

    Butternut Squash and Vanilla Bean Risotto, 150–151

    Creamy Roasted Pumpkin, Sherry, and Tarragon Soup, 119–120

    Fire-Roasted Pumpkin, Hazelnut, and Black Cumin Pie with Vanilla Bean Crème Fraîche, 211–213

    Pumpkin Tartare over Chickpea–Black Cumin Crepe Crisps with Vegan Sage and White Ale Browned Butter Sauce, 155–157

    Quinoalenta and Rosemary Squash Chips with Wild Mushrooms and Vegan Mascarpone, 83–85

Strawberries: Eggplant Parmesan Ravioli with Heirloom Tomato, Strawberry, and Chocolate Marinara, 46–48

Stuffing: Roasted Chestnut, Marble Rye, and Pancetta Stuffing with Sherry, Leeks, and Blue Foot and Shiitake Mushrooms, 140

Summertime Heirloom Tomato and Herb Salad, 176

Sunchoke Caponata, Veal Chops with, 66–67

Sushi Roll, Spicy No-Tuna, 125–127

Sweet Baguette Hazelnut French Toast with Vegan Aunt Jemima Syrup, 205–206

Tacos, Coffee-Rubbed Vegan Steak, with Grilled Lobster Mushroom, Heirloom Cherry Tomato, and Corn Salsa, 105–107

Tahini: White Pepper Vegan Turkey Shawarma with Chipotle-Tomato Relish and Roasted Garlic, Sage, and Artichoke Tahini Paste, 173–175

Taiwanese Minced Pork and Garlic Chive Chow Mein, 129–131

Tapenade: Mini Vegan Veal, Black Peppercorn, and Basil Sliders with Artichoke and Avocado Tapenade, 160–161

Tempeh:

    about, xxi

    Pan-Roasted Tempeh with White Bean Broth, Cilantro Pesto, and Roasted Shallots with Sautéed Kale, 48–50

Thai Tofu, Vegetable, and Coconut Soup, 113–114

Tofu. *See also* Scallops
  about, xxi
  Bacon, 15
  Chicken-Fried Tofu Steaks with Rosemary-Thyme Chicken Gravy, Two Ways: Gluten Free and Regular, 108–111
  Clams and Clamshells, 18–19
  Crispy Vegan Prosciutto, 14
  DIY Vegan Mozzarella That Melts!, 21–22
  Eggplant Parmesan Ravioli with Heirloom Tomato, Strawberry, and Chocolate Marinara, 46–48
  Fontina, 24
  Goat Cheese (Solid Cheese), 23–24
  Herbes de Provence and Roasted Garlic Pizza with Melting Vegan Cheese Blend, 100–102
  Kugel with Broccoli Rabe and Chanterelles, 137–138
  Lemon-Artichoke Cavatelli in an Heirloom Tomato–Cream Vinaigrette with English Peas and Vegan Prosciutto, 78–80
  Mascarpone, 23
  Pancetta, 14
  Pineapple Five-Spice Bun with Pineapple-Orange Sherry-Glazed Tofu, 35–37
  Rainier Cherry, Lemon, and Sweet Ricotta Gratin, 202–203
  Ricotta, 22
  Scrambled Eggs, 27
  Sea Bass, 20
  Thai Tofu, Vegetable, and Coconut Soup, 113–114
  White Lasagne with Basil Ricotta, Spinach, Young Rocket, and Diced Vegan Pancetta, 70–71

Tomatillos:
  Carnitas and Caramelized Shallot and Mushroom Enchiladas with Tomatillo,

Green Apple, and Avocado Sauce and Lime Crème Fraîche, 82–83
  Harvest Time Salsa, 186

Tomatoes:
  Cheesy Sweet Onion and Heirloom Tomato Pie, 120–121
  Coffee-Rubbed Vegan Steak Tacos with Grilled Lobster Mushroom, Heirloom Cherry Tomato, and Corn Salsa, 105–107
  Cumin and Avocado Oil–Rubbed Portobello Tortas with Dragon Fruit Pico de Gallo and Purple Basil–White Peppercorn Mayo, 178–179
  Eggplant Parmesan Ravioli with Heirloom Tomato, Strawberry, and Chocolate Marinara, 46–48
  Hatch Chile Chicken Cacciatore with Black Garlic–Tomato Sauce, 56–57
  Heirloom Tomato, Black Garlic, and Marsala-Roasted Chickpea Panzanella, 177
  Orzo with Vegan Chicken-Apple Sausage, Asparagus, Baby Tomatoes, and Ricotta Salata in a White Tomato Sauce, 40–41
  Summertime Heirloom Tomato and Herb Salad, 176
  White Pepper Vegan Turkey Shawarma with Chipotle-Tomato Relish and Roasted Garlic, Sage, and Artichoke Tahini Paste, 173–175

Tomatoes, sun-dried:
  Free-Form Wild Mushroom Lasagne with Champagne-Lemon Cream Sauce and Sun-Dried Tomato and Roasted Red Pepper Salsa, 68–69
  Goat Cheese, Spinach, and Sun-Dried Tomato–Stuffed Pork Chops with Roasted Garlic Fingerling Potatoes and Pearl Onions, 38–39
  Red Chard, Roasted Garlic, and Ricotta–Stuffed Peppers with Sun-Dried Tomato and Toasted Pine Nut Marinara, 76–78

INDEX

Tortas, Cumin and Avocado Oil–Rubbed Portobello, with Dragon Fruit Pico de Gallo and Purple Basil–White Peppercorn Mayo, 178–179

Tostadas, Black Cumin Crab, over Cabbage Salad with Lime, Mint, and Wasabi Dressing, 185–186

Truffle oil:
   Mini Vegan Veal, Black Peppercorn, and Basil Sliders with Artichoke and Avocado Tapenade, 160–161
   Quattro Formaggio White Truffle Macaroni and Cheese, 91–92

Tuna:
   Canned Tuna Packed in Oil, 19–20
   Spicy No-Tuna Sushi Roll, 125–127
   Tuna and Garlic Cannellini Bean Salad, 188

Turkey:
   Turkey-Style Seitan, 8
   White Pepper Vegan Turkey Shawarma with Chipotle-Tomato Relish and Roasted Garlic, Sage, and Artichoke Tahini Paste, 173–175

Turkish Pomegranate Meatball Soup, 64–65

Twinkies, 198–199

Veal:
   Mini Vegan Veal, Black Peppercorn, and Basil Sliders with Artichoke and Avocado Tapenade, 160–161
   Veal Chops with Sunchoke Caponata, 66–67
   Veal Chop–Style Seitan, 10

Vital wheat gluten, xvi

Waffles, Belgian, 203–205

Walnuts:
   Crab and Oyster Mushroom Mezzelune in a Roasted Hatch Chile and Walnut Cream Sauce, 58–60
   Egg Mix, 28
   Parmesan Blend, 22

Wheat berries: Heirloom Bean, Red Russian Kale, and Wheat Berry Chili, 117–118

White beans. See Cannellini beans (white beans)

White Lasagne with Basil Ricotta, Spinach, Young Rocket, and Diced Vegan Pancetta, 70–71

White Pepper Vegan Turkey Shawarma with Chipotle-Tomato Relish and Roasted Garlic, Sage, and Artichoke Tahini Paste, 173–175